Python Programming
for Linguistics and
Digital Humanities

Python Programming for Linguistics and Digital Humanities

Applications for Text-Focused Fields

Martin Weisser

WILEY Blackwell

Library of Congress Cataloging-in-Publication Data
Names: Weisser, Martin, author.
Title: Python programming for linguistics and digital humanities :
    applications for text-focused fields / Martin Weisser.
Description: Hoboken, New Jersey : Wiley-Blackwell, 2023. | Includes index.
Identifiers: LCCN 2023025982 (print) | LCCN 2023025983 (ebook) | ISBN
    9781119907947 (paperback) | ISBN 9781119907954 (adobe pdf) | ISBN
    9781119907961 (epub)
Subjects: LCSH: Python (Computer program language) | Computer programming.
    | Computational linguistics.
Classification: LCC QA76.73.P98 W45 2023 (print) | LCC QA76.73.P98
    (ebook) | DDC 005.13/3--dc23/eng/20230612
LC record available at https://lccn.loc.gov/2023025982
LC ebook record available at https://lccn.loc.gov/2023025983

Set in 9.5/12.5pt STIXTwoText by Straive, Pondicherry, India

SKY10063485_010224

To Ye,
without whose constant support over the years
writing books like this would not have been possible

Contents

List of Figures

About the Companion Website

This book is accompanied by a companion website.

https://www.wiley.com/go/weisser/pythonprogling

This website includes:

1) Text
2) Codes

1

Introduction

This book is designed to provide you with an overview of the most important basic concepts in Python programming for Linguistics and text-focussed Digital Humanities (henceforth DH) research. To this end, we'll look at many practical examples of language analysis, starting with very simple concepts and simplistic programs, gradually working our way towards more complex, 'applied', and hopefully useful projects. I'll assume no extensive prior knowledge about computers other than that you'll know how to perform basic tasks like starting the computer and running programs, as well as some slight familiarity with file management, so no in-depth knowledge in mathematics or computer science is required. All necessary concepts will be introduced gently and step-by-step.

Before we go into discussing the structure and content of the book, though, it's probably advisable to spend a few minutes thinking about why, as someone presumably more interested in the Arts and Humanities than technical sciences, you should actually want to learn how to write programs in Python.

1.1 Why Program? Why Python?

Nowadays, more and more of the research we carry out in the primarily language- or text-oriented disciplines involves working with electronic texts. And although many tools exist for analysing such documents, these are often limited in their functionality because they may either have been produced for very specific purposes, or designed to be as generic as possible, and so that they may also be applied to as great a variety of tasks as possible. In both cases, these tools will have been created only bearing in mind the functionality that their creators have actually envisaged as being necessary, but generally don't offer many options for customising them towards one's own needs. In addition, while the results they produce might be suitable for carrying out the kind of ***distant reading*** often propagated in DH, without any in-depth knowledge of how these programs have arrived at the snapshots or summaries of the data they have produced – as well as which potential errors may have been introduced in the process – one is never completely in control of the underlying data and their potentially idiosyncratic characteristics. To illustrate this point, let's take a look at the analysis output of a popular DH tool, the ***Voyant Tools*** (https://voyant-tools.org), displayed in Figure 1.1.

Python Programming for Linguistics and Digital Humanities: Applications for Text-Focused Fields, First Edition. Martin Weisser.
© 2024 John Wiley & Sons, Inc. Published 2024 by John Wiley & Sons, Inc.
Companion website: https://www.wiley.com/go/weisser/pythonprogling

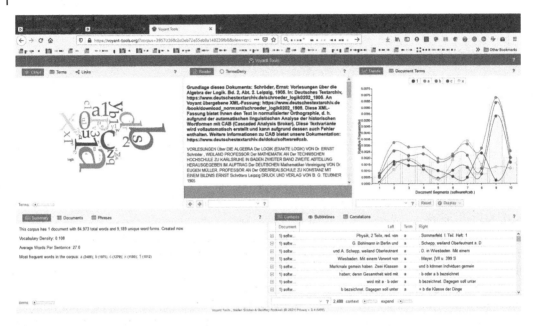

Figure 1.1 Sample text analysis in the Voyant Tools.

The text in Figure 1.1 is part of the *German Text Archive* (*Deutsches Textarchiv*; DTA), which provides direct links to the Voyant Tools as a convenient way to visualise prominent features of a text, such as the most frequent 'words' and their distribution within the text. For our present purposes, it is actually irrelevant that the language is German because you don't need to be able to understand the text itself at all, but merely observe that the tool 'believes' that the most prominent words therein are *a*, *b*, *c*, *x*, and *1*. This can be seen in the ***word cloud*** on the top left-hand side, the summary below it, and the distributional graph on the top right-hand side. Now, of course, most of us would not see these most frequent items as words at all, but rather as letters and a number, all of which hardly represent any information about the content of the text, which is usually what the most frequent words should do, at least to some extent, as we'll see in Chapter 8 when we learn to create our own frequency lists, and then develop them further to fit our needs in later chapters. The reason for these items occurring so frequently in the different visualisations in Figure 1.1 is that the text is actually about mathematics, and hence comprises many equations and other paradigms that contain these letters, but, as pointed out before, have relatively little meaning in and of themselves other than in these particular contexts. To be able to capture the 'aboutness' of the text itself in a form of distant reading, we'd need to remove these particular high-frequency items, so that the actual content words in the text might become visible. However, the Voyant Tools simply don't seem to allow us to, and hence appear to be – at least at first glance – designed around a rather naïve notion about what constitutes a word and how it becomes relevant in a context. Only if you hover over the question marks in the interface do you actually see that there are indeed options provided for setting the necessary filters. In addition, if you look at the distributional graph on the top right-hand side, you may note that the frequencies are plotted against "Document Segments", but we really have no indication as to what these segments may be. It rather looks like the document may simply have been split into 10 equally sized parts from which the frequencies have been extracted, but such equally sized parts don't actually constitute meaningful segments of the text, such as chapters or sections would do. Furthermore, the ***concordance*** – i.e. the display of the individual occurrences in a limited context – for the "Term" *a* displayed on the bottom right-hand side is misleading because the first four lines in fact don't represent instances of the mathematical variable *a* that accounts for the majority of instances of this 'word', but instead constitute the initial *A.*, which appears to have been downcased automatically by the tool, something that is fairly common practice in language analysis to be able to count sentence-initial and sentence-internal forms together, but clearly produces misleading results because this particular type of abbreviation is not treated differently from other word forms.

This example will already have demonstrated to you how important it is to be in control of the data we want to analyse, and that we cannot always rely on programs – or program modules (see Section 7.4) – that others have written. Yet another reason for writing our own programs, though, is that, even if some programs might allow us to do part of the work, they may not do everything we need them to do, so that we end up working with multiple programs that could even produce different output formats that we'd then need to convert into a different, suitable, form before being able to feed data from one program into the next. Moreover, apart from being rather cumbersome and tedious, such a convoluted process may also be highly error prone.

In terms of what we might want to achieve through writing our own programs, there are a few things that you may already have observed in the above example, but in order to make such potential objectives a little clearer and expand on them, let's frame them as a series of "How can we ..."-questions:

- ... generate customised word frequency lists or graphs thereof to facilitate topic identification/distant reading?
- ... gather document/corpus statistics for syllables, words, sentences, or paragraphs, and output them in a suitable format?
- ... identify (proto-)typical meanings, uses, and collocations of words?
- ... extract or manipulate parts of texts to create psycholinguistic experiments, or for teaching purposes?
- ... convert simple documents into annotated formats that allow specific types of analysis?
- ... create graphical user interfaces (GUIs) to edit or otherwise interact with our data?

We certainly won't be able to answer all these questions fully in this book, but at least work towards developing a means of achieving partial solutions to them.

Having discussed why we should write our own programs at all, let's now think briefly about why Python may be the right choice for this task. First of all, despite the fact that Python has already been around for more than 30 years at the time of writing this book, it is a very modern programming language that implements a number of different programming paradigms – i.e. different approaches to writing programs – about which, however, we won't go into much detail here because they are beyond the scope of this book. More importantly, though, Python is relatively easy to learn, available for all common platforms, and the programs you write in it can be executed directly without prior compilation, i.e. having to create one single program from all the parts by means of another program. This makes it easier to port your programs to different operating systems and test them quickly.

In terms of the programming paradigms briefly referred to above, it is important to note that Python is object-oriented (see Chapter 7) but can be used procedurally. In other words, although using object orientation in Python provides many important opportunities for writing efficient, robust, and reusable programs, unlike in languages like Java, it's not necessary to understand how to create an object and all the logic this entails before actually beginning to write your programs. This is another reason why the Python learning curve is less steep than that for some other popular programming languages that could otherwise be equally suitable.

Despite my initial cautionary note about using other people's modules, of course we don't always want to reinvent the wheel when it comes to particular tasks that someone else may already have solved in an appropriate way. Thus, as long as we can ensure that these modules in fact do what we expect them to do, there are many additional modules available for Python that may simplify specific problems, such as parsing out the content of web pages in order to extract only the parts we may require, etc.

Last, but not least, another important advantage of Python is that it is becoming increasingly popular with linguists and computational linguists, so that you may a) be able to find many suitable modules to simplify your tasks, and b) – more importantly – there are many opportunities to cooperate with like-minded researchers in your programming efforts or get advice from more experienced programmers.

1.2   Course Overview and Aims

In this section, I'll first present an overview of the book. As many of you are probably less familiar with issuing commands in text form to interact with their computer's operating system, prior to delving into our actual programming efforts, I'll first introduce the most important concepts involved in working with the computer in this way, and installing the software required for our purposes. Following this, Chapters 2 and 3 will introduce you to programming fundamentals – statements, variables, control structures, etc. – thereby enabling us to develop strategies for solving language-related questions computationally in their most basic form. In Chapter 2, you'll also learn some of the basics of working with strings, which represent the most useful data type for our language-related purposes.

Chapter 4 is designed to allow you to grasp more intermediate concepts in string processing, laying the foundation for processing words and short pieces of texts to do basic morphological analysis, clean up data, break sentences into words, as well as create formatted output as the most elementary form of visualising language data. In Chapter 5, you'll then learn how to work with longer pieces of data, stored in the form of text files, for handling and saving results, including a discussion of how to handle the folder structure on your computer efficiently and in a platform-independent manner.

The next chapter will introduce you to regular expressions, a powerful way of recognising simple to highly complex linguistic patterns, and processing them. This knowledge will enable you to perform tasks that are especially relevant to advanced language processing, and go way beyond the options provided by Python's basic string processing methods, such as searching through one or more files in order to extract and display information based on more or less complex patterns you'll learn to specify.

In Chapter 7, we'll move on from learning about the essential concepts towards applying these in developing our own applications, even if these may initially still be relatively simplistic. We'll start this part of the book by discussing the essentials of modularity and object orientation, thereby providing a foundation for writing more efficient programs and reusable components for increasingly complex and repetitive programming tasks. Here, for instance, we'll learn how to design user-defined functions that allow us to handle simple lexica for performing (equally basic) word-class annotation tasks, or how to set up our own object to model the behaviour of specific types of words. Chapter 8 will then turn to creating word and frequency lists, and developing an understanding of different sorting options. This will allow us to create useful objects to quantify and identify linguistic phenomena in various ways, as well as to display them in ways that are appropriate for different analysis tasks.

In Chapter 9, I'll introduce you to creating graphical user interfaces (GUIs) as a means to facilitate handling and interacting with data. While this may seem like something you don't really need for analysing language data, in my experience it is invaluable in providing yourself – as well as any potential users of your programs – with ways of interactively outputting and exploring data in forms that are often not possible on the command line, especially if you're dealing with different languages or older forms of language. By necessity, though, we'll have to restrict our endeavours here to producing relatively simple GUIs, but hopefully you'll be able to use the information provided here to develop your understanding further independently, so that you'll later be able to create more complex ones that fit your exact analysis needs or those of any projects to which you may be contributing.

In Chapter 10, we'll learn how to download and handle web data, and produce – as well as work with – annotations. As more and more data these days originates from the web, and many levels of language analysis require some form of interpretive coding, these two areas also represent very important aspects of programming for language analysis purposes. The final section also includes an introduction to the annotation scheme of the Text Encoding Initiative (TEI), a scheme commonly used for corpora and other texts in DH.

The final main chapter will introduce some basic concepts in creating visualisations, such as producing frequency plots using the matplotlib library or generating word clouds.

1.3   A Brief Note on the Exercises

Other programming books may provide you with the necessary theory, walk you through code/coding examples step by step, and then give you some more advanced exercises that essentially send you off on your own to explore things further, but then never offer any solutions. In my experience, such an approach is less effective because it runs the risk that you may simply end up doing simpler exercises mechanically, or end up learning only half of what may be relevant because the main exercises are too limited.

My approach in this book is rather different from this – perhaps more academic – because I generally start by introducing the most essential aspects of the programming constructs covered first, but then ask you to apply these concepts immediately to particular questions or projects in processing textual data, as and when necessary or relevant even introducing additional details inside the exercises. This way, you'll not only be forced to apply the concepts, but also to think about how this can best be achieved in solving language-related issues. The more we progress through the book, the more complex these mini-projects may get, and they will frequently also be designed to build upon many concepts covered in prior sections, so, in a sense, they also serve as a kind of repetition for you.

However, because the exercises may get rather complex, I will also provide detailed discussions of them at the end of each chapter. Here I not only show you the code that I consider most appropriate, based on your current level of knowledge, or perhaps even some possible alternatives, but will also explain important issues pertaining to these solutions. In addition, I'll discuss potential pitfalls or any error messages you may encounter, especially in the earlier chapters. Hence, even if you may be able to complete the exercises without any help, you should probably still read through the discussion each time you've completed an exercise to learn about these additional aspects before continuing with the main text.

All programs we produce as part of these exercises are listed in complete form in the Appendix, and will also be available, along with any other resources, from the book's companion website at http://www.wiley.com/go/weisser/pythonprogling. To challenge you a little more, I'll frequently also provide suggestions as to how you can develop the programs we devise together into more advanced little projects that you can carry out on your own in order to develop your programming skills further independently.

1.4   Conventions Used in this Book

In this book, I'll use the general conventions for representing different types of information for linguistics purposes, as well as a few other ones designed to make it easier for you to distinguish between the descriptive text and the coding constructs presented. Language samples or passages used as examples are represented in *italics*. To distinguish between different linguistic levels of description, if necessary, I use the appropriate bracketing, e.g. curly brackets ({...}) for morphology and angle brackets (<...>) for graphemes. In Chapter 10, however, the latter will generally represent parts of the syntax of the markup languages HTML and XML.

Key terminology will be highlighted **like this**, so you can identify it more easily, and expressions that deviate slightly from the standard meaning will appear in scare quotes ('...'). To facilitate distinguishing between descriptive text and programming constructs, I will use `this font`, with variable elements in the code, especially in syntax descriptions, being marked through italics. Syntax summaries are further distinguished via a box with a | drop shadow |.

To be able to make coding examples stand out even more clearly, in many cases, I'll write these on a separate line, even if they form part of a longer sentence. In such cases, I'll frequently also omit some punctuation marks, such as commas or full stops, so that these don't appear to be part of the program code.

1.5   Installing Python

Installing Python on your computer should – on the whole – not represent a big problem because installation packages for the different platforms can conveniently be downloaded from https://www.python.org, and the installation itself presents no major obstacles if you observe a few simple points, of course provided that you have administrative rights on the computer you're using. If you're using a shared computer and have no administrative rights yourself, then you'll need to consult your administrator.

Python is frequently already preinstalled on Linux and macOS, but unfortunately often only version 2, which also tends to be required by the operating system (OS), and is therefore non-replaceable! In these cases, the solution is to carry out a parallel installation of 3 alongside version 2 because we'll be using Python 3 for this book. If you're running such a parallel installation of Python 3, you'll also need to set up the so-called *shebang line* (explained in Section 2.5) correctly, so that your OS will know which version of Python to use for running your programs. In the following sections, I'll describe the installation process for the different OSes covered here one at a time. At the time of writing, Python 3.11, which is supposedly much faster than previous versions, had already become available. However, not all of the Python modules used in later parts of the book were available for this version, so that I'd currently still recommend maximally installing Python 3.9, which I've tested with all modules.

1.5.1   Installing on Windows

From Python 3.8 onwards, Python will be set up in your user directory by default, e.g. 'C:\Users*username*\AppData\Local\Programs\Python*Pythonnumber*', where *username* is your own username and number the version number without the dot, i.e. 38 for version 3.8, and 39 for 3.9.

As an administrator on your computer, you can also switch this to installing it for all users by checking the customisation option shown towards the bottom of Figure 1.2, in which case it would normally be installed into the folder 'C:\Program Files\Python39'.

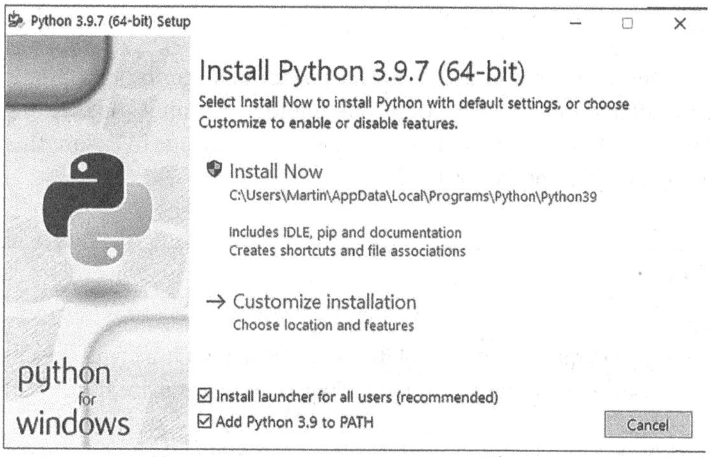

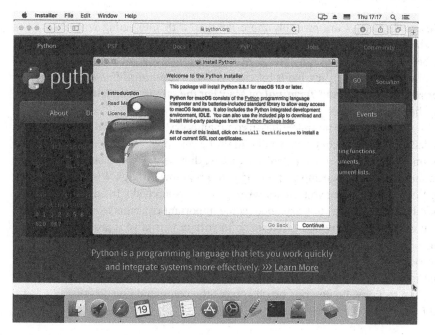

Figure 1.2 Python installer running on Windows.

You should also ensure that the box for "Add Python X to PATH" – where X stands for the version number – is checked in order for Windows to be able to find the Python interpreter, the program that converts your Python instructions into executable code, and allow you to launch Python programs by double-clicking from Windows Explorer.

1.5.2 Installing on the Mac

On the Mac, you just need to follow the basic instructions shown in Figure 1.3.

Figure 1.3 Python installer running on macOS.

When installing Python on macOS, there is no issue associating your files with an interpreter or setting the path because macOS and Linux handle the execution of programs differently from Windows, through the *shebang line*, through which you tell the OS which interpreter to use.

1.5.3 Installing on Linux

To install Python 3 on a Linux system, you should use whatever packet manager is appropriate. However, as Linux distributions differ rather strongly from one another, I cannot describe the installation process in any detail here. As on the Mac, Linux uses the *shebang line* to ensure that the right version of Python will execute your programs later.

Exercise 1   Installing Python

Go to https://www.python.org.
Find the most up-to-date Python 3 version for your OS. Note: If you're using Linux, you won't find an installer on this website, but you should use your package manager for locating one instead.
Download and install Python, making sure that you select the option for adding Python to your path if you're on Windows, and installing certificates on the Mac after completion!

Now that you should have a copy of Python 3 on your computer, we can verify that the installation process ran correctly, and then start investigating how to use it. Before we can do so, though, we first need to explore how it is possible to issue the right commands to your computer in the form of text you type in, which may well be something that you're still unused to.

1.6   Introduction to the Command Line/Console/Terminal

Most computer users these days are probably more familiar with interacting with their OSes through windows-based systems, i.e. so-called **Graphical User Interfaces** (**GUIs** – /guːiz/ – for short). However, before such GUIs became prevalent in computing, it was customary to interact with the OS by typing in commands at what is referred to as the **command line** on Windows, as the **console** or **terminal** on Linux, and **Terminal** on Mac. For the sake of simplicity, from now on, I'll refer to this as the command line.

The command line allows users to input text-based commands via the **command prompt**, which is generally signalled via a flashing cursor, and will initially be your only way of running Python or any simpler programs written in Python that don't have a GUI themselves. We'll later learn another, slightly more comfortable, way of starting and testing your programs through WingIDE Personal, the program that I'm recommending you use for writing your Python code. In addition, working with the command line will allow us to learn about some important concepts related to handling files and folders on your computer, which will form an important part of your programming once you start working with stored data from Chapter 5 onwards.

In order to issue commands to all three OSes, you type their name, plus any potential arguments, i.e. other required information such as filenames, etc., and then press Enter to trigger the command. In the next two sections, I'll describe how to access the command line, first for Windows, then for Mac and Linux.

1.6.1 Activating the Command Line on Windows

To activate the command line on Windows, there are multiple options. Perhaps the simplest one for most users initially is to press the ⊞ key or click on the Start (⊞) button, type cmd next to the magnifying glass symbol, and click on Command prompt in the dialogue box shown in Figure 1.4.

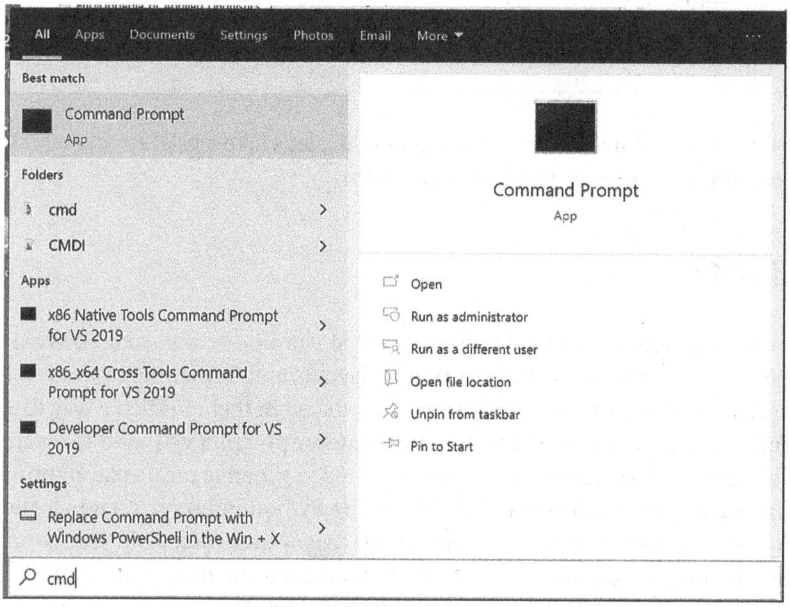

Figure 1.4   Activating the command prompt via the Windows Start menu.

Depending on how many programs or files Windows finds that start with the letter *c,* this option may already be presented to you even if you only press c or cm. As you can see, there are multiple actions available for the command prompt on the right-hand side of the start menu, other than just clicking to open it. To simplify opening the command prompt, you could for instance pin the icon to your taskbar if isn't already too crowded, and then have it available with one single mouse click. Another, more important, option you may need later if you've installed Python as an administrator, is that you can also run the command prompt in that capacity, which will then allow you to install additional packages for all users.

Another quick way to access the command prompt is to press ⊞ + r, then type cmd in the 'Run' dialogue that will open, and press the Enter key (⏎) or click on 'OK'. If you hold down the 'Shift' key (⇧) and the 'Ctrl' key while pressing 'Enter', you can also open the command prompt as an administrator.

If you're already looking at a folder that contains your programs in Windows Explorer, it's even more convenient to type cmd in the Explorer address bar and press the Enter key. This will open up a command prompt directly at the folder location, so you won't actually need to navigate there once the command line has been opened, which we'll nevertheless soon practise.

1.6.2 Activating the Command Line on the Mac or Linux

To activate the command line on the Mac or Linux, you need to start Launchpad (Mac) or click the start button (Linux), search for Terminal (or a similar name), then execute Terminal. On the Mac, you can also add the Terminal to the dock for convenience. This is usually also the case for Linux panels, but may depend on your exact Linux version.

Exercise 2   Verifying That Python Is Installed

Open a command line for your OS.
Type in `python -V`, and press Enter. You should then see the version number of your Python installation reported at the prompt.

Now that you know how to issue commands on the command line, let's take a brief look at which types of programs you can use to write your Python programs in.

1.7   Editors and IDEs

For most writing tasks on the computer, we tend to use dedicated word processors like Microsoft Word® or LibreOffice Writer that enable us to apply appealing layouts and formatting to whatever we write. These programs, however, generally store the texts produced in them in such a way that they can more or less only be opened and edited further by whatever program was used to create them, apart from containing many formatting instructions required to generate the display or print them. For writing program code that needs to be readable by the Python interpreter, and ideally editable by different programs available on the different OSes we may want to use, word processors are therefore not useful. The kind of text we need, which contains no formatting or fancy layout apart from perhaps line breaks or indentations, is called *plain text*, and the programs we can use to edit them are called (plain text) *editors*. Examples of these would be Windows Notepad®, or TextEdit on macOS. Some of these editors even offer special support for programming languages, such as syntax highlighting for different programming or markup languages (see Section 10.1), but this support, if it exists at all, still tends to be fairly limited.

Better suited to programming tasks are so-called *Integrated Development Environments* (*IDEs*, for short). These offer additional programming support, such as finding errors in code (*debugging*), advanced syntax highlighting and indentation, syntax completion, etc., sometimes for multiple programming and/or markup languages.

1.8   Installing and Setting Up WingIDE Personal

One such IDE that is optimised for Python and markup languages is the WingIDE. It exists in different versions, and is available for Windows, MacOS, and Linux. The version that is of interest to us here is the Personal edition, as it's freeware, just like Python, so that you won't have to invest anything other than your time into learning how to program in Python, but can still enjoy a number of features that will greatly simplify your programming tasks. Of course, there are also other freely available IDEs, or you may already have a preferred IDE, so using WingIDE is only a recommendation I'd like to make having evaluated a number of other IDEs. In case you (or your instructor) decide to use a different IDE, you can of course skip the remainder of this chapter, and move straight on to the next one. Before you do so, though, you should at least check to see if the output encoding for your chosen IDE has been set to UTF-8, which is usually done in the IDE's program preferences. Read on just a little to find out why this may be sensible to do.

The Personal edition of the WingIDE can be downloaded from https://wingware.com/downloads/wing-personal. The exact installation routine depends on your OS, but is generally quite straightforward, so we won't discuss it here, instead carrying it out as part of our next exercise. However, there may be a few settings to modify after the installation. The most important of these is that, at least prior to version 8, the default encoding (see Section 2.3.1) in which files are saved is automatically set to the local encoding on your computer, which is not an optimal choice. Hence, you'll minimally want to change this, setting it to UTF-8 via 'Edit → Preferences → Files → Default Encoding' in order to be able to use non-English characters properly as well in your code. It's also possible to customise many of the display options, such as setting a larger font, changing the editor background to make it easier on your eyes, displaying line numbers, or even setting a different display language, but these are largely questions of preference, so, again, we won't discuss them here.

Exercise 3   Installing and Getting to Know WingIDE Personal

Download the version of WingIDE Personal appropriate for your OS and install it.
Change the settings for the encoding if necessary.
Familiarise yourself a little with the features and functions of the IDE by looking through the menus, etc.

As we've now covered all the preliminaries, in the next chapter, we can finally begin to learn about some of the essential concepts required to allow you to begin programming.

1.9   Discussions

Discussion 1   Installing Python

Provided that you've followed my instructions carefully, there are only a few things that could have gone wrong during the installation, unless of course you're not authorised to install any software on your computer at all, in which case you'll need to ask your administrator to set up Python for you. At the time of completing this book, the most recent Python version was 3.11, but you may need to install a version lower than 3.9 if you should still be running Windows 7, which I wouldn't recommend, anyway.

On Windows, should you have forgotten to tick the box to add Python to your path, ensuring that Windows finds the Python interpreter and that your programs will also run if you double-click on them in Explorer will get a little complicated. To do so, you need to go into the Windows settings, most easily accomplished by pressing ⊞ + i, typing *path* into the search box (see Figure 1.5), and selecting either 'Edit the environment variables for your account' (for non-administrators) or 'Edit the system environment variables' (for administrators). As a non-administrator, you can then select the Path option in the box at the top, click on 'Edit...', and add the path to your Python installation to the end of the path. As an administrator, there's one intermediate dialogue, where you need to click on 'Environment Variables...' first, and then follow the same steps as just described above.

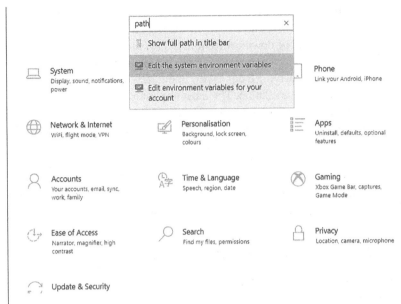

Figure 1.5   Finding the Path settings.

Installing the certificates on the Mac, if you've omitted that step, may unfortunately prove necessary in order to be able to download files from the internet as part of the exercises in Chapter 10, so if you should have forgotten to do so, please install them asap.

Discussion 2   Verifying That Python Is Installed

Provided that your installation was successful, using the command `python -V` should output the Python version number, e.g. Python 3.9.7 on my computer, which indicates that I'm running version 3, with minor version 9, sub-version 7.

Should you inadvertently have typed the wrong program name, perhaps *pythion,* you'll get an error message from the OS, indicating that the program name is not recognised. If you type a different capital letter after `python`, Python will display some usage information, but in case you've typed a small v or forgotten the argument completely, you'll end up with a different prompt that starts with >>>. This means that you've started the interactive **Python interpreter**, called the **Python Shell**, where you can actually already type in the Python commands we'll learn about later, and test different Python constructs. To close this interpreter and return to the OS prompt, simply type in `exit()` and press Enter.

Discussion 3   Installing and Getting to Know WingIDE Personal

Downloading, installing, and editing the encoding settings, if required, should be relatively straightforward, provided you download the right installer, follow all the instructions, and of course, have the necessary permissions to install programs on your computer.

When you open WingIDE Personal to explore, you should see that there are multiple sections or panels that offer different types of functionality over and above simply being able to create and edit program code. Initially, the most important part of the interface will be the editor window itself on the top left-hand side below the menu and toolbars, although we'll later also make use of other components of the IDE window. This window can actually be split, so that you can view multiple files side-by-side in order to compare them or copy and paste from one to the other, or also view different sections of a longer program.

On the right-hand side, spanning all the way from top to bottom of the program window, you'll see a window with a few 'utility' tabs that allow you

- to manage a project ('Project') – something we won't discuss here;
- get help on specific Python programming constructs ('Source Assistant');
- explore or jump to different sub-parts of your program ('Source Browser');
- and potentially manage indentation issues ('Indentation').

The 'Indentation' tab, however, is something you'll probably only need to use if you work with code that may have been created in other editors or by other people.

The bottom left-hand side is split into two panes, each containing multiple tabs, with the left-hand pane containing tabs for searching (and replacing, if activated) in the currently active file or a number of files at the same time, as well as the 'Stack Data' tab, which is used for advanced debugging purposes we won't discuss in this book. In the right-hand pane, the two tabs we'll discuss and use later on are 'Debug I/O' and 'Python Shell', whereas we won't cover the other two again.

The menu bar at the very top, as well as the toolbar below it, contain a number of familiar entries or buttons that essentially exist in most GUI programs, but also a few items that you'll probably still be unfamiliar with, and which relate to various aspects of handling the programming code. If you haven't done so already, I'd suggest that you at the very least try to read through the menus to see which entries you understand and may be useful to you in handling code, and also possibly which keyboard shortcuts you may want to use to increase your efficiency. Of course, there'll be quite a few things that won't make sense to you yet, but you can always try to understand them later, once you've made some progress in your programming career.

2

Programming Basics I

In this chapter, we want to start discussing the first essential elements of (Python) programming. These will already enable you to carry out some very basic programming tasks, create simple output, and hopefully help you to develop a sense of how to provide instructions to the computer through the Python interpreter. The first of these tasks will not yet take the form of real programs, but only short sets of instructions we'll be trying out through the Python Shell. However, we'll already turn to writing real, albeit short, programs towards the end of the chapter.

2.1   Statements, Functions, and Variables

Now let's get started by looking at how we can tell Python to do things, i.e. how to write instructions. Instructions in Python, as in other programming languages, take the form of **statements**, although, from a linguistic point of view, they of course really represent imperatives. Normally, we write one instruction per line, e.g.

```
print('Good morning!')
```

which simply outputs the greeting *Good morning!* to the command line. In some rarer cases, we can also write multiple statements, each separated by a semi-colon, on the same line, e.g.

```
print('Good morning!'); print("Or is it already evening?")
```

but generally only if they're really simple and, as in our example, more or less do the same thing. Many other programming languages require a semi-colon at the end of each statement, but Python avoids this overhead, so the above use really represents an exception.

A ***function*** is a special kind of instruction that generally takes one or more ***arguments*** in round brackets, and, instead of saying that we use a function, we actually say that we're ***calling*** it. The arguments represent the 'things' the function is supposed to do something with, and either come in the form of comma-separated lists, variably determined by position, or as argument–value-pairs with named ***keyword arguments***. In the latter case, the arguments and values are linked to each other via an equals (=) symbol. As we've already seen above, for instance, the print(...) function, in its basic variant, displays some text on the screen in the form of a string (more on this soon) as its argument, adding a line break at the end.

Python Programming for Linguistics and Digital Humanities: Applications for Text-Focused Fields, First Edition. Martin Weisser.

Statements in Python can be tested interactively in the Python Shell, which is normally activated via the command line as described in Discussion 2. However, it's also integrated into the WingIDE, so that we can conveniently use it from there without even having to open a command line. Furthermore, using it in this way, it'll also automatically be closed when we close the IDE, so we don't need to exit it, either.

Exercise 4   Basic Statements

Start your WingIDE or preferred IDE.

Find the sub-window for the Python Shell. If your IDE doesn't have an integrated Python Shell, open one from the command prompt by simply typing in `python` and pressing Enter.

Enter the statements from above one at a time in the Shell, exactly as shown, and inspect the results carefully.

Modify the strings in any way you like, and test them again.

Also try to output the two `print` statements in one go by providing two arguments inside the round brackets as explained above.

How does this output differ from the one with two separate print statements?

In case you're using the Python Shell from the command prompt, type in `exit()` and press Enter to close it.

Programs essentially 'calculate' and modify different types of values. To be able to store and change such values, we need memory locations as 'placeholders', called *variables*. These variables have to be assigned (ideally telling) names via *declaration*, so that they can later be addressed or referenced correctly. We normally declare variables by *initialising* them, i.e. giving them their first value, through an *assignment*, e.g.

```
message = 'Good morning!'
```

The assignment is here achieved using the *equals operator* (=), with the value `'Good morning'` to the right of the = being assigned to the variable `message` on the left-hand side. We can also assign the contents of one variable to another, e.g.

```
message2 = message
```

In a similar way, more complex *expressions* – or rather their results – can be assigned to a variable. To be able to picture this better, let's take a look at an example using numerical variables where we first declare and assign values to the variables a and b, and then perform an addition using these variables to assign the result to a third variable c.

```
a = 3
b = 5
c = a + b
```

One thing that is very important to remember is that – because variables simply represent memory locations – a renewed assignment to the same variable often overwrites the original contents, or even initialises, depending on the data type, a new variable, with the original one being deleted. Once a variable has been initialised, we can not only access its value, but also use it in other statements, or as an argument for functions, e.g.

```
print(message)
```

where the contents of the variable message are simply used to create output through the print function.

Although I've already stated before that variable names should ideally be as telling as possible, we haven't yet discussed how this may be achieved and whether Python imposes any constraints on us in this respect. As a matter of fact, there are some constraints, since variable names in Python may be composed of letters, underscores, and digits in general, but mustn't start with a digit and should ideally not start with an underscore, either, as this is reserved for Python-internal variables by convention. In addition, 'special' characters, i.e. characters not part of the Latin character set, ought to be avoided, due to potential locale settings that could lead to incompatibilities. We'll soon learn a little more about why this may be the case.

Telling variables may consist of multiple words, though they must also not contain spaces, and should ideally describe the function of a variable as clearly as possible. To accomplish this, we can use one of two different naming variants:

a) *underscore form*: first_word, word_1;
b) *camel-case form*: secondWord, wordTwo.

In (a), the underscore essentially acts as an unobtrusive replacement for the disallowed space, whereas in (b), capitalising each follow-on word shows the boundary between the words. In all of the above examples, it is hopefully immediately clear that the variables refer to words that occur in a certain position and order.

2.2 Data Types – Overview

Python offers different simple and 'compound' data types for different purposes, i.e. to represent different types of variables. All data types in Python are objects (see Section 7.7) with associated *methods*, which are functions associated with particular types of objects. We'll here only look at the ones that are most important for us (shown in Table 2.1), which will be introduced properly step-by-step and discussed in more detail in the following sections or chapters.

Table 2.1 Most useful data types.

Data type	Use
str	String: represents words, word parts, or longer stretches of text
int	Integer, i.e. whole number
float	Floating point number, i.e. number with decimal positions
bool	Binary truth values: True or False
list	Ordered, but not necessarily sorted, combinations of other data types; multiple occurrences possible
tuple	Ordered, fixed, 'list' of values
set	Unordered combinations of other data types; multiple occurrences not allowed
dictionary	Combinations of keys and their associated values

As stated above, all data types have their own associated methods, which are called via

```
variablename.methodname()
```

Some of these methods may also be shared by data types that exhibit some degree of similarity, as we'll see later. To find out which data type a variable holds, you can use the `type` function with the variable as an argument, as in the following example:

```
greeting = 'Good evening!'
type(greeting)
```

If you try this out in the Python Shell, the output would be `<class 'str'>` because our variable has been initialised with a string.

2.3 Simple Data Types

2.3.1 Strings

We'll begin our exploration of data types with strings, as these arguably represent the most important type for tasks in linguistics and language-oriented DH. They're used with methods for handling characters, for instance the ones shown in Table 2.2, where variable elements are indicated in italics.

Table 2.2 Some useful string methods.

Method	Functionality
string.split()	Splits strings at separator as argument
string.join(*list*)	Joins multiple strings, provided as arguments, using the string it's called on as an element appearing between them
string.splitlines()	Splits strings/files into lines at line breaks
string.find(*string*)	Finds index of a string in another
string.count(*string*)	Counts how often a string occurs in another
string.startswith(*string/tuple*)	Tests if a string starts with another, or one out of a tuple
string.endswith(*string/tuple*)	Tests if a string ends in another, or one out of a tuple
string.lower()	Produces a copy of a string in all-lowercase (i.e. small) letters
string.upper()	Produces a copy of a string in all-uppercase (i.e. capital) letters

The list in Table 2.2 is non-exhaustive, and we'll introduce a few more methods as and when we'll need concepts that require their use. However, the regular string methods are often too simple for the more complex types of analysis we later need to carry out, so we'll explore better options of dealing with language patterns in Chapter 6.

To be able to indicate to the Python interpreter that we want to declare a string, we normally write it in paired single (`'...'`) or double (`"..."`) quotes. However, triple quotes can also be used for longer strings including multiple line breaks, especially as so-called `Docstrings` for documenting programs. Quotes contained within quotes either have to be different or need to be masked via a backslash (\), e.g.

```
"They said \"Hello\""
```

or

```
'They said "Hello"'
```

Strings containing special characters, e.g. \, can be marked as raw by prefixing them with an `r`, which we'll also return to in Chapter 6.

To be able to understand some of the character representation issues I referred to in the context of naming variables, we need to delve a little deeper into how characters are in fact handled by the computer. Computers don't really store text, as one might perhaps expect, as sequences of characters or words, but as numbers that take up a specific number of bits or bytes. This is referred to as their *encoding*. The first, simple *character sets*, single-byte character sets, either used up to 7 (ASCII; up to 128 characters) or 8 (Latin-1) bits (up to 256 characters). Within these character sets, all Latin characters are encoded as single numbers in the ranges shown in Table 2.3.

Table 2.3   Character positions in ASCII and Latin 1.

Range	Positions
Control characters	1–32
Punctuation, digits, etc.	33–63
Capital letters	64–90
Lowercase letters	97–122

The higher positions in such character sets are variable, depending on locale, which already leads to compatibility problems for older (legacy) encodings, even for Western languages. On top of this, it's impossible to store Asian languages with many thousands of characters in single-byte encodings, which eventually led to the development of double-byte character sets. However, these only introduced further incompatibility problems, thus hampering the exchange of data from different areas around the world, including multilingual data. The solution to this was a set of encoding schemes called **Unicode**, which come in different flavours that use either fixed or variable-byte length encoding, and essentially make it possible to store all possible multilingual content. The different (main) types are UTF-32, UTF-16, UTF-8, with the latter being ideal for language-related analysis tasks, partly also because Python internally uses it by default, but also because it's rapidly becoming the standard for encoding on the web. UTF-8 uses up to 6 bytes to encode characters, and the simple Latin characters cover exactly the same positions as in ASCII or Latin-1, so that it's easy to handle documents encoded in them when opening them in Python, too.

Strings in Python are composed of single characters, each in turn representing a string object. The code for a character can be found via the `ord` function, and, conversely, be produced using the `chr` function. One thing we should always bear in mind, too, is that they are *case-sensitive*, so that uppercase characters occur at lower positions than lowercase characters, something that is especially important for comparing words or longer phrases in sorting operations (see Section 8.3).

Now that we know a little bit more about variables, let's practise using them in a short exercise.

Exercise 5 Swapping Variables

Return to the Python Shell, either in your IDE or on the command line.

Set up two string variables for the words *there* and *is*.

Choose your own variable names, and also test to see what happens if you try to use a variable name starting with a digit.

Use two `print` statements with two arguments to output both words, the second time round reversing the order of the arguments. What did you simulate here?

Now try to achieve the same effect by swapping the contents of the two variables through assignments and outputting the results via `print` again. What can you observe here?

Try to solve the problem using a third variable named `temp`, first instantiating the first variable again with the right word, then initially storing its contents temporarily in `temp`, and then carrying out the swapping operation.

Finally, determine which letter has the code 72 in UTF-8, and which letter you get when you type 72+32 inside the round brackets of the function you used.

As pointed out earlier, strings represent the most important data type in language-related analysis. However, since we frequently need to be able to count the phenomena we're investigating, numbers may also play an important role in writing our programs, so that we'll discuss the relevant data types in the next section.

2.3.2 Numbers

Python has a variety of numerical data types, but only two out of these are really important for our purposes. These are `int` (integer, whole number), which can be used to perform basic counting of the phenomena we observe, and `float` (floating point numbers), which allows us to calculate relations or relative frequencies (see Section 11.4) of such phenomena. Regarding the latter, Python uses an Anglo-Saxon number format, so that the . represents the decimal separator, and not the comma, as in European formats.

When we want to create output by joining strings and numbers together, the numerical types generally need to be converted (***cast***) to strings using the `str` function or formatted using special format statements we'll discuss in Section 4.6. Table 2.4 introduces the two most useful functions we may need for working with numbers. Arguments presented here in square brackets are marked as optional, but the square brackets are not part of the syntax.

Table 2.4 Important functions for working with numbers.

Function	Use
`int(n)`	Converts floating point numbers to lowest basis; casts string to integer
`round(n, [precision])`	Rounds floating point numbers to the nearest integer or, optionally precision of *n* digits

---

Exercise 6 'Rounding' Numbers

Return to the Python Shell.

Set up a variable `float_num` and initialise it to the value `1.758`.

Output its value using the `int` function.

Do the same using the `round` function, once using only the variable as a single argument, and once specifying the precision of `1` as a second argument.

2.3.3 Binary Switches/Values

Binary switches or values are represented through the `bool` data type, which marks whether a condition is true, or a property of an object exists. If the value is `True`, a condition is fulfilled, or a particular property does exist. Conversely, if it's `False`, then the condition isn't fulfilled, or the property doesn't exist.

Boolean values – named after the logician George Boole – are normally returned from conditional statements or loops, which we'll discuss in Section 3.5. They can also be set 'manually', i.e. programmatically, to mark conditions, e.g. to indicate that something has already been processed and therefore can be ignored in further processing steps.

Now that we have an understanding of the basic data types, we of course need to find out which types of operations can be carried out on them, and how we can indicate these operations to the Python interpreter, which we'll do in the next section.

2.4 Operators – Overview

As their name says, *operators* enable us to perform operations on data. So far, we've already discussed the assignment of a values to a variable via the = operator, or how two numerical values can be summed by using the + operator. In their most basic form, operators can trigger mathematical, logical, or string operations, as well as a few more, again discussed later as required. Some operator symbols are 'polysemous', i.e. their exact function depends on the data type(s) they're being used with.

2.4.1 String Operators

Since we've already established that strings represent the most important data types for us, let's start our discussion of operators with those that allow us to perform operations on these, as listed in Table 2.5.

Table 2.5 String operators.

Operator	Function	Example
+	Concatenation	`message = 'Good ' + time_of_day + '!'`
*	Repetition	`print('-' * 50)`
%	Simple formatted output (all Python versions)	`print('5/3 rounded to 2 decimal places: %.2f' % (5/3))`
==	Test for equality	`'Ab' == 'ab'`
!=	Test for inequality	`'Ab' != 'ab'`
<	Less than (regarding character code)	`'Ab' < 'ab'`
>	Greater than (regarding character code)	`'Ab' > 'ab'`

The concatenation operator (+) is mnemonic in the sense that we can associate it with the mathematical concept of adding things together, only that, in this case, we're adding one or more strings or string variables to each other. Something similar goes for the repetition operator (*), which simply multiplies the number of times the string preceding it will occur, usually for some printed output. For instance, the example in Table 2.5 draws a line of 50 characters width using as many hyphens. The % operator, however, is not mnemonic in the same sense, but simply acts as a place-holder to be filled with the current content of a specific variable, formatted according to specific criteria that we'll discuss in more detail in Section 4.6.

The remaining operators all revolve around comparisons between strings, based on the code points of the characters they consist of, as well as potentially their length. They don't return numerical values, but instead Boolean ones, i.e. True or False. We'll only really see the useful-ness of this in Section 3.5, but most of the comparisons are self-explanatory, so that I really only need to draw your particular attention to the test for equality, as this misleadingly looks like an assignment, due to the symbol simply being reduplicated, which may lead to problems when inad-vertently used incorrectly. A very common mistake you might make when you actually want to test for equality in a control structure (see Section 3.5) is to use a single equals symbol, which will lead to the statement always being true because making a successful assignment always returns True. An exception to this rule would – of course – be if you were trying to use variables in the assign-ment that have never been declared or – for instance – the right-hand side of the assignment con-tained an expression where a value is divided by 0 (see Section 2.4.2 for division operators), which will always cause an error because division by 0 is disallowed. The operator in the test for inequal-ity can be read as 'not equal', with the ! symbolising the negator. The final two operators should be familiar to you from mathematics, only that, as stated above, the mathematical comparison here is based on code points.

To develop a better understanding of how these operators work, let's do a quick exercise again.

Exercise 7   Trying Out the String Operators

Test the string operators by trying out the examples from the above inside the Python Shell. Experiment by changing the examples as you see fit.

Especially try to understand the results of the comparisons.

Tip: If you make any mistakes, or simply want to change some of the details of a statement, you don't need to type everything in again because the Python Shell actually retains a his-tory of all the commands you've typed in. To access this, all you need to do is use the up-arrow key (↑) until you find the command you want, edit it, and then run it again. If you've accidentally gone too far back, you can also move forward again by using the down-arrow key (↓).

2.4.2   Mathematical Operators

You'll already be familiar with many of the mathematical operators from your mathematics classes in school because the same symbols that were used there generally also indicate the same mathematical operations in programming languages. However, you will also encounter a few operators you've never heard about, as well as see a few special cases of assignments combined with these mathematical operations. The latter are alternative, shorter, options, and indicated here in the second row of each field. A summary of mathematical operators is presented in Table 2.6.

Table 2.6 Mathematical operators.

Operator	Functionality	Example
+=	Addition without assignment Addition with assignment	`number = number + 3` `number += 3`
-=	Subtraction without assignment Subtraction with assignment	`number = number - 3` `number -= 3`
*=	Multiplication without assignment Multiplication with assignment	`number = number * 3 }` `number *= 3`
**	Exponential function	`number = number ** 2`
/=	Division without assignment Division with assignment	`number = number / 3` `number /= 3`
//	Integer division (no decimals)	`number = 5 // 3`
%	Modulo (remainder of division)	`number = 5 % 3`
==	Test for equality	`number1 == number2`
!=	Test for inequality	`number1 != number2`
<	Less than	`number1 < number2`
<=	Less than or equal to	`number1 <= number2`
>	Greater than	`number1 > number2`
>=	Greater than or equal to	`number1 >= number2`

Out of the operators in Table 2.6, you should definitely be familiar with +, -, *, /, <, <=, >, and >=. Getting used to the forms combined with assignment may require some more explanation, so let's illustrate this using + and +=. In the long form, `number = number + 3`, on the right-hand side, we take the value that's currently stored in the variable `number`, add 3 to it, and then assign the result of this expression back to `number`, thereby overwriting the original value and actually recreating the variable. In the short form, `number += 3`, the + before the assignment operator signals to the interpreter that we're using the value already stored in `number`, and that the value to the right of the assignment operator simply needs to be added to this original value, thereby providing a convenient shorthand where we don't need to type the name of the variable `number` twice.

For the exponential function, the notation ** will most likely be unfamiliar to you, but it's simply a convenient replacement for the ^, which is more difficult to type on the computer. If you perform an integer division, all you essentially do is 'chop off' all decimal places, truncating the result to the integer only. The modulo operator performs a division, but then returns the remainder, i.e. everything that's left over if the first number cannot be cleanly divided by the second. For example, performing a modulo operation using the numbers 12 and 6 would return 0 because 12 is cleanly divisible by 6. However, if we apply it to the numbers 12 and 7, the latter only fits into the former once, with a remainder of 5. This operator is e.g. useful if one wants to extract every nth element from a list, such as every 5th word, because then one can simply take the position of the word, divide it by n, and if the remainder is 0, pick the word.[1]

So that you can get a feel for how the mathematical operators work, let's now do another short exercise.

---

1 There's only one slight glitch here: programming languages like Python don't start indexing list positions at 1, as we would normally expect, but at 0, so that any program we might want to write to extract every nth word would need to be adjusted accordingly.

> **Exercise 8   Trying Out the Mathematical Operators**
>
> Test the mathematical operators by trying out the examples from the previous page in the Python Shell.
> In doing so, you can first initialise the variable `number` at will, and change it as many times as you like.
> You can also simply output the respective values after the operation inside the Shell by typing `number` and pressing the Enter key, so there's no need to use the `print` function.
> Always observe the return value (i.e. result) in the Shell closely and try to understand its meaning.

2.4.3 Logical Operators

Logical operators are normally used with conditional statements, or in other control structures (see Section 3.5), in order to determine the state of variables and influence program flow.

Table 2.7 Logical operators.

Operator	Function	Example
`and`	Joins conditions/comparisons, i.e. both need to return `True`, otherwise `False`	`a != 0 and b < 5`
`or`	Distinguishes between alternatives, i.e. at least one of the two needs to return `True`, otherwise `False`	`word1 != 'maybe' or word2 == 'perhaps'`
`not`	Negates a condition	`not condition_true`

As these operators are plain English words, they're essentially not difficult to understand, apart from the fact that `or` here indicates an ***inclusive or***, where both options can theoretically be true, whereas in natural language, only one alternative would normally be applicable, as in e.g. *I'll either come at three or five o'clock*.

We'll get much more experience in using logical operators later, with more realistic examples, but for now, let's just do the usual exercise.

> **Exercise 9   Trying Out the Logical Operators**
>
> Test the logical operators, trying out the examples from Table 2.7 in the Python Shell again.
> Again, choose the values for the variables yourself and change these until you've had at least one `True` and one `False` as results.
> Always try to understand how the different values affect the conditions.

You should now have developed a basic understanding of which string, mathematical, and logical operators there are, and how to use them. In addition, you'll have gained some practice in working with variables and statements in the Python Shell, but will probably have realised that, despite the fact that you can issue statements here, and the history function is fairly convenient for editing them, this still doesn't feel like you've written a proper program that you can edit and modify until it does exactly what you might want to achieve. How you can write and save actual programs will be the topic of the next section.

2.5   Creating Scripts/Programs

As we've just seen, the Python Shell is highly useful for testing code snippets and executing shorter statements, but it's not really practical for designing longer programs that are also meant to be run repeatedly. The solution to this is to create storable programs in the editor or IDE you're using, and which can then be executed directly using the Python interpreter.

The files you create for your programs normally have the extension `.py`, although you may sometimes also encounter `.pyw` for GUI-based programs that should be executed without opening a command line when double-clicked on in your file manager. In Windows, these programs are associated with the Python interpreter via their extension during the Python installation process, provided you've chosen the right option. In addition, Python is added to path of folders containing executable programs.

In Linux/macOS, no extensions are associated in this way. Instead, the 'association' is created via the **shebang line** `#!/usr/bin/env python3`, which the operating system reads first when executing the file, thereby determining which program should be used to run the actual code. Furthermore, your programs generally need to be made executable via the command `chmod +x filename` or setting the appropriate property through the file manager on Linux or Finder on the Mac.

The source code for programs needs to be stored as plain text and should ideally be encoded in UTF-8 to allow you to use characters beyond the standard ASCII or Latin1 range. Any deviation from this default should be marked, e.g. adding the line

```
# -*- coding: iso-8859-15 -*-
```

for Latin-1 after the shebang line. Just to be on the safe side, the appropriate encoding should also be set in the editor/IDE as discussed in the previous Chapter.

Empty lines in your code are normally ignored, and can sometimes make your program code easier to read, so feel free to add them, especially between sections that perform different tasks.

Editors like the WingIDE normally wrap longer lines automatically if line wrapping is enabled in the program preferences, so that you'll still be able to see the complete code without the need to scroll. To improve the readability of code further, for instance for printing purposes, it's also possible to break longer lines manually. To do so, it's best to wrap the relevant parts in round brackets, unless they already appear in them, and then add a line break prior to each operator, e.g.

```
print('This is a test for breaking a slightly longer'
    + 'line, which otherwise may be harder to read.')
```

We can still simplify the above example because two strings that follow each other will automatically be concatenated. This makes it possible to easily distribute longer strings across multiple lines. Used excessively, though, it may also make your code decidedly less readable, as no operators are visible then.

If the bracketed expression constitutes a multi-argument list, the individual elements can also be written one beneath the other. However, in this case, the comma between the elements should remain on the incomplete line to help express the list character more clearly.

Apart from these three options, there's also a final – yet dispreferred – one, which is to mark the line as incomplete using a \ at its end. This, however, may lead to errors in case one has inadvertently typed/left a space behind the backslash, something that may be difficult to spot. In order to increase the readability of the program code in this book, from now on, I'll always use the most suitable option. For lines of code that have unambiguously and correctly been marked as incomplete, it's also permissible to indent each follow-on line for readability, even if Python is otherwise extremely sensitive where indentation is concerned. This is another option I'll take advantage of as and when useful.

Exercise 10   A Program for Swapping Variables

Using your file manager, create a folder called `programming` in your home folder.

Write the swapping operations of the two string variables from Exercise 5 as a program called `01_swap.py` that you create from scratch in your IDE and store in the folder you just created. Don't forget to add a shebang line as the very first line in the file, so that your program could also run on macOS/Linux, even if you're only working in Windows.

To be able to recognise the values that the variables have prior to and after swapping, add informative `print` statements as appropriate.

If necessary (on MacOS/Linux), set the necessary permissions to make the file executable.

Open a command line in your folder and run the program:

- Windows: `01_swap.py` + ↵
- MacOS/Linux: `./01_swap.py` + ↵ (We'll find out what the `./` are for in Section 5.1.3)

The first programs you'll write will be relatively short, like the one you've just produced, but the more you gain in experience and will be able to write useful programs, the longer these will get, too. And, along with their length, their complexity will also rise, which is why it may become important to have little indications inside them that show you – or others – what's happening when and where. How to achieve this in a sensible way will be the topic of the next section.

2.6   Commenting Your Code

All programming languages allow us to add comments to our code in some form. These comments in your code facilitate understanding the code for other programmers who may need to use of modify your code, but also allow you to handle code better that you haven't worked with for a while. One of the reasons for the latter is not only that – as I've stated above – the complexity and size of your programs is bound to grow over time, but also that your own idiom is likely to change with experience, so that you'll end up approaching different programming problems in different ways, ways that may become less and less familiar over time.

At the same time, however, you'll learn to read code more easily, so that you'll end up needing fewer comments for certain constructs that you've become more familiar with. Commenting your code therefore always means striking a balance between usefulness and cluttering code. To develop your understanding of your own code, I'd therefore recommend that you start out adding lots of comments in the beginning of your programming career, describing your code in a way that enables you to develop a better understanding, but then gradually phase out adding comments for simpler constructs that you encounter repeatedly over time and are likely to be familiar to other programmers who may be using your code, starting to concentrate only on describing the most important stages and subparts of your program. Once you start writing more modular code, which we'll be discussing from Chapter 7 onwards, and especially if you start sharing your code with other people, you need to ensure that anyone who wants to become familiar with you modules has sufficient information about which functionality they provide, and especially which arguments may be required in user-defined functions or object methods, and for which purposes they are used.

Python provides two different forms for adding comments. Simple comments start with a hash mark[2] (#), and everything following this will simply be ignored by the interpreter when it executes your program. For slightly longer comments, these usually occur at the beginning of line, e.g. like for the shebang line or encoding info we discussed above. In general, they still tend to be fairly short, though, although of course you can also use them to document information that spans multiple lines, using another # at the beginning of each line.

Because the hash marks cause everything that follows them to be ignored, another use for them is to temporarily 'switch off' parts of your code that you don't need (but potentially want to retain for later), `print` statements you use to display interim results for testing, etc. As this form of 'commenting out' is so useful, most IDEs also provide shortcut keys for them, the one in the WingIDE being 'Ctrl + .' (i.e. Ctrl + the period key).

Triple quotes start multi-line comments, primarily for advanced documentation purposes. Although they can also be used to create string variables that contain line breaks, they are frequently used without assigning them to such variables to create so-called ***docstrings*** for generating documentation automatically for the user-defined functions and objects that we'll discuss in Chapter 7.

Exercise 11   Commenting Code

Add comments to the program you wrote in the previous exercise to explain what happens in each step.

Only use the simple comment form and write the comments in such a way that you yourself can understand them best, ideally considering at the same time if and how this may be comprehensible to others.

Add your name as author as a comment, too, and also document when you created the program.

As how you comment your own code is really also your own choice, I won't provide any solution to this exercise here.

In this chapter, we've explored the most basic concepts you need in programming, from issuing statements to working with variables. At the same time, we've seen how we can perform very basic language-related tasks, such as swapping initial words to simulate a syntactic inversion that allows us to create basic English yes-no questions from simple forms of declaratives. Of course, many declaratives in English don't actually start with simple adverbs or NPs that may be inverted in this way, so I'll leave it up to you as an additional exercise to think about whether you could already write a program that simulates slightly more complex syntactic inversions in this way.

---

2 . . .or pound symbol if you speak American English.

2.7 Discussions

Discussion 4   Basic Statements

Starting the IDE should represent no problem, and – as described earlier – the sub-window for the Python Shell can easily be found on a tab in the right-hand pane at the bottom of the program window that you simply need to activate by clicking on its tab.

If you enter the single and double `print` statements, each time triggering them by pressing the Enter key, you should easily be able to see that the print statements are all output to a single line followed by a line break. However, if you output the two in one go by specifying them as two arguments to a single `print` statement separated by commas, i.e.

```
print('Good morning!', "Or is it already evening?")
```

you should hopefully have observed that now the two messages appear on the same line, only automatically separated by a space, despite the fact that your statement didn't even contain this extra space. In other words, what we can see here is that the `print` function, if called with multiple arguments, simply outputs all of them, each time inserting a space between them.

Discussion 5   Swapping Variables

Although it would be possible to set up the variables as empty strings, and then initialise them in the next step, the easiest way is to declare and initialise them in one go. Which names you choose for them is really up to you, but as we've got two words we want to represent through these variables, perhaps `word1` and `word2` are most suitable, so that our first two lines of code would be:

```
word1 = 'there'
word2 = 'is'
```

Of course, you need to press Enter each time you've completed a line of code here because otherwise your instruction won't be passed to the Python Shell. If you've accidentally forgotten one of the single or double quotation marks to mark the strings, you'll receive an error message similar to this:

```
Syntax Error: EOL while scanning string literal: <string>, line
1, pos 12
```

The exact number for the position will depend on your variable name and whether you choose to have the spaces around the assignment operator, which I'm using for clarity, but aren't really required. You can probably expect to see many such errors, especially in the beginning of your programming career, and the important thing is to learn how to interpret them instead of panicking.

If you try to use a digit at the beginning of the variable name, you should receive the following error:

```
Syntax Error: invalid syntax: <string>, line 1, pos 2
```

Creating the two `print` statements should be relatively easy because we already practised using `print` with two arguments in the previous exercise. And, when examining the output, you'll hopefully have realised that we've simulated the syntactic inversion we normally encounter in yes/no questions, even if we'd customarily expect the first word to be capitalised in standard orthography.

When you'll try to swap by exchanging the variables, you'll probably write something like

```
word2 = word1
word1 = word2
```

Of course, you could also write it the other way round, but even then, the result would probably be rather disappointing because, instead of having swapped the contents of the two variables, you'll have ended up with one of the two words reduplicated. This only goes to show that what we can easily do in our heads or by simply accessing the values of the variables in reverse order will go badly wrong if we carelessly 'mess with' our placeholder slots instead.

To solve this problem using a temporary variable, we should write something like the following:

```
temp = word1
word1 = word2
word2 = temp
```

Here, we ensure that the contents of `word1` are first preserved in `temp`, so that we can safely overwrite the variable with those of `word2`, and then overwrite the contents of `word2` with the original contents of `word1` that we can now recover from `temp`. Of course, this requires a bit more planning, is slightly cumbersome, and requires an extra variable, so that Python, being an elegant and efficient programming language, actually offers us a better way of doing this through tuples, which we'll learn about in the next chapter. The main purpose of this exercise was to raise your awareness of potential issues when dealing with variables without thinking about any potential consequences.

The final part of the exercise should again be relatively easy if you remember that the `chr` function is used to 'translate' a code point into its corresponding character, and that lowercase characters are 32 points higher than their corresponding uppercase equivalents, so that you could theoretically always calculate the value of each lowercase character from that of the uppercase one. I say 'theoretically' here because, again Python already offers a more convenient way of doing just that that we'll find out about later.

Discussion 6   'Rounding' Numbers

Setting up and initialising the variable to the specified value should not present any problem. We do this so that we can reuse the value three times in a row, thereby saving ourselves the effort of having to type the same value repeatedly, and also to avoid accidentally mistyping it.

In order to display your results, you of course need to use the `print` function, but instead of simply outputting a single string or the contents of a string value, you have to specify the relevant functions as arguments to `print()`, in turn providing one or more arguments to these functions, essentially practising how to chain function calls. The four statements should therefore be:

```
float_num = 1.758
print(int(float_num))
print(round(float_num))
print(round(float_num, 1))
```

The results of the first two output operations should of course be different, even though we're converting the values to integers in both cases. The first result should be 1 because int() effectively only uses whatever precedes the decimal point, but the second result should be a genuine rounding as we're used to from mathematics, yielding 2. And last, but not least, the result of the last statement ought to be 1.8.

Discussion 7   Trying Out the String Operators

Trying out the string operators should present no real problem, unless, of course, you forget to use the right paired quotes, etc. When performing concatenations, you need to ensure that your variable time_of_day is initialised to a sensible value, such as 'morning' before trying out any examples. What you'll hopefully also have noted is that you need to manually add a space between words or phrases when concatenating them, which is different from when you use the print function with multiple arguments, where spaces are automatically added. Hence, if you simply wanted to print out *Good* and a variable value for the time of the day in a greeting, you could just provide two arguments to the print function. However, to add the exclamation mark at the end, you couldn't simply add this as a third argument because it would then equally be preceded by a space. Hence, you'd still need to concatenate time_of_day and the punctuation mark before using the result as the second argument.

The example for repetition, as already stated above, simply draws a line consisting of 50 hyphens, something that may be useful in separating output in something like a simplistic tabular format, or to separate results of operations more clearly from some explanatory text that may precede them.

If you've played around with the formatted output, you'll hopefully have realised that the result of the expression in round brackets following the second percent sign will be output with two decimal places, which is specified through the .2f following the first percent sign. Here, the dot marks the number following it as specifying the decimal places and the f that the output to be filled in is of type float. If you were to change the calculation 5/3 inside the brackets to any other values, you'd obviously also need to change the information provided at the beginning of the string to reflect this.

While carrying out the comparisons, you'll hopefully be reminded again that these are always case-sensitive. In the tests for equality and inequality, you need to ensure that the two-symbol operators are always written together because otherwise you'll get a syntax error. Should you forget to write one of the equals symbols in the presumed equality test, instead of a Boolean value being displayed, you would again get an error message, this time saying that you cannot assign to a literal, which makes sense in this context because you cannot assign one string to another, but only a string to a variable.

Discussion 8   Trying Out the Mathematical Operators

The only mistakes you can make in this exercise are essentially to forget to initialise one of the variables, or that you try to perform a division by 0. In the first case, you should see a `NameError`, and in the second a `ZeroDivisionError`. To illustrate some of the operators you will probably not have been familiar with yet, let's take a look at some examples that demonstrate what you would get to see in the Python Shell.

```
number = 7
number += 3
print(number)
10
number = 5 // 3
print(number)
1
number = 5 % 3
print(number)
2
```

In the beginning, we initialise number to the value of 7, and then increment this value by 3 using the compact form of addition, as opposed to the slightly more verbose `number = number + 3`. We then print out the current value of `number`, which, as should be expected, is now `10`. In the following line, we directly assign the result of a division without remainder to our variable, thereby overwriting it with the resulting value `1`, which we again print out in the next step. This result is due to the fact that we essentially throw away the decimal places, as the result of a normal division would have been 1.6666666666666667, which you can also verify in the Python Shell if you want to. Finally, we use the same numbers in an expression where the modulo operator is used to identify the remainder after we've established that 3 fits into 5 once, but that 2 remain afterwards when 3 has been deducted from 5.

Discussion 9   Trying Out the Logical Operators

Before trying out the operators, you of course need to initialise the relevant variables again, so that you don't get any errors related to names. For the examples for `and`, as well as `or`, this should be straightforward enough, but to be able to test the negation operator, you either need to initialise the relevant variable to `True` or `False`, and then either `print()` its value or type the name of the variable and press `Enter`. Let's take a look at an example to illustrate the use of the `not` operator.

```
story = False
print(story)
False
print(not story)
True
```

In the above example, we first assume that the story being discussed is `False`, so that we assign that value to it, and then test the assignment by `print`ing the value. To test what the result would be if we negated this, we then simply prefix the argument to print by the `not` operator, which changes the value to its opposite in the output only, but of course without affecting the original value.

Discussion 10   A Program for Swapping Variables

Unless you made mistakes typing the program name, or forgot to set the permissions in Linux/ on the Mac properly, starting your program should present no problem, obviously provided that there aren't any errors in your code. The finished product should look approximately as follows, where I'll provide separate comments on the individual program parts.

```
#!/usr/bin/env python3
```

The shebang line above should be the first one inside your program, allowing Linux or macOS to identify the correct Python interpreter. As pointed out in Section 1.5, on Windows, the extension ought to be associated with the interpreter, anyway, allowing it to interpret the line as a comment to simply be ignored.

```
word1 = 'this''
word2 = 'is''
```

Declaring and initialising the variables is something we've already practised beforehand, and so should present no problems as long as there are no typos in the code.

```
print('Prior to swapping, beginning of declarative sentence: Word 1 =',
      word1 + '; Word 2 = ', word2)
```

This simply `print`s the contents of both variables, along with a suitable description. Note how I've combined using several arguments to the `print` function and concatenation in creating the output.

```
temp = word1
```

Here, we temporarily store the contents of `word1` in `temp`.

```
word1 = word2
```

In this step, we assign the value stored in `word2` to `word1`, thereby changing the value of `word1` to is.

```
word2 = temp
```

At this point, we assign the value of `temp`, originally stored in `word1`, to `word2`, hence changing `word2` to here.

```
print('After swapping, beginning of interrogative sentence: Word 1 =',
      word1 + '; Word 2=', word2)
```

Finally, we output the result of the swapping operation, along with another suitable comment. Hence, the output for the user should approximately look like this:

```
Prior to swapping, beginning of declarative sentence:
Word 1 = there; Word 2 =  is
After swapping, beginning of interrogative sentence:
Word 1 = is; Word 2= there
```

Of course, it's equally possible to store the contents of `word2` temporarily to perform the swapping correctly. How you'd need to modify the above code to make this work is something I'll leave up to you to figure out, though.

3

Programming Basics II

In this chapter, we want to explore the remaining programming basics, which will already allow us to perform far more interesting language-related tasks than simply dealing with individual words. To achieve this aim, we first need to learn something about the more complex-structured compound data types Python offers. Next, rather than always 'hard-coding' values for our variables inside our programs, we want to discover basic forms of interacting with our programs and/or users through collecting input from the command line to enable you to create basic tests or perform interactive exploration of data. Following this, we'll develop some ideas about how to solve simple to slightly more complex problems in programming, as well as avoid some of the most basic errors. Last, but not least, we'll find out about making decisions regarding the way our programs should proceed, e.g. in choosing relevant output, or to repeat specific steps with different parts or types of our data.

3.1   Compound Data Types

The simple data types we looked at in the last chapter can only contain a single value, but of course the constructs we need to deal with while processing language aren't generally as simple as individual words only. And although we can easily store a complete text, such as a whole poem, play, article, or book inside a single string variable, generally we don't want to treat these texts in such a 'holistic' fashion. Instead, we want to be able to split them into their individual hierarchical parts, such as sections, chapters, paragraphs, sentences, or words, to be analysed separately and usually also retain some information about the order they appear in. Likewise, linguistic 'objects' of interest don't only exist at or above the level of words, but may also constitute parts thereof, such as affixes or even individual letters that we might want to manipulate or quantify.

To be able to handle the multiple levels of elements present in language, we essentially need two things: containers for multiple items of data, and ways of creating or manipulating these. Here, we primarily want to discuss what the container objects Python puts at our disposal look like in terms of their properties and most useful methods for working with them. In later sections and chapters, we'll explore these in more detail as and when useful, and I may introduce further particulars relevant to our specific language-processing tasks.

One very important concept we still need to discuss before looking at a list of compound data types is that of **mutability**. Mutability refers to the ability of objects to be changed directly without creating a new slot in memory for them. For all the simple data types we discussed earlier, this is

Python Programming for Linguistics and Digital Humanities: Applications for Text-Focused Fields, First Edition. Martin Weisser.
© 2024 John Wiley & Sons, Inc. Published 2024 by John Wiley & Sons, Inc.
Companion website: https://www.wiley.com/go/weisser/pythonprogling

not the case, so for instance whenever you assign a new value to a string variable, you're not in fact changing its value, but discarding the variable and creating a new one by the same name. The memory slot for the old one will then automatically be emptied by the interpreter through a mechanism called *garbage collection*. You don't need to be able to understand the exact reason for why this is the case, but simply that some of the compound elements we're discussing here are mutable, while others aren't. Table 3.1 shows a list of compound types, what they may contain, as well as their mutability.

Table 3.1   List of compound data types.

Complex type	Contents	Mutability
Lists (list)	Sequence of elements, following insertion order; multiple occurrences of elements possible	Mutable
Tuples (tuple)	Fixed, ordered sequence of elements; multiple occurrences of elements possible	Immutable
Sets (set)	Unordered sequence of elements; elements are unique	Mutable
Dictionaries (dict)	Unordered sequence of key–value pairs; keys are unique	Mutable

As you can see, most of the compound types are in fact designed so that their elements can be changed in some way, apart from tuples, which are normally used to represent 'lists' of properties we want to record as being unchangeable, such as the word classes a given word may belong to or the positions it might occur at inside a text. Accessing individual elements of lists and tuples to read their values can be achieved via their *index positions*. However, unlike in the natural world, in programming languages – including Python – these index positions commonly begin at 0, not 1, which initially represents a frequent source of error until you get used to this! Because lists are mutable, we can also assign values to specific index positions, while we cannot do so for tuples. Items in dictionaries or sets cannot be accessed via index positions. We'll later learn how to access items in these two types.

Because compound data types are objects, and can contain other objects as well, it's also possible to create even more complex, nested, data structures by storing one or more compound data types inside each other. Lists, tuples, and strings (the latter despite being basic data types), also belong to a special group of variables collectively referred to as *sequences*[1]. We'll talk more about this as required, and will explore specific ways of working with sequences that tend to be common to them in Section 4.3, but for now, let's spend a little more time thinking ahead as to how the specific compound data types may be used for different language processing and analysis tasks.

Exercise 12   Brainstorming the Potential of Compound Data Types

Look at the properties of the different data types in Table 3.1, and think about which types of linguistic objects may be stored in them and how.

While doing this, also bear in mind the types of linguistic objects I mentioned prior to introducing the table, as well as whether these objects may require nested structures.

---

1 Python also defines some other data types as sequences, but these aren't relevant to us here.

Now that you hopefully have some initial ideas about which compound data types may be useful for our purposes, we can start discussing the most basic one, the list.

3.2 Lists

Lists represent the simplest form of container, used, for instance, to store the words in a text or corpus. To assign to a list variable, you use paired square brackets ([...]) with a comma as separator between the individual list elements you want to insert, e.g.

```
words = ['this', 'it', 'a', 'sentence']
```

Lists can also be produced by using the list function, e.g.

```
emptyList = list()
```

to create an empty list. Empty lists are normally created if one doesn't yet know which elements exactly will be stored in them and how many, for example if texts are split into words in order to create word (frequency) lists. You can also use the list function to produce lists with content, but unless you use a function that returns words as an argument to list, this is really more cumbersome than using the form shown in the beginning because you essentially need to write the same thing, apart from also adding the function to your declaration, as in

```
words = list(['this', 'is', 'a', 'sentence'])
```

Once the list exists, individual elements can be accessed via *listname*[*index*], e.g.

```
words[1]
```

which would of course return is from our list of words above, bearing in mind that the index positions start at 0. Table 3.2 provides a short summary of some useful list methods.

Table 3.2 Useful list methods.

Method	Functionality
list.append(*element*)	Adds an object to the end of the list
list.extend(*elements*)	Adds elements of another list-like object to the end of the list
list.pop(index)	Removes an element at position provided by index; if index is missing, 0 is assumed as default
list.insert(*index, element*)	Inserts an element at a specified position; index may also be negative to insert *n* positions before the final element
list.sort(*arguments*)	Sorts the list according to specific criteria provided as arguments (more on this in Section 8.3)
list.len()	Returns the length of list
list.clear()	Empties the list

The difference between append and extend is extremely important to remember because it may affect the way you need to process the individual items in the list later. Let's imagine you append a list of words to a list of existing words, and then want to access each of the words again in turn. In this case, you can't directly print out each word, since, once you've reached the appropriate index where the nested list is stored, you need to start accessing the sub-indexes of that list until you've reached its end, instead of simply printing out each word in turn. If, however, you use extend with the existing list to add the other list, this will add all the new words individually, which is exactly what we would want. To illustrate the difference 'graphically', let's take a look at a few lines of code from the Python Shell that simulate this, where I've highlighted the most relevant parts in bold to make the issues easier to see:

```
sentence_list1 = ['this', 'is', 'a', 'sentence']
sentence_list2 = ['this', 'is', 'another', 'sentence']
sentence_list1.append(sentence_list2)
print(sentence_list1)
['this', 'is', 'a', 'sentence', ['this', 'is', 'another', 'sentence']]
print(sentence_list1[4])
['this', 'is', 'another', 'sentence']
```

In the first two lines of code, we set up two lists of words to represent the words in two simple sentences. In the third line, we use append to add the second list to the end of the first. However, if we print out the first list now, we can already see in line 5 that there's a nested set of square brackets in the output. To make it even clearer where the problem lies, we print out the element at position 4 in the list, which should be the first word of the second sentence if append didn't actually add an object to the list. However, as we can clearly see in the final line, the output is not a single word, but the whole list representing the second sentence.

The type of error we've introduced above by using the wrong method is known as a semantic error, i.e. an error that affects the meaningfulness and logic of the results your program produces. As such, it's quite distinct from the syntax errors we get if we, for instance, forget to close a bracket for a function call or don't use paired quotes for a string.

Running the same code again, but this time using the extend method, we can easily see in line 5 of the output, shown below, that there are no nested brackets, and that printing out the item at index position 4 now indeed shows the initial word of the second sentence.

```
sentence_list1 = ['this', 'is', 'a', 'sentence']
sentence_list2 = ['this', 'is', 'another', 'sentence']
sentence_list1.extend(sentence_list2)
print(sentence_list1)
['this', 'is', 'a', 'sentence', 'this', 'is', 'another', 'sentence']
print(sentence_list1[4])
this
```

The remaining functions will hopefully make sense to you intuitively, so we'll only discuss them as and when needed. To get some practice in using lists, let's do another exercise now.

Exercise 13   Simulating Simple Syntactic Inversion (Sentence Version)

Create a new program called 02_sentence.py.
First declare a list of words as shown earlier.
Then use a print statement in which you output the individual elements as arguments, and concatenate a dot with the final element, as discussed under string operations in the last chapter.
Add a further print statement in which you swap the first two arguments and concatenate a question mark with the final element instead of a dot.

We've now moved on from using only simply variables containing single values, and you can hopefully see that, despite the effort still required to initialise all the values in our list, at least we can already do something more useful with such complex variables. Of course, we'll later also discuss more efficient ways for populating such lists from actual data, but before doing so, we first want to discuss how to interactively obtain data from the users of our programs, including ourselves, which will allow us to move away from hard-coding everything inside our programs.

3.3 Simple Interaction with Programs and Users

Additional functions from internal and external modules can be embedded in Python via `import` statements. We'll learn how to create our own modules in Section 7.4, but for now we'll discuss how to use the ones that already come with the standard installation of Python, i.e. the internal ones, so that you won't need to know how to install any additional ones yet. One such module that we'll frequently need is the `sys` module. Amongst other things[2], this module offers functionality for interacting with the interpreter by providing access to the command line arguments that users supply, and can easily be 'embedded' into our code with the statement

```
import sys
```

Once we've imported the module and start the program, the `sys.argv` list contains all the program's arguments, with `sys.argv[0]` always holding the program name, and the remaining index positions the actual command-line arguments typed by the user. The use of `sys.argv` makes sense if a user is familiar with the program, but if not, it isn't usually practical without suitable error handling (introduced in Section 5.5) that checks the input and alerts the user to the arguments the program expects.

An alternative to using command line arguments is to prompt the user for one or more values via the `input` function, which then retrieves these values in turn and stores them in corresponding variables, e.g.

```
subject = input('What are you studying?\n')
```

This function, which is available without first importing it, is e.g. useful for creating simple tests or retrieving other pieces of information. Please note that, in the above example, the prompt ends with `\n`. This causes a line break after the prompt because otherwise the user would need to start typing immediately after the prompt, which would look odd. With both approaches – the use of the `sys` module or the `input` function, program arguments should normally be checked for validity, at least if it's possible to provide incorrect or too few arguments. We'll test both options, without doing much else useful, in the following exercise. This will provide a basis for later, more useful and elaborate programs that make use of these approaches, especially from Chapter 6 onwards, though.

---

2 ... most of which even advanced programmers may never use.

Exercise 14   Retrieving Input

Create two programs, `03_get_args_argv.py` and `04_get_args_input.py`.
In the first, two arbitrary words should be passed as program arguments. In the second, the user should be prompted for the same number of words via `input` statements. In both cases, these two words should be stored in suitable variables.
In the first program only, start by outputting the program name with a suitable message. In both programs, the values of the two word variables should then be output, again with suitable descriptive messages.
Open a command line and test the programs, for the first one ensuring that you actually provide two words as command line arguments.

3.4   Problem Solving and Damage Control

As you'll already have noticed from my descriptions of the simple programs we've created above – as well as how these programs may be suboptimal in some respects – more complex programs require targeted, sometimes fairly advanced, approaches. However, at least in the beginning stages of your programming career, the approaches you might take may still end up representing only fairly 'clumsy' problem-solving strategies, at least partly due to the fact that you haven't learnt more elegant techniques yet, or aren't aware of all the options a programming language like Python has to offer. To ultimately achieve your aims in creating more sophisticated and elegant programs, you often need to split these programs into distinct logical steps that perform individual tasks and then later bring their results back together. This is known as a ***divide-and-conquer*** strategy. Learning how to program requires targeted training of your algorithmic thinking and problem-solving skills to develop such strategies through trial and error, as well as to for you to develop your own personal idiom in writing Python code.

In this process, you'll frequently create buggy code, and some of the semantic errors you'll produce can lead to endless loops, where the program can no longer be stopped. In such cases, often the ultimate solution is to press 'Ctrl+c' on the command line, which will interrupt the program at OS level. We'll find out more about loops and other control structures in Section 3.5, but for now, I first want to raise your awareness as to how you can easily avoid some of the most common issues by allowing your IDE to help you develop your code and 'point out' any potential errors through syntax highlighting and simple forms of debugging.

3.4.1   Getting Help from Your IDE

The more sophisticated your IDE is, the more it will show you things that might be wrong in your code. However, even basic, simplified, versions of IDEs – such as the Personal Edition of the WingIDE I've recommended for the course – will provide you with a considerable amount of help in writing your programs if you pay attention to what they display and how they 'format' part of your code. For instance, when you declare a new string variable in the editor window in the WingIDE[3] and want to assign a value to it, once you start typing an opening quote, this quote,

---

3 . . . though not the Python Shell.

along with any text you type, will be highlighted until you add the closing quote. Something similar will happen if you start writing the opening brackets for function arguments, index positions in lists, etc., where each time you pause typing for a few seconds, the initial bracket will be highlighted in red, but once you've typed the closing counterpart, both parts will be marked in green. Once you start typing some code and this code is recognised as a potential keyword, function, or existing variable name, this IDE – as well as many other IDEs – will provide options for possible completions to you. Such completion options often also have little symbols next to them that indicate whether they may constitute a keyword, built-in data type, function, etc., which allows you to choose the appropriate conventions to write in working with them or, in the case of keywords, which words to avoid using as variable names. A good example of this would be the `int` function discussed earlier. As soon as you've typed the three letters of its name, you'll see an indication that there is indeed a built-in function by that name, and once you've selected it, the name of the function will also be highlighted in a different colour from the variable names you've created yourself. In a similar way, different data types will also appear in different colours that you can often also customise to your own liking, and may differ from IDE to IDE, which is why I'm here generally not referring to specific colours.

In addition to syntax completion, most IDEs will also incorporate some form of syntax help that allows you to highlight a specific construct and then display detailed information on it. In the WingIDE, this information is displayed in the 'Source Assistant' tab on the right-hand side of the program window. If you e.g. highlight the `print` keyword in your editor window, you'll get information displayed about the fact that it represents a function, its potential arguments, whether these are optional or not, etc., which is highly useful for refreshing your memory or exploring new options. In other IDEs, there may be a similar tab present, or possibly only a tooltip displayed.

When you write multiple lines of code and the syntax of one of these is incomplete, for instance if there is a closing bracket missing to a function, then all follow-on lines in a good IDE will normally be underlined with the kind of wavy lines you're used to from spell checkers in word processors, so that you should immediately be able to see which line the error occurred on. In more complex constructs, the error location may not always be so obvious immediately, but having an indication that there is an error will already take you a long way towards identifying it.

3.4.2 Using the Debugger

Another extremely useful feature that most IDEs will provide is some form of access to Python's **debugger**, a tool that helps you identify program errors. This tool can normally be started from any active IDE window, which is quite convenient, as we'll soon see. Fully explaining the debugging options is beyond the scope of this book, though, but I'll introduce at least the most basic concepts to allow you to see how you can profit from using the debugger.

In the WingIDE, the debugger is started either via the relevant menu item on the 'Debug' menu or a button that looks like the start button on a DVD player (▶). In other IDEs, there's usually a similar option, but possibly no dedicated 'Debug' menu. Instead, there will often be a 'Run' menu that incorporates debugging options. To identify potential problems, for instance related to the values a variable may take on while the program is running, you can set so-called **break points**. These allow you to run your programs only up to this point and then inspect the variable values, etc., and then usually step through or over follow-on statements, thereby controlling which parts of your program are executed and observing the changes that have occurred after each step. Once the debugger's running and has been interrupted in such a position, you can usually stop it by pressing a stop button that again looks like the corresponding control button on a DVD player (■). This is also the way to stop the kind of 'misbehaved' programs that produce empty loops that I referred to above.

We won't explore 'active' options for debugging any further here, but instead only discuss how you can make more 'passive' use of the debugger. Because the debugger allows you to run your programs, we can actually 'abuse' it as a replacement for the command line. This already saves us some time opening the latter each time we want to test a new program. Hence, from now on, we'll start running our programs from within the IDE. When you start the debugger in the WingIDE, either from the menu, via the button, or by pressing 'F5', the IDE will first pop up a special dialogue, displayed in Figure 3.1, that allows you to specify command line arguments in the textbox in the middle, amongst other, more advanced options not discussed in this book.

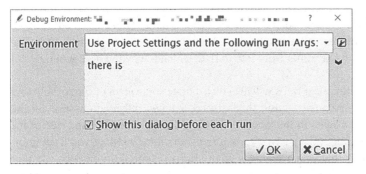

Figure 3.1   The Debug Environment dialogue in the WingIDE.

Other IDEs may not provide such a convenient dialogue, but instead run the debugger immediately, so you'll need to explore other ways of providing command line arguments to them, or, in the worst case, still resort to using the command line. Once you click on the 'OK' button in the WingIDE, the program in the currently active editor window will get started and its output redirected to the 'Debug I/O' tab in the bottom right-hand pane of the IDE window. For our most recent program, this tab is also where the user would need to type in the values elicited by the prompts, so that you need to ensure that your cursor is inside that window before typing in any values. Again, in other IDEs, the input and output may be redirected elsewhere, or dialogues may pop up for the `input` function.

If the program you're running in this way is 'well-behaved', i.e. doesn't contain any buggy code, it will simply execute as planned. However, if there are any errors, the debugger will stop the program on the line where the first error occurs, highlighting this line for you, so that you can immediately try to identify and fix the error. In the WingIDE, errors will also activate the 'Exceptions' tab in the bottom right-hand pane and display what kind of error has occurred, along with any other relevant information. We'll discuss more elegant methods for handling predictable errors in the next section, and especially in Section 5.5, but for now you at least have a convenient way for getting them reported and taking action based on this.

3.5   Control Structures

Control structures are an essential part of any programming language because they allow us to make decisions based on the values variables take on, or on the current program state, as well as to perform specific tasks repeatedly without any need to write a new statement each time.

3.5.1 Conditional Statements

Since we frequently need to check on values or program states, perhaps the most important control structure you need to know about is the one that makes it possible to test conditions. Just as in natural language, if you want to specify such a condition (or even multiple ones), you use the keyword `if`, and, depending on the condition(s) stated and whether they're fulfilled, your program will return a Boolean value, i.e. either `True` or `False`.

Before we find out how to actually state such conditions in our program code, let's first do some brainstorming about their use in dealing with language-related issues again.

Exercise 15   Brainstorming the Usefulness of Conditions

Briefly think about where, in dealing with language, you may need to test for specific conditions.

As pointed out above, conditions in Python are expressed using `if` statements followed by one or more conditions and a colon, e.g.

```
if word1 < word2:
```

for a simple comparison of two words. If multiple conditions are to be evaluated, these need to be joined by the logical operators we discussed in Section 2.4.3. Any statements that should be carried out if the conditions are fulfilled have to be listed in a block following the colon, which is indented by one level. It's not only possible to specify single conditional statements, though, but also alternative conditions. If present, these are normally introduced by

```
elif condition(s):
```

where of course `elif` is short for *else if*. To cover all other conditions that haven't been specifically defined, a final block prefixed by an

```
else:
```

statement can be used, so that the general syntax is:v

```
if condition(s):
    statement(s)
elif conditions:
    statement(s)
else:
    statement(s)
```

However, neither `elif` nor `else` blocks are required if no alternatives are present. This may for example be the case if the program absolutely expects a command line argument, but none has been provided, so that it doesn't make sense to run the remaining code. In this case, we can terminate the program directly using the `exit` function from the `sys` module, which also allows us to provide our own error message or usage information to the user as a string argument.

When the final conditional block has been processed, and all alternatives have been handled, the program flow continues again, with any further code un-indented by one level. The indentations in Python 'replace' the bracketing used in other programming languages, and absolutely need to be consistent, as inconsistencies cause syntax errors that will generally prevent your program from running. The indentation level should ideally be four spaces, but better IDEs, such as the WingIDE, automatically convert Tab key (→|) presses, or even add indentations automatically following specific keywords, based on their syntax checking.

Sometimes, you know that you'll need to include further conditional branches, but aren't yet sure exactly how to implement them. In such cases, you can already add the conditional statement, but need to mark the associated block using the keyword `pass`, allowing the interpreter to ignore and skip it, so that you'll be able to test the program without it. To practise working with `if` statements and multiple branches, let's do another exercise.

Exercise 16   Comparing Words

Write a new program (`05_word_comparison.py`), in which the user should provide two words as command line arguments that can then be tested, checking on whether they're equal or one comes before or after the other alphabetically.

Before you write the program, first think about how you would need to go about creating the appropriate control structures and which operators you may need.

Inside this program, use a conditional statement to first test if both words are equal and if so, output a message to that effect, including both words.

After that, test if the first word (based on character codes) occurs before the second, again with a corresponding message.

Finally, as a last alternative, add a message stating that the second word comes after the first. Pay particular attention to consistent indentation of the blocks.

Try the program using different words, sometimes simply changing their case as well.

As you'll no doubt have noticed, this example covers one of the cases you could have identified during our earlier brainstorming exercise, i.e. the comparison of words required for sorting. However, as we'll see in Section 8.3, Python actually provides functions or methods for doing alphabetical sorting, so that we don't usually need to implement this kind of comparison ourselves. What this exercise should still be useful for is to demonstrate that the basic comparison by code points clearly makes a distinction between upper- and lowercase characters, so if you provide the same word, once in small and once in capital letters, as arguments, there will never be equality between them. And just in case this now makes you wonder how exactly the words are compared when they of course contain multiple characters, this is also easily explained. The comparison starts with the first letter, then, if there is no difference, moves on to the next, and so forth, until it has either identified that there are no differences or, once it has actually found one, it reports what makes the words different.

3.5.2   Loops

Having covered how you can specify conditions to control program flow, we can now move on to discuss how to run specific program parts repeatedly in so-called ***loops***. Python essentially offers two different types of loops, one that runs as long as, or *while*, conditions are true (***while loops***), and one where we can iterate over all elements of sequential compound data types (`str`, `list`, `tuple`, `set`, and `dict`) individually and process them (***for loops***).[4]

---

4 In addition, it's also possible to combine features of the two concepts through a process called *comprehension*, which is often more efficient and elegant than loops for filtering or manipulation. As this is a slightly more complex topic that already requires some experience with loops, though, we won't discuss comprehension until Section 10.5.

As in conditions, loop bodies, i.e. all the statements that follow the line controlling the loop – which we can refer to as the *loop head* – also need to appear in a block structure. To be able to exercise further control over the loops, if a condition applies inside a loop body, the loop can be stopped prematurely using the keyword break, or the next loop cycle initiated via continue. To test for such conditions inside the loop body, we can of course use if statements.

3.5.3 while Loops

As stated before, while loops run for as long as one or more conditions are fulfilled. Their general syntactic form is:

```
while condition(s):
    statement(s)
```

Please note here that, even though you're actually testing for one or more conditions, there's no need to use the keyword if because use of the keyword while already 'implies' that everything that follows it up to the colon will be conditions that need to be tested. Such loops can for instance be used to request user input repeatedly to elicit specific information, such as in acceptability tasks, testing their knowledge of appropriate vocabulary, or in order to process/skip specific text segments, such as the front matter of a book. We'll produce a simple example for eliciting vocabulary knowledge in the next exercise.

Exercise 17   Collecting Collocates from the User

Write the program 06_collect_collocates.py, in which you prompt the user for three collocates of the word *cause*, only allowing them to quit the program once they've done so, and then showing them the list again for verification.

Before you start writing the program, think about how you could achieve this task given what you already know about getting user input, testing whether it actually contains any content, collecting this input in a list, and how to use conditions to control the flow of the loop.

Once you're ready, start by prompting the user for an initial collocate, and store it in a suitable variable.

Set up a list to store all the user responses.

Start a while loop that tests whether the length of this list is shorter than three elements.

Inside the loop block, first test to see if the user may not have typed anything, i.e. simply pressed Enter. If so, prompt the user again, telling them that they haven't provided any valid input.

Otherwise, append the valid input to the list of collocates, then test whether the list is already complete. If so, end the loop using the appropriate keyword, and if not, prompt the user to provide another collocate.

After the end of the final loop blocks, output a suitable message, as well as the collocates.

Now that you know how to do things repeatedly based on various criteria, you can learn how to process lists or other types of sequences one item at a time.

3.5.4 `for` Loops

Using `for` loops enables us to access all elements of a compound data type via a variable. This process is normally referred to as *iterating* or *iteration*. The basic syntax to use with `for` loops is this:

```
for variable in compound_type:
    statement(s)
```

Some of the most common actions that can be carried out with such iterations are e.g. to output each item one-by-one, test all elements for specific properties, or transform them, as we'll practise in our next exercise.

Exercise 18   Transforming a List

Write the program `07_uppercasing.py`, where you split a sentence into individual words, then transform each of these to uppercase, add it to a new list, and finally output the newly created 'sentence'.

Before you write the code, think about how you could go about carrying out this task, and whether you already know how to perform each sub-task. Hint: to help you find at least one method you might need here, you can take a look at Table 2.2.

When you're ready to write the program, as a first step, prompt the user for sentence.

Next, use the `split` method of the `str` object (shown in Section 2.3.1) without any arguments, and assign the result to a word list.

Set up a new empty list that will later hold all the uppercased word forms.

Write a `for` loop iterating over all words in the wordlist. Inside this loop, transform each word using the `upper` method of the `str` object, and 'add' it to the list.

Finally, join the uppercased words, and output the modified sentence together with an appropriate message.

In this chapter, we've found out about complex data types, and explored one of these, the list, in some more detail. In addition, we've learnt about how to achieve basic interaction, discussed how to solve some common programming issues, and how to control the flow of our programs. And although the short programs we've written were still very basic in terms of what we can achieve with them from a language-processing point of view, you should now have a basic knowledge of how to carry out the most basic programming tasks, as well as at least some little experience in developing your algorithmic thinking. This way, we can now continue and gradually learn more about specific details that are even more relevant towards handling language-related data tasks, and work towards developing more useful programs that you may either be able to apply directly to your analysis needs or that you can later extend to fit your own needs or those of any larger project you may be a part of.

If you already want to practise extending your programming skills further independently as an advanced exercise, you can modify our collocation collector in a number of ways. You can make it more flexible by adding command line arguments for both the node word, i.e. the one you want to collect collocates for, and the number of collocates the user is supposed to input. And if you want to tackle an even harder problem, try to make the number of words to collect open-ended, so that the informant would need to input at least *n* collocates, but could provide as many as they want. I won't provide solutions for these optional tasks, but will continue to offer ideas for such extensions to our programs at the end of each chapter to provide you with additional challenges.

3.5.5 Discussions

Discussion 12   Brainstorming the Potential of Compound Data Types

Because lists are relatively simple containers, but allow you to store multiple elements, they're ideal for storing linguistic objects that contain words or textual positions associated with individual words. The most common use for them is to store the elements that may make up a single sentence or text. More complex, nested, lists can also contain other objects in the textual hierarchy, such as chapters that may contain lists of paragraphs, which in turn may contain sentences, and these, again, words. To access elements within such nested lists, you'd then need to use multiple levels of indexes. How this may be achieved will become clearer as we learn more and more about working with such sequences.

Tuples, as pointed out above, are useful for recording specific properties of words or other objects that can never change. For instance, a word can normally not change the word class or classes it may represent, unless of course it undergoes a word formation process such as conversion, in which case we could create a new tuple also listing the newly acquired word class property. Similarly, when we record the positions of a word in a text, we might not only want to record a pure index position, i.e. the number of the word in the text, but instead a tuple that represents its exact start and end in terms of character positions. These positions are of course unlikely to change over time, even if they may potentially be different in different editions of a book.

Sets, due to the fact that each element can only occur in them once, are ideal containers for storing special types of lists, such as vocabulary lists. In addition, they can be used to store information pertaining to category membership, for instance storing a list of closed-class items, such as prepositions, or semantic classes. Other lists can then be checked against such sets, which is e.g. useful for counting how many words in a text may belong to these specific categories, etc.

Dictionaries, as their name already implies, are useful for e.g. storing words and their associated properties, where the property names may again represent dictionary keys. For simpler purposes, as we'll see in Chapter 8, they can also be used to quantify the occurrences of words in texts or whole corpora.

Discussion 13   Simulating Simple Syntactic Inversion (Sentence Version)

Creating the new program should hopefully have presented no problems to you, and neither should setting up the list containing the words of the sentence, ideally in this form:

```
words = ['this', 'it', 'a', 'sentence']
```

Writing the `print` statement to output the original sentence unfortunately at this point still requires you to add all the index positions one-by-one because we don't know how to process lists efficiently for this purpose yet, which we'll learn in Sections 3.5.4 and 4.5, respectively.

If you've overlooked my explicit instruction relating to "argument*s*" for `print`, you could now be tempted to use four individual `print` statements, but of course you'd then not output something that (more or less) looks like a sentence, but have all the words appearing on separate lines because we don't know yet how to use `print` without adding a line break yet. Hence, the proper way to achieve this sub-task is to use multiple arguments to the function, which would look as follows:

```
print(words[0], words[1], words[2], words[3] +'.')
```

If you've mistakenly added the punctuation symbol as a fifth argument instead of concatenating it with the fourth, you'll have ended up with a space between the final word and the dot. The final statement that simulates the inversion with a full sentence now is almost identical to the above, only that the first two index positions need to be swapped and the question mark added at the end instead of the full stop:

```
print(words[1], words[0], words[2], words[3] +'?')
```

The only problem here remains that the initial word of each sentence still isn't capitalised as we'd expect from standard orthography.

Discussion 14   Retrieving Input

For the first program, we need to start by importing the `sys` module as described in Section 3.3. If you forget to do so, when you run the program, you'll get an error message saying

```
builtins.NameError: name 'sys' is not defined
```

If you forget to provide either one or both arguments, the program name will still be output, but then the program will terminate with the message

```
builtins.IndexError: list index out of range
```

because the Python interpreter will notice that the argument list does not contain enough arguments once it tries to access them. If you provide more than two arguments, anything after the second one will simply be ignored because we don't access the index positions from within our program. Retrieving, storing the arguments in suitable variables, and outputting a sensible message should not present any problem, and could look like this:

```
word1 = sys.argv[1]
word2 = sys.argv[2]
print('word1:', word1 + '; word2:', word2)
```

In the second program, since we don't import the `sys` module, we also don't have access to the program name. However, as stated before, you can use the `input` function directly without importing anything at all. Here, it's important to provide a telling prompt, as well as ideally to allow the user to type in the value on the next line as shown in the example above. Bearing these things in mind, the program itself can be a little shorter than the previous one and could look like this:

```
word1 = input('Please input 1st word...\n')
word2 = input('Please input 2nd word...\n')
print('\n\nword1: ' + word1 + '; word2:', word2)
```

Please note that, in the above, code, I've added two more line breaks before the output, simply to make it easier to see where the prompted values appear and where the output begins. This wasn't necessary in the previous program because all we got to see there was the output. However, we could actually have shortened the previous program to two lines, the `import` statement and the output line, as we didn't really need to store the arguments in variables at all, and could simply have used the index positions from the `argv` list in the output, something that isn't possible in the second program because we retrieve the two values from the user separately.

There's one more important thing I need to mention here. If you ever use one of the two approaches to work with numbers, you need to ensure that you're casting the arguments or values you retrieve from the user to whichever data type you actually want to use because the original values will all be strings.

Discussion 15   Brainstorming the Usefulness of Conditions

Essentially, when dealing with language, some of the conditions we may want to test for are whether

- we've found a specific word while processing a text, perhaps out of a group of words, such as function words,
- a word has a specific length, either as a measure of complexity or to see whether any affixes may be present that need to be stripped to arrive at base forms or lemmata,
- a given word has a specific property – perhaps if it's a noun or a verb, a positive or negative adjective, etc.,
- a word occurs inside a dictionary or not,
- a word comes earlier in the alphabet than another, so that we can sort it into its proper place when creating a vocabulary list or dictionary,
- a sentence ends with a specific type of punctuation, indicating its potential pragmatic function,
- a specific word or type of phrase, or sentence, occurs more frequently than other types, hence possibly indicating its semantic salience,
- etc.

At least some of the above cases will play a role in our future exercises.

Discussion 16   Comparing Words

To get the words from the command line, we of course need to import the `sys` module again, so the beginning of this program is basically identical to `03_get_args_argv.py`, apart from the fact that we're not outputting the program name. Hence, you could either simply copy the relevant parts from there, or save it under the new name and then modify it to meet the remainder of the instructions. The first three lines, with an extra one to separate the import statement from the rest of the code, would therefore be:

```
import sys

word1 = sys.argv[1]
word2 = sys.argv[2]
```

After retrieving the words from the command line and assigning them to the variables, we can start comparing them. The first statement is supposed to test for equality, so that, looking back in our list of string operators, you'll hopefully have found that we need to use == for our comparison, thus making the initial if statement

```
if word1 == word2:
```

and the following, suitably indented block containing the print statement something like

```
    print("The words are equal.\nword 1\t" + word1
            + '\nword 2\t' + word2)
```

Please note that I've formatted the code here in a specific way to increase its readability, following the rules discussed in Section 2.5. In addition, to separate the descriptive texts from the words' values, I've also inserted a tab (\t) before outputting each variable. The alternative condition needs to test if the first word is, numerically speaking, less than (<) the second, so that the corresponding if statement and block would look like this:

```
elif word1 < word2:
    print("Word 1 comes before word 2.\nword 1\t" + word1
            + '\nword 2\t' + word2)
```

The final branch can of course simply start with an else, as it covers the remaining option, so we can write it in this way:

```
else:
    print("Word 1 comes after word 2.\nword 1\t" + word1
            + '\nword 2\t' + word2)
```

If you make any indentation mistakes, you'll probably see an error like

```
builtins.IndentationError: expected an indented block
```

However, if you're using the WingIDE, whenever you use inconsistent indentation, it will underline the line that is improperly indented with a wavy yellow line. This will already prevent you from making at least some indentation errors, although it may not catch all potential errors if you're using multiple nested conditions, in which case making a mistake in your indentation may well constitute a semantic error, anyway, which not even the interpreter may identify when you run the program. Please note, too, that not all IDEs will highlight potential indentation errors for you.

Discussion 17   Collecting Collocates from the User

While thinking about how you might write this program, you'll hopefully have realised that you've already learnt how to prompt the user for input, how to set up an empty list, and how to express conditions. What you haven't practised yet is how to establish the length of the list, but if you look at Table 3.2, you should easily be able to see that you can use the len function for this, using the name of your collocates list as an argument. From the same table, as well as the discussion below it, you should have been able to see that, in order to add the collocates you retrieve from the user input to that list, the most suitable way is to use the append method of the list. As far as working with the `while` loop is concerned, what you need to bear in mind is that, within its body, you need to be able to 'skip' over empty strings the user has provided, as well as to end the loop once the number of collocates that actually ended up inside the list reaches the required number 3.

Now that you're aware of all the above points, let's take a look at the actual implementation stages again. As a first step, we collect an initial input from the user and store it in a variable, ideally named `collocate`. Next, we need to set up the empty list that will hold the – presumed – collocates, which you can simply name using the plural form `collocates`, befitting a list. I say 'presumed' here because of course there's no guarantee that the user will in fact input genuine collocates, unless of course we already had a list to check against and could reject invalid ones on input. However, as even such a list may be incomplete and we might in fact be trying to compile one by eliciting potential collocates from many informants, we really don't want to constrain the options here. Hence, the first two lines prior to starting the loop could look like this, where, again, the first line is simply broken so that it'll fit the printed line:

```
collocate = input(
        'Please type in 3 collocates of the verb \'cause\'.\n')
collocates = list()
```

Now we can start the loop, to run as long as the number of collocates in the collocates list is less than three, making the loop head

```
while len(collocates) < 3:
```

When we first enter the loop, of course this list is still empty, so it's guaranteed to run. The first thing we need to check inside the loop body then is whether the user has really typed anything useful and not mistakenly simply pressed the Enter key. Given our current knowledge of how to handle string content, the only thing here we can sensibly test for is whether the string is empty, making our condition

```
if collocate == ":
```

Obviously, the above line needs to be indented by one level, as it occurs inside the block structure of the loop body. If our condition is `True`, we need to elicit another potential collocate from the user, making the statement inside the block associated with the condition[5]

```
collocate = input(
        'No collocate provided!\nPlease type one in.\n')
```

Otherwise (i.e. `else`), if the user input is assumed to contain a valid word, we can add this to the list of words, making the next two lines

```
else:
    collocates.append(collocate)
```

Inside the `else` block, however, we now need to test `if` we already have three collocates in our list, in which case we can end the loop, making the next two lines, naturally again at the right level of indentation,

---

5 From this point onward, I'll simply indent longer lines without referring to the reasons we already discussed.

```
if len(collocates) == 3:
    break
```

Make sure that you use two equals symbols in a row for comparison because otherwise you'll get a syntax error when you try to run the program. However, the IDE should already indicate that error to you via a red wavy line before you even start the program. Then, if we haven't yet collected three words, prompt the user for another collocate again, so that the alternative block should be

```
else:
    collocate = input('Please provide another collocate.\n')
```

The above lines complete the loop, so that we need to decrease the indentation level all the way again. All that's left to do now is to output the message and the collocates. The only thing you have to observe for this is that you need to provide the collocates list as the second argument to the `print` function. Concatenating the list with the message itself won't work because a string and a list are incompatible data types, so that if you tried to do so, you'd get an error message. If you absolutely wanted to use concatenation here, you could use the `str` function to create a string representation of the list, which, however, you get 'for free' automatically if you provide the list as an argument, so that this saves you additional typing. What we don't know at the moment is how to elegantly output the different elements of the list without having the list enclosed in square brackets with all the elements quoted. We'll learn about one way to do this in the next section, and about another, even more elegant one, in the next chapter.

Discussion 18   Transforming a List

This time, you won't necessarily know how to perform each of the sub-tasks of this exercise because we haven't discussed the string methods introduced in Section 2.3.1 in any detail yet. There, you'll find the `split` method listed, which is exactly what we'll need to transform the original input sentence into a list. Another string method you'll still be unfamiliar with, but which is not listed in that table, is the `upper` method. This allows us to transform the words into their uppercase equivalents. We'll discuss this, and some similar methods, in more detail in Section 4.6. What you should already be familiar with, though, is how to get the input from the user, as well as how to iterate over a list, based on the `for` loop syntax model. Now that we've discussed some of the basic requirements, we can again go through the steps in your program.

Prompting the user is something you've now done repeatedly, so it will no longer present any problems to you, and it would make sense to call the variable to hold the sentence just `sentence`, making the first line

```
sentence = input('Please input a complete sentence.\n')
```

If you've remembered that methods are called by attaching them to their object variables via a dot, you should also have had no problem in splitting the sentence into words and assigning them to a word list like this:

```
words = sentence.split()
```

As you might have guessed, if you provide no argument to the `split` method, the string is simply split at spaces, which is exactly what we wanted here. However, it's also possible to provide other strings as separators, e.g. for splitting a string of comma-separated values into its component parts. Creating the new empty list should be easy for you. You could simply write

```
cap_words = []
```

or

```
cap_words = list()
```

where `cap_words` is short for 'capitalised words'. Based on the syntax description, you can just as easily write the loop head as

```
for word in words:
```

and the simple loop body, containing only a single statement, as

```
cap_words.append(word.upper())
```

To add the words to the list, we had to use the `append` method here because we're only adding a single word object to the list each time. If you'd used `extend` instead, all the individual letters of the words would have been added separately to the list, and you would later not have been able to recreate a proper sentence. Feel free to try this out on your own.

Outputting the final uppercased sentence shouldn't represent a problem, provided that you'd picked up on my hint using the word *join* in the instructions, and used the corresponding method in creating the output like this:

```
print('The sentence in all-caps is:', ' '.join(cap_words))
```

Instead of using `join` here, you could of course have written a `for` loop to assemble the modified sentence. However, to achieve this aim, you would have had to concatenate all the words to a new string, each time adding the uppercased word and a space to the original variable, leaving the final variable with an additional space at the end. This space would still need to be deleted at the end, so that you'd have to write a few extra lines of code. How you could remove this extraneous space will be something you'll find out about in the next chapter.

4

Intermediate String Processing

We've been using string variables from the very first programming steps we took, and already know a fair bit about which methods and operators can be used with them. However, as pointed out before, this certainly isn't all there is to know about strings, so in this chapter, we want to expand our knowledge of how to process them, starting with a look at removing unwanted 'noise' in the shape of extraneous spaces that may interfere with our processing, etc. Next, we'll take a closer look at processing compound data types, as strings essentially consist of lists of characters, allowing us to understand how we can deal with sub-strings, i.e. parts of words that may constitute affixes, opening the door to morphological analysis. In these sections, we'll not only learn how to extract parts of strings, but also further options for handling case, as well as different ways of formatting our output. The latter essentially represents our first step in presenting potential results of our analyses, and can therefore equally be seen as a first step towards very basic data visualisation.

4.1 Understanding Strings

As there's no data type for characters in Python, strings always represent a sequence of 1-element Unicode code points. This makes them iterable like any other compound data type, i.e. it's possible to run a for loop over all characters, so that we could, if Python didn't already have a method for doing so, count all occurrences of a specific character or capitalise each one in turn. As the characters of strings form a fixed sequence, it's also possible to access them via their indexes, and even extract parts of the string using a general list operation called ***slicing***, which we'll discuss in Section 4.3.2.

Because strings are objects, they also have their own methods, some of which we've already used in our programs or shown above. Table 4.1 repeats some of these, but also adds a few more, without being fully exhaustive, though.

Table 4.1 More string methods.

Functionality	Methods
Enquire about properties of characters or strings	`islower()`, `isupper()`, `isdigit()`, `isalpha()`, `startswith()`, `endswith()`, etc.
Search through strings	`find()`, `rfind()`, `count()`, etc.
Manipulate strings	`upper()`, `lower()`, `split()`, `join()`, etc.

Python Programming for Linguistics and Digital Humanities: Applications for Text-Focused Fields, First Edition. Martin Weisser.
© 2024 John Wiley & Sons, Inc. Published 2024 by John Wiley & Sons, Inc.
Companion website: https://www.wiley.com/go/weisser/pythonprogling

Strings may also contain special characters, unless they're marked as ***raw***, which we'll discuss in more detail in Chapter 6. Two of these special characters that we've already encountered in our exercises are \n and \t. The former marks a line break, which is normally represented differently on different operating systems as:

- \r\n, i.e. (carriage) return + newline (Windows)
- \r (Linux/macOS)
- \n\r (older macOS)

However, when Python reads in a plain text file, even if it has been created on a different platform, it normally converts these to \n automatically, making it easier to use the same program on different OSes[1]. The latter inserts a (horizontal) tab(ulator) character, usually the equivalent of either 4 or 8 spaces, depending on the interpretation of the OS or any program displaying it, though many programs such as IDEs generally allow you to change the default value. As already hinted at earlier, this can be used for simple alignment in tabular form, or as a separator for data fields in file formats such as '.csv', where the extension is an acronym for comma-separated values despite the fact that most programs not only accept the comma as a separator, but will often handle data better if a tab is used. Sometimes, though, we may also encounter the lesser-known extension '.tsv', where the data is really expected to occur in tab-separated form.

Armed with this knowledge now – and before we continue looking into how to clean up strings –, let's spend some time again on which kinds of operations on strings may be useful in language-related processing tasks.

Exercise 19   Brainstorming the Potential of Strings

Think about which language-related operations you may possibly be able to carry out using strings, especially bearing in mind the methods listed and/or described earlier. Hint: It may be useful for you to look at some books or electronic texts to see which kinds of operations may need to be carried out to retrieve only the words making up the text, etc.

4.2 Cleaning Up Strings

As you'll have seen in the discussion of the previous exercise, the data we might want to work with isn't always as clean as we'd like it to be. This is why one of the most common tasks in dealing with strings that encompass units larger than words is to perform some kind of cleanup operation prior to being able to process them. Simple cleanup of strings is possible using one of three techniques, two of which we'll introduce here, deferring the third until Section 4.3.2.

The first is using the built-in strip method. This method removes items from both start and end of string at the same time. If used without arguments, it will remove all whitespace, e.g.

```
word = 'Word  '.strip()
```

to remove the two trailing spaces after Word in the above string. This also makes it ideal for removing any line end markers because these count as whitespace, too. If used with specific characters

---

1 An exception to this rule seem to be program files, which don't seem to get executed on some Linux systems if they originate on Windows.

as a string argument, all instances of the set of characters contained in this string will be removed, e.g.

```
heading_text = '2.3\tChapter 1 --...'.strip('23.\t -')
```

will produce the heading text Chapter 1 only from the original string, as all the characters specified in the set will be removed, regardless of the order they appear in. The variants lstrip and rstrip, respectively remove characters on the left (i.e. the beginning) or right (i.e. end) of the string.

The second option is to use the replace method to alter specified parts of strings regardless of where these parts occur, for instance replacing all line breaks by spaces, e.g.

```
'Line 1\nLine 2\nLine 3'.replace('\n', ' ')
```

Both techniques have (serious) limitations and can generally only be used if exact initial start and end conditions apply or can be tested for.

Exercise 20 Simple String Cleanup

Write the program 08_cleanup.py, in which you test the two different cleanup techniques for removing spaces.

First initialise a string with two words and two spaces at either end, as well as in the middle.

Use the print function, applying the strip method without arguments to this string (including a suitable message). The string variable itself should not be changed in the process.

Next, use a print statement, in which you also apply the replace method, this time with two spaces for the first argument and one space for the second, to this string (again with a suitable message).

In a third print statement, use the replace and the strip method, applying these to the string in turn.

In all three print statements, you should mark the beginning and end of the result in such a way that it would be apparent if any leading or trailing spaces remained.

Which conclusions can you draw from the results?

Now that you know a little more about simple forms of cleanup, we can move on to looking at how to deal with parts of strings in various ways.

4.3 Working with Sequences

4.3.1 Overview

Although I've already provided some basic information about sequences – i.e. lists, tuples, and strings – in Section 3.1, and we've gone into some more detail about one particular type, the list, in Section 3.2, we have by no means discussed everything that may be relevant in terms of the specific functions, methods, or possible operations they have in common. As we've already seen above, we can use the len method to determine their length, for instance to see how many characters there are in a word, how many words in a sentence, or how many lines in a poem, etc.

To perform simple counting operations on specific elements of sequences, we can employ the count method, e.g. to see how frequently a specific character occurs in a text stored as a string.

This may give us an indication as to the language the text may (or may not) be in, or, in the case of phonemic data, possibly if a learner uses an appropriate number of reduced forms in the reading of a set text if we test for a shwa or other possible vowel reductions.

Similarly, it's also possible to establish the highest or lowest values in a sequence via the max and min methods. Hence, if we had a list for storing the length of individual texts in a corpus, we could immediately tell how many words the longest and shortest texts contain, albeit not which texts these were. Interestingly, this will also work for non-numerical sequences, such as lists of words, where max would identify the word that occurs the furthest into the alphabet, whereas min would find the earliest.

To establish whether an element exists inside a sequence, we can make use of the in operator or its negation not in to see if it doesn't. Being able to do so not only allows us to compare e.g. word lists for the occurrence of specific words easily, but also has the advantage that we don't need to set up a separate loop to iterate over such lists in order to determine this.

All elements in a sequence can be accessed via their index positions, but what's even more important for us here is that we can also extract specific parts thereof, i.e. multiple elements, via so-called *slices*, where the name is of course a metaphor for cutting off/out specific parts. How to do so is what we'll discuss in the following section.

4.3.2 Slice Syntax

The basic syntax for working with slices is

```
sequencename[startposition:endposition(:stepwidth)]
```

where – as indicated through the round brackets – the step width is always optional, i.e. the second colon and value may be absent. Unless you ever have occasion to only extract every n^{th} item from a sequence, it's fairly unlikely that you'll use the stepwidth argument much using a positive integer value. However, as all arguments can also take on a negative values, using -1 for this argument will actually allow you to reverse a word, which is useful in creating lists of words or longer units of text that are sorted by their endings. This is something we'll discuss in Chapter 8. To present an example for the general usage, though,

```
word[2:6]
```

will extract four characters from a word, starting from third and up to the sixth, as the end position is always exclusive, which is important to remember. Hence, if our word were *impossible*, we would get the stem poss as a result. To illustrate this graphically, Table 4.2 shows the word and index positions, where those positions that are not part of the extracted slice are greyed out.

Table 4.2 Index positions for slices.

i	m	p	o	s	s	i	b	l	e
0	1	2	3	4	5	6	7	8	9

If the start value is absent, the beginning of string is automatically assumed, e.g.

```
word[:6]
```

yielding imposs. If the end value is absent, automatically the end of string assumed, so e.g.

```
word[2:]
```

will return everything from third character onwards, making the result `possible`. If the start value is negative, a position to the left of the end of the string is assumed, e.g.

```
word[-4:]
```

will produce the last four characters of the word, in our case the suffix `ible`. Now that you know that both start and end position can also be left empty, I can also present the full syntax for reversing the word, e.g.

```
word[::-1]
```

would produce the output `elbissopmi`. This output on its own of course doesn't make much sense to anyone reading it, but we'll learn in Chapter 8 how it may be employed for creating more sensible-looking output for reverse-sorted word lists.

Before we can embark on our next exercise where we'll practise how to use the slicing technique to work with prefixes, we first need to find out a little more about tuples, which we haven't discussed in any detail yet.

4.4 More on Tuples

Essentially, tuples represent a special form of list, that, unlike normal lists, is immutable. Hence, once we've created them, they cannot be modified without creating a new memory slot. Now, this may seem to only be a disadvantage considering that they basically share the same methods with lists, but their real advantage lies in the fact that, because they can never change, we'll always know their size and what positions all elements will occur in.

Tuples can be created by enclosing their comma-separated elements in round brackets, so e.g.

```
tags = ('adjective', 'adverb')
```

would assign the two word classes to a tuple, which could then be stored as a property of a word like *hard* once you've learnt how to do this. Alternatively, using the `tuple` function e.g. allows us to create a tuple from a list.

As we've already seen in the above example, tuples are particularly suitable for storing information that belongs together, e.g. fixed properties, or passing a number of fixed arguments, as we'll see in the next exercise, where we'll use a tuple as the argument to the `startswith` method of the string object. In addition, they also allow us to perform certain operations more efficiently, such as swapping the variable values from our very first real programming exercise, where the swapping operation could simply have been written as

```
(word1, word2) = (word2, word1)
```

without the need for a temporary variable. Forgetting about the immutability of tuples, however, is a not uncommon error, so that you may for example be tempted to write this

```
tags[1] = 'noun'
```

to add the word class to an existing tuple for the verb *run*, which would lead to the following error

```
builtins.TypeError: 'tuple' object does not support item assignment
```

Armed with our new knowledge about tuples, we can finally do the next exercise.

Exercise 21   Stripping 'Prefixes'

Write the program `09_strip_prefix.py`. In this program, the stem of words with selected 'prefixes' should be displayed to see if it's still recognisable after the operation and whether the presumed 'prefix' actually constitutes a prefix at all. The words to test should be hard-coded into the program in a single string for convenience, while the prefixes ought to be provided as one single argument on the command line, where the individual words are separated by commas.

As usual, before you start writing, think about how you could achieve this task given your current knowledge.

Then, in the first statement, retrieve a string from the command line containing comma-separated prefixes, use `split` to create a list from this, but immediately turn it into a tuple before assigning it to a tellingly named variable.

Next, create a string containing words with these prefixes, this time separated by spaces, and assign this to a suitable variable. Make sure that, for each prefix, you have at least two words. Also ensure that your string contains words that start with the prefixes {un} and {under}, {de} and {dis}.

Use a `for` loop in which you first `split` the string and then iterate over all elements.

Inside the loop, only stems for words containing the relevant prefix should be output (via slices).

To test this, you can first use the `startswith` method with the prefix tuple as an argument to weed out all cases in which the word doesn't contain a relevant prefix

Then use another nested `for` loop to iterate over all prefixes and test if the prefix actually occurs with the current word before outputting the presumed stem.

Test your program with different prefix combinations, at least once using the combinations listed under 3b) above. Which issue(s) do you encounter?

As we've just learnt and practised, the slice syntax makes simple extraction of strings of known length and position possible. However, apart from the fact that we need to be careful in assuming that given parts of strings we do extract actually represent the morphological constructs we're interested in, sometimes the exact position of such constructs may also be unknown, for instance with infixes. The solution to this problem is to use the `index` method to determine the starting position of the embedded string, and then apply the slicing, as we'll practise in the next exercise.

Exercise 22   Making Negative Statements Positive

Write the program `10_negative_to_positive.py`, in which the negator *not* should be deleted from negative-polarity sentences.

First, think about how you may be able to achieve this, given our newly developed experience in using slicing, as well as the information about infixes I just gave you above, even if the negator is not really an infix in the true morphological sense.

Start by defining a variable for the negator.

Again, set up a string in which you list a few declarative sentences, all containing *not*. Make sure that each sentence, apart from the last, ends in a full stop and a space, as you would do in normal writing. The final one should simply end in a full stop.

As in the previous program, iterate over a list of these sentences that you create using `split` with an appropriate argument.

Inside the loop, first test to see if the sentence still ends in a full stop. If not, append one to it.

Establish the index position for the beginning of the negator inside the sentence using the `index` method and store it.

To make it easier to see how we'll 'cut out' the negator later, set up two string variables with appropriate messages as parts of our final output. The first one should simply contain an indication that we're displaying the negated sentence, as well as the original, unmodified, sentence. The second one should equally contain an appropriate message, but followed by the modified sentence.

To extract the relevant parts to add to the second part of the message, use two slices, one from the beginning of the original sentence to the index position, and one starting after the end of the negator and running to the end of the sentence. Make sure, though, that you also 'delete' the remaining space after the negator.

Finally, use a single `print` statement with the two message parts as arguments to create the output. In order to separate the results for the different sentences better, add `end='\n\n'` as a third argument.

Now that we know multiple ways of 'splitting' strings, we can turn towards learning how to put them back together in more efficient ways than the ones discussed before.

4.5 'Concatenating' Strings More Efficiently

We already discussed the operators + and * for concatenating and repeating strings in Section 2.4.1. However, as I pointed out before, concatenation is not actually a very efficient means of combining strings as – due to the immutability of strings – each concatenation leads to a new variable being created. A better way of doing this, for instance in order to assemble lists of strings, such as word lists or 'sentences', is to use the `join` method I already showed you in Discussion 18, but am now formally introducing here. The syntax for this method takes some getting used to, though, as this method, unlike most of the other methods we've discussed so far, takes an arbitrary string as the basis for joining, and inserts it in between all elements of a sequence that is provided as an argument:

```
'string'.join(stringlist)
```

To get properly used to this unusual syntax, let's do another quick exercise.

Exercise 23   Joining Strings Efficiently

In the Python Shell, set up a list of words, and use the `join` method with different separators to `print` out different joined combinations of the words.

Try at least commas, line breaks, and tabs as separators to see how the results change. Otherwise, think of your own ways of linking the items together.

4.6   Formatting Output

Although we can of course join strings to use as intermediate values in our analyses and later discard them, sooner or later we'll usually end up creating some form of output from them that may need additional formatting to make the results stand out more clearly or be aligned to enable us to compare specific values at one glance. This is why programming languages like Python generally offer specific options to create such formatted output that not only allow us to take care of spacing and alignment of the values, but also to interpolate these. In other words, they allow us to insert the values of one or more variables in specific places in an output string, which is especially useful if you're re-using the same variable inside a loop.

Python essentially puts three options for this at our disposal that were added to the language at different times, and later options therefore often contain more flexible or advanced features. But even if I specifically advocate in this book that you use one of the latest versions of Python 3, you may sometimes also encounter older code written for Python 2 that you'll need to understand or convert, so that we'll discuss all options here, pointing out their advantages or disadvantages. This discussion will initially focus on the syntax of the individual options, while the detailed formatting choices that are possible are presented in Section 4.6.4 because they're common to all options.

4.6.1   Using the % Operator

Use of the % operator is the oldest and least flexible option for creating formatted output. It allows us to interpolate variable content from simple variables, tuples, or even calculated expressions into a formatted string by inserting % placeholders into a string and then providing a tuple of arguments following the % operator. This makes the general syntax options

```
'[string]%format' % value
```

for interpolating a single variable. The string in square brackets here, as well as in the following syntax options, represents optionality. An example would be

```
'The current word being processed is %20s.' % word
```

where the current value stored in the variable `word` is interpolated into the message string as another string, but padded with spaces on the left until a length of 20 characters is reached. Hence, if you're outputting words from a list in a `for` loop, these would be right-aligned below each other, making it easier to recognise them, and creating the impression of a simple table. The following syntax can be used for interpolating a tuple of values or a calculated expression:

```
'[string]%format' % (value(s)/expression(s))
```

Where of course multiple % placeholders in different places would be needed for a tuple of values, e.g.

```
'%s\t%5d' % (word, frequency)
```

which outputs word, a tab, and an integer frequency value padded to 5 digits. When multiple values are provided as input, it's important to have the corresponding number of placeholders in the string, as well as to remember that the values are interpolated in exactly the order they appear in inside the tuple. For expressions, the brackets are important because otherwise whatever gets interpolated may not end up being the result of a calculation, as can be seen in the following example, again copied from the Python Shell:

```
number = 10
'%d' % number * 2
'1010'
'%d' % (number *2)
'20'
```

Here, we take the number 10 as our starting point and first use this as an argument to interpolate into the output string without using the brackets. However, what this does is that it 'misinterprets' the * operator as being used for string repetition, rather than multiplication, thereby producing what looks like the number 1,010 that also gets interpolated into the output with that value, which is unlikely to be what we'd intended. If we use bracketing here, the multiplication is successful, so that we do indeed get the doubled value of the original number interpolated.

It's also possible to insert multiple items based on key–value pairs from a dictionary. The syntax for this, for the sake of presenting complete information, as we haven't really discussed dictionaries yet, would be

```
'%(key_1)s\t%(key_2)5d' % {'key_1':variable_1,
        'key_2':variable_2}
```

where each key on the left-hand side of the colon represents a name for a placeholder to be inserted. Note that, in this case, the order of our arguments is actually irrelevant because the value to be interpolated into the slots is always the one associated with the given key used as a placeholder.

4.6.2 The format Method

The second option, which was introduced with Python 3, is the more flexible format method of the str object. This method uses (numbered) placeholders in curly brackets, with optional format specifications following a colon:

```
'string {argument_index[:format]}'.format(argument(s)
        [,keyword_arguments])
```

Re-using the example of a word + frequency information from above, we could write:

```
'{0:{length}}\t{1}'.format(word, frequency,
        length=longest_word)
```

which outputs the word from position 0 in the argument tuple, left-aligned and padded to length of longest word, a tab, and the integer frequency value from position 1 in the tuple. Here, the keyword argument length – which we've defined ourselves – links to the variable longest_word. Due to the option for numbering the arguments in the formatted string, we already gain more flexibility in specifying the arguments, but also being able to specify variables for the format options increases the flexibility even further.

4.6.3 f-Strings

The third formatting option, introduced in Python 3.6, are *f-strings*. These are highly flexible, and allow interpolation of existing variables or expressions via curly brackets directly in string, so that no arguments are required at all. In order to create one, you write an ordinary string and simply prefix it by f or F, so the general syntax is

```
f'string {variable[:format]}'
```

where the format is, again, optional. An example would be

```
f'{word:{longest_word}}\t{frequency}'
```

which produces the same output as for `format` method we used above, only more elegantly.

4.6.4 Formatting Options

We've already used a few formatting options in the examples above, but so far without fully explaining any of the specifics. The first thing we need to know is that we can specify more precisely what data type the variable should represent inside the formatted output, so that suitable rendering options will become available. These data type indicators are

- s for string,
- d for integer, and
- f for floating point number.

For all of the above, it's possible to indicate the desired length and specify alignment indicators. Length values specify how much space should be reserved for a variable, and include spaces for padding. Length is indicated to the left of data type indicator, e.g. 25s for a string expected to be maximally 25 characters long, which would cover most word forms in English.

For floating point numbers, it's possible to indicate both precision and an overall expected length, e.g. 10.5f. If the overall expected length is not reached, then the string will also be padded by spaces; if it's exceeded, the number won't be truncated, though. If you want to pad by zeroes instead, you can use 010.5f. The same padding options also work for integers.

In order to achieve alignment, we can use the following – largely mnemonic – markers:

- < for left,
- > for right, and
- ^ for centred.

Using these alignment options represents a great way of achieving the impression of a proper tabular output, although it's always important to judge properly how much space is required for one's output. We'll especially see just how useful these options can be once we start creating word frequency lists in Chapter 8, but of course you can also make use of them for simpler tasks.

Sadly, being the least flexible formatting option, use of the alignment options is not possible using the % operator. To achieve alignment here requires you to employ the ljust, rjust, or center methods used on the respective arguments, with the appropriate length or padding specified.

4.7 Handling Case

Python offers different string methods for handling case. They're mostly useful for caseless comparison, i.e. to ensure that uppercase and lowercase characters are sorted together in alphabetical sorting, such as for creating dictionaries. We've already used one of these in Exercise 18, but Table 4.3 presents a more extensive list.

Table 4.3 Case handling methods.

Method	Functionality
`upper()`	Produces an all-uppercase copy of the string
`lower()`	Produces an all-lowercase copy of the string
`casefold()`	Like `lower()`, but also converts special characters like German *ß* to their equivalent spellings, e.g. *ss* for the former; umlaut characters are not converted to their equivalents, though
`swapcase()`	Produces a copy of a string where all upper- and lowercase characters are changed into their opposites
`capitalize()`	Produces a copy of a string where the first character is uppercased
`title()`	Produces a copy of a string where all-lowercase words are changed into words with initial capital

We'll explore the specific use of some of the above further in Chapter 8, but for now, let's just practise applying these methods to a single variable or string.

Exercise 24   Trying Out the Case-handling Methods

Again using the Python Shell and a slightly longer string of your choosing that contains both upper- and lowercase characters, test the case-handling methods described above in order to develop a sense of how useful they might be, and in which situations you may want to use them.

In this chapter, we've delved deeper into the particular properties of strings and their usefulness for linguistic processing, especially in terms of morphology. In addition, we've explored features that sequences in Python have in common, learnt more about one type of them, tuples, and investigated options for outputting formatted strings to improve the representation of our data. Last, but not least, we've discussed different ways of handling case, something that now allows us to work with one feature of standard orthography better, along with the basic knowledge of cleaning up strings we've developed. Now that we understand far more about strings, we can go on to start working with longer strings that represent whole files and are stored on our computers in the next chapter.

4.8   Discussions

Discussion 19   Brainstorming the Potential of Strings

As we've already seen and/or pointed out above, in the first instance, strings can be used for storing short items of text, such as words, affixes, or even only individual characters, as well as storing numbers as text, which then, however, need to be converted to a number if used in numerical operations. However, string variables can also contain considerably longer pieces of text, ranging from phrases via sentences, paragraphs, sections, chapters, to even whole texts. In some corpus formats that contain samples from different categories, e.g. the very first computerised corpus, the ***Brown Corpus***, some of the files even contain multiple sub-texts to arrive at the envisaged number of words in the sample. Likewise, it's possible for a whole corpus to be stored in a single plain text file, provided that the divisions are clearly marked.

To be able to extract pieces of text from such longer strings, we obviously need to have ways of splitting them using different criteria, such as textual elements that mark their divisions, e.g. spaces between words, but also such markers for longer divisions, such as the string *Chapter*, followed by a number, somewhere inside the text of a novel or other type of book. However, even if we may often be able to use markers like spaces to do the splitting, we still don't always just end up with the words only, as at least some of them will be followed by punctuation or enclosed in quotation marks. Likewise, clitic forms, such as *isn't* or *she's*, are joined by apostrophes, and we may variably want to treat these as one or two words.

At other times, there might be extraneous spaces or line breaks in the text, especially if the text has been extracted from a format such as PDF, which only describes its layout, but not the logical structure. This might require us to first (re-)assemble the relevant passages so that they actually become coherent, and we may then be able to extract the sentences or other textual units contained in them. Sometimes, such noise in the data could also come from the text having been scanned and automatically converted to readable text, but where the programs that produce the text may, depending on the state of the original text and their quality, not produce a desired outcome. Furthermore, even if we may already have electronic text, this text might have been formatted according to specific in-house rules by a publisher that aren't conducive towards extracting the words. One such convention, for instance in printed books that have been converted to an electronic form, is that long dashes may either be represented by two short dashes in a row (--), or that parenthetical structures may not contain spaces around hyphens, to try and retain an impression of the original layout. To understand some of these issues better, you can look at the following sample, where I've highlighted critical issues by using boxes around the relevant constructs.

Example 4.1   Extract from the Project Gutenberg Text of *The Glimpses Of The Moon* by Edith Wharton, Published 1922

⟨IT⟩ rose for ⟨them--their⟩ ⟨honey-moon--over⟩ the waters of a lake so famed as the scene of romantic raptures that they were rather proud of not having been afraid to choose it as the setting of their own. 'It required a total lack of humour, or as great a gift for it as ours, to risk the experiment', Susy Lansing opined, as they hung over the inevitable marble balustrade and watched their tutelary orb roll its magic carpet across the waters to their feet.

⟨'Yes--or⟩ the loan of Strefford's villa', her husband emended, glancing upward through the branches at a long low patch of paleness to which the moonlight was beginning to give the form of a white house-front.

In the above extract, we find two problematic issues. The first is that the initial word of the paragraph has been completely capitalised, which, as we've learnt before, essentially makes it different from the two forms of the pronoun *it* we might expect to find and handle in such as text. The second is what I already described above – i.e. that two dashes meant to symbolise long hyphens are simply fused with the words surrounding them –, so if we extracted words from this text based on spaces, we'd end up with rather strange compounds.

Once we have words or longer constructs, we may want to quantify these or parts of them. Here, we can of course, as we've done above, break sentences into words and then use the `len` function to see how many words are in the sentence, or test the length of each of the words using the same function to identify which one is the longest, or in order to extract only words of a given length or above. The results of both analyses can then be used as crude measures of complexity. Similarly, the length of a word may also give us an indication as to whether there could be any inflectional affixes present, as a word that is only three or four characters long is hardly likely to contain any affix. Hence, if we encounter the word *fish*, we'll hardly assume that it's possible to stem this to *f* in order to remove any potential derivational adjective suffix {ish}.

Looking more closely at what we can do with affixes, it should be obvious that, in order to identify or remove them, we first need to know whether they're present in a string or not, and if so, where they start and end. And once we know their start and end positions, we need to have ways of specifying which parts of the words should be removed or otherwise manipulated, e.g. in identifying the stem or base of a word, or to adjust them in such a way that we can add an affix, for instance in changing the adjective *happy* to the adverb *happily* where we first need to arrive at the stem {happi} and then add the suffix {ly} to it.

We'll still discuss means of carrying out some of these tasks in this chapter, but will defer some more complex tasks or efficient techniques for string manipulation until Chapter 6.

Discussion 20 Simple String Cleanup

Writing this program should now hardly present any challenges to you, as you've already repeatedly initialised strings and used them in `print` statements. Essentially the only thing that's really new for you is how you can 'chain' method calls in the third `print` statement in order to avoid an extra step involving a variable. In addition, you now also had to mark the string somehow in the output. Hence, the final code, as usual formatted for readability, could be:

```
string = '   word1   word2   '
print('strip method without arguments: >>'
      + string.strip()
      + '<<')
print('replace method: >>'
      + string.replace('  ',' ')
      + '<<')
print('both methods: >>'
      + string.replace('  ',' ').strip()
      + '<<')
```

Note how I use the double opening and closing angle brackets to highlight the beginning and end of the output string. In this way, it immediately becomes apparent that, in the second subtask, the replace method only succeeds in reducing the spacing between the two words in an appropriate manner, but still leaves an additional leading and trailing space in the output. This can be seen in the output listed for reference below.

```
strip method without arguments: >>word1   word2<<
replace method: >> word1 word2 <<
both methods: >>word1 word2<<
```

This way of highlighting information in the text by using doubled (or tripled) characters that rarely form part of ordinary texts already represents a very simple form of markup, which we'll discuss in greater length in Chapter 10, but will make more use of in a similar way in Chapter 6.

Looking at the output more closely, essentially the conclusion you can draw from the results is that neither method on its own may be ideal for genuine, everyday cleanup purposes, as such features as doubled, leading or trailing spaces are in fact very common in electronic texts, and you should constantly be aware of them, as well as which means you can employ for cleanup operations. However, as chaining string methods in this way is still rather cumbersome, and potentially also error-prone, we'll discuss far more efficient and flexible techniques for cleaning our data in Chapter 6, where we learn about more advanced options for string processing. Nevertheless, you'll still frequently find yourself making use of the `strip` method for removing unwanted line endings when dealing with files that are being processed line-by-line.

Discussion 21   Stripping 'Prefixes'

You certainly already know how to retrieve command line arguments and set up variables, so, basically, these two parts of the program should be easy to handle, although we'll possibly do so in ways you're still not used to. When you've thought about how to test for the potential prefixes, you'll probably also have realised that we'll need to iterate over the list of words and test – using an `if` statement – whether the current word in fact starts with one of our prefixes, and then, provided that this is the case, you extract the stem by removing the relevant prefix and displaying whatever we would assume to be the stem. So much for the 'theory', but let's now again look at how we can handle the actual implementation.

Before starting the main program body, you of course need to ensure that the `sys` module has been imported, making our very first line (excluding comments)

```
import sys
```

In the next line, you retrieve the argument from the command line – stored of course in `sys.argv[1]` –, apply the `split` method to it with a comma as its argument, and – in turn – make this the argument to the `tuple` function, storing the result in a suitably named variable. This line could hence look like this:

```
prefixes = tuple(sys.argv[1].split(','))
```

Here, you absolutely need to use the tuple function because the `split` method only creates a list, but the `startswith` method either expects a string or a tuple as argument, and we want to test for more than one string at the same time, so that we cannot use a single string. Thus, if you'd forgotten to use the `tuple` function, you would have received the following error:

```
builtins.TypeError: startswith first arg must be str or a tuple of
str, not list
```

Don't be confused by the reference to 'first arg' in the error, as the other arguments you could provide – but we'll ignore here – are a start and end position for the search. Naturally, it would also be possible to type a number of command line arguments that could then have been retrieved as `sys.argv[1:]`, excluding the program name, and turned into a tuple, but since I specified that they should be provided as one single argument, this wouldn't have been the correct way for this exercise. One other thing that's important in the solution I asked for is that there aren't any spaces after the commas because otherwise merely using the comma as an argument to `split` would have potentially returned words preceded by spaces that could never match any of the prefixes.

Which words to be tested for prefixes exactly you include in the hard-coded string variable is up to you, but my definition of the string variable looks like this:

```
word_string = 'delete destroy disappear disentangle dispel
download downsize overload overheat prefer preload reflect repeat
unheard unknown understand underwrite upend upload'
```

Note that, in the above, I've here kept the string as one single run-on line, rather than breaking it down into different lines, purely for the sake of convenience.

Setting up the `for` loop should not really present any problems to you anymore, bearing in mind that you ought to create the list to be iterated over on-the-fly via the `split` method for the sake of efficiency, rather than first creating a list variable and then iterating over that. The loop control should then look as follows:

```
for word in word_string.split():
```

Inside the loop body, we now test to see if any of the prefixes match the current word, which we do like this:

```
if word.startswith(prefixes):
```

because the `startswith` method allows us to test for the whole tuple of prefixes at once. This test allows us to establish whether the current word contains any of our prefixes, but not which one exactly, which is why we need another for loop to iterate over the prefixes like this:

```
for prefix in prefixes:
```

Note that we're here iterating over the tuple, just as we did for the list. However, since not all prefixes are likely to match the current word, even if multiple ones might, provided that one of these is longer than the other, but otherwise identical, and the extra character(s) still match the start of the word, we now need to test again to see if the presumed prefix is part of the word-start.

```
if word.startswith(prefix):
```

If the condition is true, we can now establish the length of the prefix using the `len` function, and use this as the starting index of a slice of the word variable, simply leaving the end index empty because we want to extract everything up to the end of the string, anyway, and output the result.

```
print('The stem of', word, 'is:', word[len(prefix):])
```

Again, it would of course be perfectly possible for you to calculate the length of the prefix first in a separate statement where you assign it to a variable. However, this being less efficient, we simply skip this unnecessary intermediate step.

One other thing you may now be wondering about is why we haven't included any `else` branches, i.e. alternative conditions, here. The simple answer to this is that we don't need to because there are no alternative actions to be taken if the conditions don't match, so we don't really need to specify anything, and the program simply continues with the next iteration. Of course, you could also add two additional `else` branches with `continue` statements in the relevant places without breaking the program, but this would only be redundant typing effort.

Looking at the output, you'll hopefully have realised that 'blindly' stripping away what we assume to be potential prefixes won't always leave us with the right stem. If you've used a similar set of words to mine, you can easily see this if you check on the 'prefixes' {un} and {under} at the same time, where, incidentally, you'll also see that two 'prefixes' of different length may match the same word, only that one of these cases won't really return the correct stem.

Discussion 22 Making Negative Statements Positive

Conceptually, this task should be relatively easy. You need to process each sentence, identify the starting position of the negator using the `index` method, extract a slice that contains everything before the negator, and concatenate that with another slice that starts at one position behind the negator and then runs until the end of the sentence. How exactly this may be done, and which issues we need to deal with along the way, we'll take a look at now.

Setting up the negator variable and the string to hold the sample sentences should present no issues, and could be done like this:

```
negator = 'not'
sentences = "This is not true. It's not a negative sentence. You
did not make a mistake here."
```

Setting up a for loop is something we've now done repeatedly, so, technically, this should also be easy. However, you need to make sure that you use the right string as a separator, i.e. `'. '` (full stop followed by one space), as this is the only criterion that will allow us to split our string into the proper elements to iterate over, making the loop control statement

```
for sentence in sentences.split('. '):
```

Unfortunately, though, this leaves us with all but the final sentences having no punctuation mark at the end, so that we're forced to add this to all pre-final sentences. This obviously requires a test to see if the full stop is not present, so that the conditional block (again usually with suitable indentation) would look like this:

```
if not sentence.endswith('.'):
        sentence += '.'
```

Extracting the starting position for the negator can easily be achieved like this:

```
indexPos = sentence.index(negator)
```

However, you definitely need to ensure that all your sample sentences in fact contain the negator; otherwise, you'll receive the following error if you try to use the `index` method on the sentence that lacks the negator, also causing your program to fail:

```
builtins.ValueError: substring not found
```

At the moment, we have no proper way to handle such errors yet, though, so we have to trust – or in this case, because we're providing the sentences ourselves, ensure – that whatever we use as input is well-formed. We'll learn how to handle such issues in Section 5.5. If you're curious and bent on solving problems independently, you might now delve into the Python documentation on strings and find out that the `find` method basically allows you to achieve the same thing as `index`, but without in fact throwing an error. Unfortunately, though, this won't work for us, either, as it'll return a value of -1 if it cannot find what it's supposed to look for, which will produce rather strange results if you try and use it to create the non-negated version of the sentence. You can test this yourself once we've finished creating the program. Having said that using `find` will not be an option to use in our program isn't entirely true, though, as at least having a return value to test against would allow you to set up a conditional block that, instead of completely causing the program to fail, would at least allow you to output a warning to the user that there's no negator present, and then use `continue` to jump to the next item in your iteration.

Returning to our original program, the next step would again be easy, as all it involves is creating a suitable message regarding the display of the original sentence, and appending this to it, hence

```
message_pt1 = 'Sentence with negation: ' + sentence
```

The really difficult part of this program then consists in using the appropriate syntax for extracting all the relevant parts form the original sentence, only leaving out the negator and the space that separates it from the following word. This step could be coded like this:

```
message_pt2 = ('\nWithout negation: '
              + sentence[:indexPos]
              + sentence[indexPos+len(negator)+1:])
```

Note that I've used brackets in the statement above in order to be able to break the individual lines to increase readability, as described in Section 2.5. In this statement, the slice in the second line takes everything from the beginning of the original sentence up to, but not including, the position where the negator starts, since the end position is exclusive, as we learnt in Section 4.3.2. To find the start position of the word following the negator, we need to add the length of the negator, which we calculate on-the-fly again, plus 1 position (`+1`) for the space after the negator, and make that the start position for the second slice, leaving the end position empty, so that – by default – we retrieve everything up to the end of the sentence.

Writing the final `print` statement is again not very difficult, and should look somewhat like this:

```
print(message_pt1, message_pt2, end='\n\n')
```

The third argument here is a so-called ***keyword argument*** for the `print` function, 'telling' the function that, instead if the default of a single newline, it should use two. We'll learn more about these keyword arguments in Chapter 7.

Discussion 23   Joining Strings Efficiently
This exercise in itself is not very challenging once you've become used to the syntax. However, it's certainly highly useful to see how the presentation of the output changes when you change the 'joiner'. If you use single spaces, you get a basic impression of a sentence, while using a tab character (`\t`) will actually make the output look like a simple table, and using the line break creates the effect of a listing or can be used to create multi-line strings.

Discussion 24 Trying Out the Case-handling Methods

This exercise should be easy to do, and you'll probably observe that, essentially, `lower` and `casefold` return the same results, unless you should have special characters like *ß* in your string. In fact, it's actually rather difficult to find good examples – other than the one already provided – for characters that will be changed because most of these will be special Unicode characters that you cannot easily type into the Python Shell. However, if you're dealing with data from complex scripts, it might well be useful to use `casefold`.

I personally cannot really see a reason for ever using `swapcase`, but its use is quite straight-forward. On the face of it, `title` appears to be a highly useful method for producing title case, e.g. in order to automatically create a heading, but as it actually capitalises every single word, including shorter function words that would never be capitalised in a proper heading, it's really not terribly useful, either. On the other hand, `capitalize` is rather useful because it'll allow us to fix the problem we had in not being able to represent our examples of syntactic inversion properly in Exercise 13 because we could now have the first word in the declarative capitalised, using `lower` to remove the capitalisation on the second word after swapping, but employing `capitalize` on the first word. The only problem that would then remain is if the first word were actually a proper name, which should of course not be decapitalised after swapping, but this is in fact a problem that could only be solved by testing to see if the word may not appear in a list of acceptable proper names before converting it to all lowercase.

5

Working with Stored Data

In this chapter, we want to explore how to access and process files that are stored on our own computer. To be able to understand better what's required in accessing such files, we'll begin with a brief discussion of the filing systems used for computer storage before moving on how to open, read, extract information from, and write files. Along the line, we'll also find out how to deal with some of the potential errors that may occur if e.g. a file name has been mis-spelt, etc., finally returning to the issue of dealing with file systems using specific modules in Python.

5.1   Understanding and Navigating File Systems

You'll probably already have encountered file systems through whatever GUI-based file manager is installed on your OS, Explorer on Windows, Finder on the Mac, and perhaps Nautilus or Konqueror on Linux. However, apart from perhaps having created some sub-folders in your user/home folder, you may not have thought much about the exact setup of the filing system on your computer. However, as I pointed out earlier, you'll soon need to understand this to be able to access files or folders from within you programs that are designed to handle any kind of stored data, which is why we'll start this chapter with a brief discussion of the most relevant facts.

All computer file systems represent the folder – sometimes still called directory – and file structures on your computer using a hierarchical arrangement as a tree. At the top-most level we always find the **root** of the file system. This, however, is initially all the three OSes discussed here have in common, as Windows uses different concepts from the other two platforms. However, even if you may not be working on Windows, you still need to understand these concepts in order to be able to write truly platform-independent programs.

Windows employs letters to refer to the **drives** or **partitions** a disk can be split into. Each of them receives a separate letter, some of which are fixed, some freely assignable. The root on each drive or partition here is abbreviated to \, and normally the main drive where the OS and programs are installed is the C:\ drive or partition. Figure 5.1 shows the folder structure for a drive with letter 'I', label 'data2', and three folders, each containing two to three sub-folders.

Python Programming for Linguistics and Digital Humanities: Applications for Text-Focused Fields,
First Edition. Martin Weisser.
© 2024 John Wiley & Sons, Inc. Published 2024 by John Wiley & Sons, Inc.
Companion website: https://www.wiley.com/go/weisser/pythonprogling

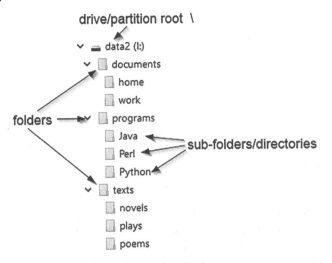

Figure 5.1 File hierarchy for a Windows drive.

macOS and Linux share the same concepts, as macOS is only a Linux system 'under the hood', but with a different GUI overlaid that actually hides many aspects of the OS from the user. On Linux, however, users generally have more access to different parts of the system, even though, for non-administrators, these may only be readable, but cannot be actively modified. On both macOS and Linux, we find no drive letters, but only mount points that are attached at different levels within the root, which is here represented as /.

5.1.1 Showing Folder Contents

Important tasks when working with the filing system on your computer are finding folders, listing their contents, and moving around between them. For these tasks, some of the commands we use on the command line may at times be quite similar between all three OSes, but sometimes also rather different.

Hence, on Windows, in order to display the contents of a folder in the command line window, we type `dir` (for *directory*) and press Enter. This will show lots of information about any files or sub-folders within the current folder, and is sometimes a little over-informative. To display more compact or targeted information, we can modify this command in different ways. To reduce the information to a minimum, we can use the /b (for *bare*) flag, which changes the output format accordingly. There are other possible flags, all equally preceded by a forward slash (/), but we don't need to discuss these here. Should you ever want to find out more about them yourself, you can always type `help dir`, and you'll be presented with a list of them. Figure 5.2 shows the output from both the unmodified (`dir`) and modified (`dir /b`) commands, one below the other.

```
 Directory of C:\Users\▮▮▮▮\programming

04/10/2022  15:19    <DIR>          .
04/10/2022  15:19    <DIR>          ..
04/10/2022  15:19    <DIR>          code
04/10/2022  15:19    <DIR>          texts
              0 File(s)              0 bytes
              4 Dir(s)  167,453,786,112 bytes free

C:\Users\▮▮▮▮\programming>dir /b
code
texts
```

Figure 5.2 Folder content display on Windows.

Which folder will initially be shown to you may depend on the exact version of Windows and who you're logged in as, but it's usually either your user folder, generally C:\Users*username*, or C:\WINDOWS\System32.

On macOS or Linux, the appropriate command is `ls` (for *listing*). In contrast to the unmodified `dir` command on Windows, this provides little additional information, and you need to use the flag `-al` to get more detailed output. Note also how the flag as a modifier here is not indicated by slash, but a hyphen. Figure 5.3 again shows the two different options.

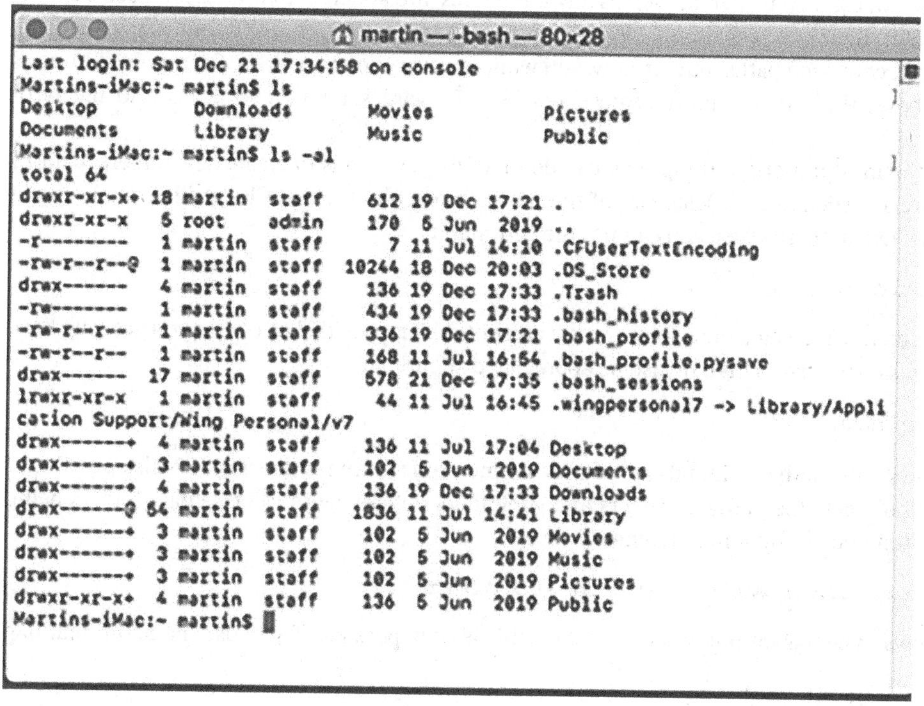

Figure 5.3 Folder content display on macOS.

On both MacOS and Linux, normally the user home folder (/home/*username*) is shown when the default terminal is opened.

By default, both the `dir` and `ls` commands output the complete contents of the current folder as a list of folders and files, apart from perhaps hidden files, but it's also possible to display the contents of other folders by providing a **path**, or to restrict the listings to files or folders that match specific criteria, such as starting with a specific letter or being of a specific file type. We'll learn more about paths in the following paragraphs, but for specifying file patterns, you should know that it's possible to use so-called **wildcards** in order to create them. These wildcards are the asterisk (*), which stands for any number of characters, and the question mark, which represents a single letter. This way, you can, for instance, only have files/folders listed that start with ex, as in *exercise*, by specifying ex* as an argument to the file name, generally following any flags. Similarly, if you wanted to find all Python files in a folder, you could type *.py? because Python programs generally have the extension .py, but sometimes also .pyw.

5.1.2   Navigating and Creating Folders

When dealing with file paths, we need to distinguish between ***absolute*** and ***relative*** ones. Absolute file paths are essentially composed of a root element, followed by any number of intermediate folders, and, finally, a file name, e.g.

- C:\temp\texts\text01.txt (Windows) or
- /temp/texts/text01.txt (macOS/Linux),

while folder paths simply lack this final element. On Windows, absolute paths start with the drive/ partition letter, e.g. C:\. Folder, as well as any file names, are attached to this after a backslash (\) as a separator, their exact location depending on their level in the tree. We'll soon start practising how to work with such paths, but for now, still want to cover the other OSes. On macOS/Linux, as we saw above, the root is simply represented by a forward slash (/), which is also the ***path separator***.

One of the most important things you can do in a filing system is to create new folders to allow you to store a particular (sub-)category of files in them, such as the text files we'll be analysing in due course. On all three OSes, you can use the command

```
mkdir foldername
```

to do so, which will create a new folder in the current folder, provided of course you actually have write permissions there. This can also be abbreviated slightly to

```
md foldername
```

on Windows only. Both commands are of course mnemonic for *make directory*. It's also possible to create a whole new hierarchy of folders and subfolders directly, with intermediate folders being created automatically, by simply typing

```
m(k)d(ir) folder\subfolder\sub-subfolder
```

on Windows, whereas on the other two OSes, this is only possible if you use the additional flag -p, i.e.

```
m(k)d(ir) -p folder/subfolder/sub-subfolder
```

on macOS/Linux. If you forget to add this flag, you'll simply receive an error message saying that "No such file or directory" can be found and the folder hence not be created. You can also delete folders again, but of course should always do so with extreme caution! The common command for this is

```
rmdir
```

on all OSes – for *remove directory* –, which can again be abbreviated on Windows to rd. As before, deleting multiple folders at once on macOS/Linux requires the -p flag, but even Windows won't allow you to delete a whole (sub)tree at once, so that you'll need to use the flag /s to achieve this, as otherwise only final subfolder in the tree will be removed.

To move between folders, all OSes use the cd (*change directory*) command, so

```
cd folderpath
```

changes to specific folder. On macOS/Linux, because there's only a single root, this can be any folder, whereas on Windows, this folder needs to reside on the active drive/partition. If it isn't, you'll need to change to the other drive first by typing the drive letter, followed by a colon, and pressing Enter, e.g. I : to change to the drive shown in Figure 5.1. To change to one's home folder, the appropriate command is either

- `cd %homepath%` (Windows) or
- `cd` or `cd ~` (macOS/Linux)

On macOS/Linux, the prompt for your home folder should show a tilde symbol (~) or the complete path `/home/username`. If the exact path is not shown, you can use the

`pwd`

(*print working directory*) command to display it. To move to the root folder, we simply use `cd`, followed by the respective path separator, i.e.

- `cd \` (Windows), and
- `cd /` (Mac/Linux).

Let's practise some of these commands, so you can familiarise yourself with navigating the folder hierarchy (see Exercise 25).

Exercise 25   Working with File Systems (a)

Open the command line for your OS.
Based on the path prior to the prompt, check to see if you're already in your home folder.
If not, change there to ensure that you've got write permission, then change to the `programming` folder where you've stored our earlier programs.
Create a new folder named `code`, open up your file manager, and move all the programs you've written so far in there.
Create a new folder named `texts` with a sub-folder `output`.
List the contents of the `texts` folder, using both the long and short forms, and see if you can understand all the information presented there.
Change into the sub-folder `output`.

5.1.3   Relative Paths

As already stated above, paths can be specified both as absolute – e.g. `C:\Users\username\texts\output` (Windows) or `/home/username/texts/output` (macOS/Linux) – or relative. We've already covered absolute paths in some detail above, so we now only need to learn about relative ones, which allow us to specify an abbreviated path, relative to current folder, and where we don't need to know the names of any parent folders. This is where the single and double dots that we encountered in the previous exercise come in. The `.` is a reference to the current folder, and you'll need to use this if you want to start your own programs on the command line on macOS or Linux; otherwise you'll get an error saying "command not found". In other words, if you wanted to start a program somewhat unimaginatively named `myProg.py`, you'd instead have to use the relative path `./myProg.py`. The `..` is the corresponding reference to the parent folder, and allows you to conveniently move up one or more levels in the folder hierarchy without needing to know, or explicitly specify, the names of any of the parent folders. For instance, in order to change to the parent folder of our `output` folder, all we need to type is `cd ..` instead of e.g. `cd C:\Users\username\programming\texts` or `cd ~/programming/texts`.

Exercise 26   Working with File Systems (b)

List the contents of the parent folder, first using an absolute path, then a relative one.
Using a relative path, change into the folder two levels above the folder `output`.

Now that we have a basic understanding of file systems and how to navigate them, we're ready to start working with data stored on our computer.

5.2   Stored Data

When we process data, the most common storage form for us is that of individual files, but sometimes the content to be analysed may also be stored in databases. Dealing with the latter, however, is not covered here because it represents a rather advanced topic. The particular files we may want to process for language analysis are normally text files, but could also be binary files, such as audio or video files, or files originating from the internet, which we'll discuss in Chapter 10, at least to some extent. As this book is focused on texts, though, multimedia data will also not be covered here.

Handling stored data generally also requires working with folder structures – i.e. reading, creating, and navigating – and partly also involves file permissions. This makes handling files a rather error-prone process because access is not always guaranteed, especially if you're working on a shared computer. Hence, without suitable error handling, handling files and folders can easily lead to errors and program crashes, which is why we'll discuss error handling in Section 5.5. First however, we'll learn how to open and close files.

5.3   Opening and Closing Files

As almost everything in Python, files are also objects (type: `file`) with their own methods. Before we can in fact work with a file, we need to ensure that we can access and work with its contents, in other words, open it. There are a number of different modes for opening files for different purposes, but we'll only introduce the ones that are most important for us. Before we do so, though, let's spend some time again brainstorming on what we may need to be able to do with files in our work, and which type of access this may require.

Exercise 27   Brainstorming the Options for Working with Files

Think about what kinds of things you may need to be able to do with files at different stages of working with them.
When you do so, perhaps it's easiest to think of them not only as electronic objects, but rather also a book or some other type of publication that you might want to work with.

Now that you should have developed some ideas about what files may be used and useful for, we can discuss the relevant basic access modes Python provides. Once we understand these, we can then go on to discuss how to actually open and close the files.

5.3.1 File Opening Modes

The file opening modes you minimally need to know about are:

- r: opened for read-only; default.
- w: opened for write access; non-existent files are created, if possible; already existing files are overwritten!
- a: opened for appending (normally to the end of the file).

The default for opening is in text mode. This can also be made explicit by appending t to the general mode. If files are to be opened in binary mode, i.e. to access a specific number of bytes at a time, b needs to be appended to prevent the file from being treated as text.

5.3.2 File Access Options

The modes described above can be specified as mode attributes to the open function, which is used to gain access to the file until it's closed. There are two different access options, one to open the file object, process its contents, and close it manually using the close method:

```
filehandle = open(filename/path
      [,mode='mode']
      [,encoding='encoding'])
processing instructions
filehandle.close()
```

As you can see in the syntax synopsis above, here we need to use a variable to store a handle on the file object that we can then refer to once we've opened it. As indicated, all you absolutely need is the file name, or rather a path to the file. If you don't specify the mode string, it will automatically default to r, and the encoding to the default encoding specified for your OS. As accepting the latter may lead to complications when exchanging files between computers set up for different countries, we'll generally specify the encoding keyword argument, setting its value to utf-8. Once the file has been opened, you can use the various methods for accessing files described further below to extract all or parts of the text, using the file handle.

With this first access option, you explicitly need to employ close on the file handle once you've accessed the file contents. If you forget to do so in a shorter program where you only open one file, this won't be a problem because the file will automatically be closed once the program ends. However, in a longer program – where the same file handle may be used multiple times – this could lead to unforeseen errors in your program, which is why it's best to either make it a habit to close all file handles explicitly, or use the more modern syntax for opening files with automatic closing:

```
with open(filename
      [,mode='mode']
      [,encoding='encoding']) as filehandle:
      block for processing
```

The option shown above involves the so-called ***context manager*** through the use of with, and linking an object to it through as. Linguistically speaking, we could say that this object then becomes the focus of attention or topic, and everything that is then being stated within the context – given in the form of a block – applies to it. Once that block finishes, the file handle is automatically closed. In this way, it also becomes possible to open multiple files concurrently, and their file contents can even be processed in parallel via the `zip` function.

In general, I'd recommend using the context-manager version, as the file not only gets closed automatically, but the block also makes it clearer what happens with the file while it's being held open. Whichever way you choose, though, both options should always be complemented by suitable error handling techniques, which we'll discuss in Section 5.5, once you know how to read file contents.

5.4 Reading File Contents

As with the mode and access options, there are different methods we can call on a file handle/ object to achieve different purposes, and depending on how much memory we can use.

Perhaps the most intuitive method of these is

```
read()
```

which, without any argument, reads the whole file at once into a string variable. This is particularly useful if we want to perform global replacements, etc., something we'll explore in more depth in the next chapter. When processing huge files, though, this may consume a lot of memory. Luckily for us, though, the files we're likely to be processing most of the time won't be huge from a memory point of view, even if they may contain a few hundred pages of text. If used with an integer number as argument, this method reads that many characters from the file, which is generally less useful for us, so we won't discuss it any further.

The next option is to read a single line from the file, and is achieved via the

```
readline()
```

method. This is particularly useful if the file contains structured information and there is certain amount of meta information present that we need to discard before being able to access the actual text proper. To be able to picture this better, you can think of the front matter of a book, which contains all sorts of information, including the title, author, year of publication, etc., as well as a table of contents, which aren't really useful for us if all we're interested in is the text itself, so we'd want to skip over those parts. However, in some circumstances, it may also be necessary to extract this meta information, for instance if we want to create some kind of bibliographical reference, or store such information in some form of database describing the texts we're working with.

Used without an argument, `readline` reads a single line (at a time)[1]. This can be useful to skip *n* lines, e.g. a file header (i.e. the 'front matter') of a fixed length, using a loop.

The third option for accessing files,

```
readlines()
```

again involves reading the whole file content, but instead of storing everything in a single string, it reads all lines at once, storing them in a list. If files are naturally structured into lines, such as in a file containing a poem, we can make immediate use of this to process each line. In other cases, because a line in a file is essentially nothing but a string of text that ends in a newline, such 'lines' might actually represent paragraphs that we may then break down into sentences using punctuation marks as splitting criteria. We'll explore options for handling cases like these in this and future chapters.

---

1 Used with an integer argument, it reads as many bytes only, which is rarely useful.

The final possibility we want to discuss here is somewhat similar to the preceding one. Rather than actually splitting the file into a list when it's read in, we can simply perform an iteration with a `for` loop over the file itself, as a text file object in fact represents a list of lines. Hence, we can simply write

```
for line in filehandle:
    block of statements
```

This is highly useful and simple for processing files line-by-line, and saves on memory, especially with larger files, as the file contents don't even need to be stored in a list or string.

The methods described above seem to be more or less straightforward ways of dealing with file contents. Yet, as I've already indicated above, processing text files isn't always as clear-cut as you might think. In some cases, such as when one has extracted text from PDF files where the line breaks don't occur at logical points in the text structure, but rather in places where the line needed to be broken in order to be able to fit the text onto a page, one has to find ways of 'gluing' the relevant pieces of text back together and then extract sensible textual units. If this isn't done properly, one may end up with similar problems to the ones I pointed out in Discussion 19.

5.5 Error Handling

Errors that occur while working with files may be based on a number of different factors, such as a wrong path or file name, i.e. path or file doesn't exist or is mis-spelt, a lack of permissions for reading and/or writing, etc. In these cases, Python will throw an `OSError` with an associated error object. To try and catch any such error before it occurs, we use the keyword `try`, followed by a block in which we attempt to open the file. Hence, if we wanted to open a file, read all lines, and simply output them again to the command line before closing the file handle, we could write

```
try:
    in_file = open('./file.txt', mode='r', encoding='utf-8')
    lines = in_file.readlines()
    print(''.join(lines))
    in_file.close()
```

Handling an error, if it does indeed occur, should be done inside an `except` block, where the error object that can be stored via

```
OSError as error objectname
```

and you can then choose to either report the error to any other parts of the program that need to deal with it or – if the file you're trying to open is crucial to the running the program – terminate the program. Storing the error in a variable is essentially optional, but different types of error also report varied types of useful information that may be presented to the user to indicate what went wrong, so it's usually advisable to do so. As the error is in fact an object and not a string, we also need to cast it to a string using the `str` function before we can use it to create any messages, e.g.

for our example above, if the file name were incorrect and the file could hence not be opened, we could trap the error by writing

```
except OSError as err:
     print(str(err))
```

which would continue running the program, simply printing out the error if the file hadn't been found, and then stop because we hadn't specified anything after the `except` block. If, instead, we'd tried to output the lines on a line following the `except` block, though, there would have been another error because then there wouldn't be any lines in the list of lines, and the program would still have crashed.

For larger programs, where e.g. a number of files may already be open or some operations need to be completed before terminating the program, sometimes also a `finally` block may be defined in order to perform 'cleanup operations', but we won't need to use this feature in our small programs.

The complete syntax for exception handling, no matter whether this concerns opening files or other activities that may cause errors, is

```
try:
     statement(s)
except [error_type as error_object]:
     statement(s)
finally:
     statement(s)
```

Table 5.1 shows a list of the most common error types you're likely to encounter, along with some explanations as to what their causes may be. This will hopefully already give you a good idea what types of issues you should learn to anticipate, even if these may only be discussed later as and when they're likely to arise in our programs.

Table 5.1 Common error types.

Error type	Description
NameError	Occurs if a variable hasn't been defined, has been mis-spelt, or when a variable or object wasn't instantiated to a correct value
SyntaxError	Indicates that markers for data types, such as quotes or brackets, haven't been used or completed properly, or that there's a colon missing before the start of a block
IndentationError	Occurs if a block isn't indented at the right level
ZeroDivisionError	Indicates an attempt to divide by 0
IndexError	Flags an attempt to access a non-existent index position, e.g. frequently if required program arguments don't exist in sys.argv because they haven't been provided on the command line
ImportError or ModuleNotFoundError	Shows that a function/method or module cannot be found or loaded
KeyError	Occurs if a key cannot be found in a dictionary
OSError	Indicates that a path or file name couldn't be found, or permissions are insufficient

Let's now use our newly gained knowledge about reading file and error handling in another exercise.

Exercise 28   Reading from a File (a)

Create a new file named `11_read_file_a.py` in your code folder.
Download the archive texts.zip from http://www.wiley.com/go/weisser/pythonprogling, extract the file called `sample_sentences.txt`, and store it in your `texts` folder. You'll be using this file for testing this program, as well as some other programs we'll write later.
In the first program step, retrieve the file name from the command line as an argument.
Try to open the file for reading using the first option described, assuming that the correct relative path to the file has been provided, and with suitable encoding.
If an error should occur while opening, store the error object in a variable and end the program inside of the block using the `sys.exit` function and the variable – cast correctly – as its argument.
If no error occurred, read the lines in the file using the `readlines` method of the file object and store these in a list.
Write a `for` loop with a tuple containing a variable for the line number and one for the respective line on the left-hand side of the `in` operator and on right-hand side the `enumerate` function with the list as its argument. This function generates a tuple consisting of a running number and the respective list element.
Inside the loop, output a suitable message, the line number and the current line, bearing in mind that the number first needs to be converted to a string using the `str` function unless you're using an f-string.
Test your program, first using the correct file name for your text file, but also once changing the name to something that doesn't exist in your folder.
When you observe the output of the correctly running program, what do you notice that could be improved and how?

Now that you've practised how to open files and then close them again manually, we can explore the next option.

Exercise 29   Reading from a File (b)

Save a copy of the last program as `12_read_file_b.py` and rewrite in such a way that the file will be opened via a context manager.
Inside the `with` block, the complete file should be read into a string.
Note that, in this case, the error handling can only occur after the end of the `with` block, with the file being closed automatically.
Rewrite the `for` loop in such a way that a list is created via the `splitlines` method of the string, again creating the tuple using `enumerate`.
When you create the output, also ensure that you reserve two spaces for the number and right-align it, so that the output looks neater. To do so, make use of the formatting options we discussed in the last chapter.

Last, but not least, let's also practise treating the file as a list of lines.

Exercise 30   Reading from a File (c)

Rewrite the previous program again (as `13_read_file_c.py`), this time iterating over the file within the `with` block, again using `enumerate`.

Which of the above forms of handling files you'll use for your own purposes will probably depend on what exactly you need to do with the file contents, but at least you should now be aware of all the options at your disposal, and we can soon move on to discussing how to write to files.

Before we turn to writing, though, we first have to cover a different way of handling errors, rather than taking immediate action as we've done in our programs so far by calling `sys.exit` with information about the error. In larger, more modular programs, we may need to pass the relevant information on to another module, which is done by using the keyword `raise` with an appropriate error type and message.

5.6   Writing to Files

As for reading from files, there are also multiple options for writing to them. To be more precise, we have two options that may be appropriate for different purposes. The first is the

```
write()
```

method of the file object, which can either be used to write a file as a complete string in one go, or add to the file incrementally line-by-line, e.g. in a loop, until you've finished creating your output. The first of these actions may e.g. be carried out if you've made global replacement to the whole file and want to store the output, or if you've written an editor using the GUI elements we'll discuss in Chapter 9, and want to save a file that has been edited in it.

The second option is to use the

```
writelines()
```

method, which takes a list of lines as its argument and writes these out in one go. Unlike `print`, though, both of these methods don't automatically add line breaks, so you need to ensure that the lines you're writing to the file are properly terminated in order to avoid creating run-on text.

Now that we know how to read from and write to a file, let's practise this by creating a little copy program. In the form our program will take, it's not really terribly useful (yet), but the exercise will at least allow you to understand the basic mechanisms of non-destructive file processing. We'll later explore more advanced ways of creating file output that are more appropriate for our language-processing tasks.

Exercise 31   Copying a File

Write a program `14_copy_file.py`, in which you open a file and output it into another. Both file paths should be passed as arguments on the command line, and both files be opened using a single `with` statement, with the individual calls to `open` being separated by a comma. Inside the `with` block, you should then iterate over the lines of the input file and output these into the other file.

When you test the program, first use a file path that points to the `output` folder inside your `texts` folder, then also pretend that you accidentally provided the same file path for both input and output, and observe what happens.

After the previous exercises, you should have a suitable grasp of how to deal with file contents, so we can now move on to learning how to work with file locations outside the current folder.

5.7 Working with Folders and Paths

As we've seen earlier, access to the program folder is generally unproblematic, but for many other operations, interaction with file system via different modules is necessary. For instance, we may need to read the contents of folders to find out which files exist, create new folders to store data in changed form, delete files or folders, etc. Just like working with file names, which essentially only represent simple, short file paths, working with longer paths generally requires error handling, and will also throw OSErrors if something goes wrong. In the following sub-sections, we'll discuss two different approaches to dealing with paths and folder structures.

5.7.1 The os Module

Perhaps the most important module to know about when handling paths and folders is the built-in os module, which can simply be imported via

```
import os
```

This module provides options for basic interaction with operating systems, but normally requires use of operating system specific path separator, i.e. / for Linux/macOS X and \ for Windows, which makes it a little inconvenient for cross-platform development. To make it easier to handle the separator, the module provides access to a special variable, os.sep, which can be used in concatenating path names. However, the os.path submodule also provides a number of functions that allow you to split or join paths more efficiently from their various components, as well as to extract specific parts of the path, so it's preferable to use those. Below, I'll describe a number of useful functions from both the top-level and path sub-module.

The listdir function returns the contents of a folder specified as its argument as list, but unfortunately doesn't distinguishing between files and folders. For example, using it on the 'texts' folder of the drive shown in Figure 5.1 earlier – of course after using import os first in my Python Shell – produces the output shown in the second line below:

```
print(os.listdir('I:\\texts'))
['info.txt', 'novels', 'plays', 'poems']
```

Here, the listing[2] shows not only the three sub-folders 'novels', 'plays' and 'poems,' but also a single file named 'info.txt' that I'd specifically created inside the 'texts' folder beforehand. Used without argument, listdir defaults to the current folder. The same goes for scandir, which returns an iterator over the folder entries as objects that can then be queried for their properties, e.g. object.name. When an individual entry is selected inside the iterator, we can also identify whether it's a folder, using the is_dir method, or a file, using is_file.

Dissecting a path can be done via os.path.split, which returns a tuple of file path and name, if the latter exists, e.g.

```
os.path.split('I:\\texts\\info.txt')
```

---

2 Note that I've here escaped the path separator for the Windows path to ensure that the \ is understood as a path separator and not as the beginning of a tab character.

will return

```
('I:\\texts', 'info.txt')
```

This is particularly useful for processing all files in an input folder and using the file names to generate modified copies inside an output folder. To generate an output folder name from an existing path, we could use the path part of the tuple and concatenate it with the name of an existing folder, to which we could then append the file name again to end up with a full file path for the output file. To perform this concatenation efficiently, and without the need to worry about separators, we can employ os.path.join with a list of path components. Of course, if the output folder whose path name we've created as an intermediate step didn't exist yet, we'd first have to create it, which we'll soon explore as well. To test if a path does exist, you can use os.path. exists. The os.path sub-module also offers functions for dealing with absolute and relative paths, etc., but we won't discuss these here.

Exercise 32   Reading from a Folder

Write a new program 15_read_folder_contents.py to output the contents of the current program folder, separated into folders and files.
To do so, first set up two lists for the two types of object after the module import.
Use scandir to process all elements in the folder in a loop, and store them, depending on their type, inside the appropriate list.
To add the elements to the lists, use the append method of each list.
Output the contents of the two lists, following a suitable message indicating each type, each time only outputting the names of the elements if any may be present.
For the print statements indicating the type, you can improve the formatting by changing the end keyword argument of this function so that two line breaks follow the message.
As an additional exercise, think about how you could re-write this program so that it would allow you to list the contents of any folder provided as a command line argument, including any potential additional error handling and/or tests.

Even though the os module functions will allow you to deal with most path-related issues, they can be a little more complex, so we'll next take a brief look at part of another module that simplifies these processes a little.

5.7.2   The Path Object of the libpath Module

The Path object of the libpath module may be more suitable for complex path operations, as it e.g. permits providing paths safely using /, even on Windows. It's imported via

```
from pathlib import Path
```

Creating a new path object can be achieved easily via e.g.

```
path = Path('./test')
```

Again, this doesn't mean that the path now physically exists on your system, but only that you have a reference for it that will allow you to find out whether it exists, using the exists method of the Path object, or to create it using the mkdir method, modelled on the OS command we're already familiar with. By default, this method only creates a single folder without parent folders, if these don't exist yet. However, by using the `parents` keyword argument and setting it to `True`, we can also force the creation of intermediate folders.

New paths can also simply be generated from old ones, e.g.

```
newDir = path / 'test'
```

where the slash acts as a concatenation operator for joining paths together. Path objects created in this way can also be used with functions of the `os` module, but first need to be cast to a string.

A few more useful methods of the `Path` object are:

- `cwd()`: find the path/name of the current folder;
- `home()`: identify the path/name of the user folder;
- `iterdir()`: iterate over folder contents;
- `rglob(pattern)`: compile a list of all files matching a specific pattern recursively, i.e. including the contents of all subfolders, e.g.
  `pythonfiles = path.rglob('*.py')`.

The methods `is_file` and `is_dir`, as well as the `name` attribute, also apply to elements identified via `iterdir`, just as with `scandir` of the `os` module.

Let's now also practise applying the `Path` object to handling file paths in a copy operation.

Exercise 33   Copying to a Backup Folder

Write the program `16_copy_to_folder.py`, in which you create a subfolder named `backup` in the current program folder and copy one of your program files there.

To do so, import the `Path` object from the `pathlib` module, and read in the file name from the command line.

Store the current program path in a suitable variable, using the appropriate method of the `Path` object (see above).

Create a new path for the `backup` folder and store it in another variable.

Create a new path for the output file from the path for the backup folder and the name of the input file.

Using the appropriate method with the folder path created above, test if the backup folder already exists.

- If not, generate it using the appropriate method of the `Path` object, and output a suitable message. Don't forget to handle a potential error in case the folder cannot be created, though.
- If it does, simply output a suitable message.

Finally, as in the previous copy program, copy the file again, only this time using the new path for the output file, first converting the path object for the file to a string.

In this chapter, we've covered the essentials of working with stored data, starting by developing an understanding of file systems on the computer and how they relate to our work with data, then moving on to how to read and write from files, and, last but not least, how we can handle file paths and folder structures for non-destructive processing of data. This will now allow us to continue developing our skills in identifying patterns worth noticing in our data that we'll then be able to extract from or mark in files.

5.8 Discussions

Discussion 25   Working with File Systems (a)

If you've followed the steps described above closely, most of this exercise should present no problems, at least up to the point where you've changed to or ensured that you're in your home folder, where you should always have write permissions. There, all you need to do is type `cd programming` and press Enter. To simplify the following explanations, I'll always use the command that is common to all OSes, simply adding specific flags as and when necessary.

In order to create the new folder structure, you of course have two options, the first being to create all the folders step-by-step, and the other to specify the tree structure for the folder containing the sub-folder directly. For the first option, there are actually multiple ways to achieve this. You can either write `mkdir  texts`, followed by `mkdir  texts/output` (macOS/Linux) or `mkdir  texts\output` (Windows), because now the intermediate folder will already exist. Slightly less efficiently, you create the `texts` folder first, then first `cd` into it, and create the sub-folder there. To achieve the second option, you simply write `mkdir  texts\ output` (Windows) or `mkdir -p texts/output`.

Listing the contents of the programming folder only requires you to change to it, and using both the long and short forms as again explained above. The results for Windows and Ubuntu Linux are displayed in Figure 5.4.

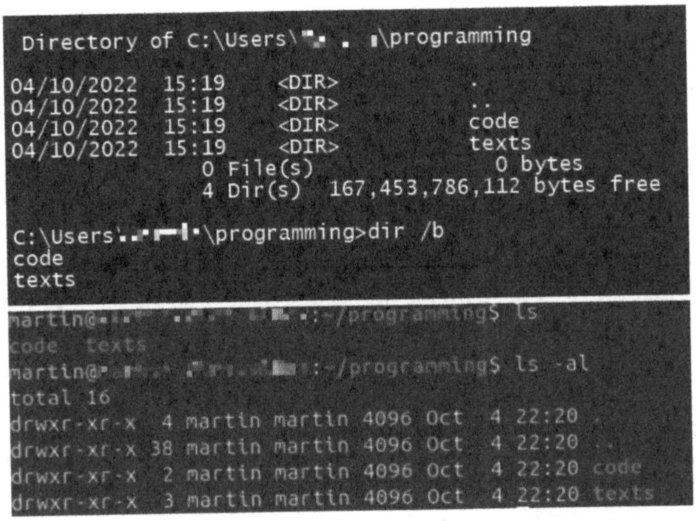

Figure 5.4   Folder listings on Windows and Ubuntu Linux.

As you can see in Figure 5.4, the output of unmodified `dir` shows that there is one sub-folder `code` and one `texts`, as we would have expected, but also two more entries, `.` and `..`, all of which are marked as type `<DIR>`, indicating that they are folders. The timestamp information to the left refers to the date and time when I last modified – in this case, created – the two main folders. Below that list, we can see that there are no files within the folder, which, unsurprisingly, also doesn't take up any space in bytes, again that there are four folders, and the amount of space left on the drive (again in bytes). Now, you may still be puzzled about the fact that there should be four folders in this folder, and especially two that you never created, but this mystery is easily explained, as the single and double dots are simply references to the current and parent folders, respectively, and we'll soon learn how to use them to work with relative paths.

The bare output – using the /b flag – only lists the name of the two actual folders we created, hiding all the other information from us. The same goes for the bare output of ls on Ubuntu Linux.

The complex -al flag here actually specifies that the information should be output in long (l), i.e. detailed, format, and that all (a) information, i.e. including hidden files, ought to be included. The first line of the output may again be confusing because we'd expect the "total" to refer to the number of files and folders inside the folder, when in fact it actually indicates the number of blocks taken up by the contents, something that you can safely ignore. The remainder of the lines again provides us with the information that we have four 'folders', which can also be seen in the d (for directory) at the very beginning of each line. This is followed by information about the access permissions to the folders, how many symbolic links there are – again, ignore –, the file size – because Linux treats both files and folders as files –, as well as the modification timestamp again.

Discussion 26 Working with File Systems (b)

Listing the contents of the parent folder of the texts folder – which you should still be in after the previous exercise – would simply require you to write dir .. on all OSes, but moving up two levels of course necessitates the use of different path separators, so you'd need to use either cd ..\.. (Windows) or cd ../.. (macOS/Linux).

Discussion 27 Brainstorming the Options for Working with Files

Hopefully, my little analogy of a book or other form of publication has helped you to imagine the options for files and file access a little better, but let's now discuss in some detail what we may do once we've opened a file. The first thing we normally want to do is read all or parts of it, which is also what we need to do if we may want to carry out any kind of analysis on the file. However, how much or little we might want to read, or which parts of the publication, is something we need to choose in some way, and we'll explore different option for making such choices as we go along, some in this chapter, some in others.

When we read through a publication and find something of interest, we often want to extract this information and store it somewhere, perhaps to use this for an academic paper, which is why we also need to have the ability to write to files. However, instead of extracting this information to store it elsewhere, if we actually own a copy of said publication, we may also simply highlight parts of it using text marker or write comments in the margin. When we do so, we in fact modify the original in some form. We'll discuss the basic operations for writing to documents for such purposes soon, and will successively learn about ways of identifying or marking up information in a number of later chapters of this book.

When we gather information from a file that we may want to retain in another document, we might also start by extracting some bits of information, storing these in a document, then read some more, and add any new information to the same file. In this case, we may need to re-open the document and append this information.

The above essentially represents everything we can do with basic file operations, but of course this doesn't cover manual editing processes where you frequently go back into the document text and make new changes. This kind of thing cannot really be achieved using the basic access methods we're covering in this chapter, but requires dedicated graphical user interfaces we can create for extracting information from and manipulating documents through editor windows. The basics of creating such interfaces will be the topic of Chapter 9.

Discussion 28   Reading from a File (a)

Creating the program files and copying the sample text file into the `texts` folder will hopefully not have presented any problems to you.

Of course, in order to be able to retrieve the file name from the command line, you first need to import the `sys` module again and then get the name from `sys.argv[1]` as we've done before. This isn't the only thing we need the module for, though, as you'll later also use the `exit` function from the same module.

To open the file with appropriate error handling, you need to set up the `try` block as follows, where of course the variable name for your text file may be different from the one I used:

```
try:
    file_handle = open(fileName,
        mode='r',
        encoding='utf-8')
```

To ensure that the file will be found, you need to 'prefix' the file name by `../texts/` on the command line to create a relative reference pointing to the correct folder in relation to your `code` folder, which, of course, isn't a part of the actual program. This block will now handle the case where the file name you've provided exists in the correct folder and you also have permission to read the file. To catch any potential error, we then add the except block as follows:

```
except OSError as err:
    sys.exit(str(err))
```

Here, I've used the variable `err` to store the error object, and the `str` function to create a string representation of it, which then becomes the argument for `sys.exit`, terminating my program in an orderly fashion and outputting a message describing the error. Using an incorrect path pointing to the program folder when I run the program, I get the error message

```
[Errno 2] No such file or directory: './sample_sentences.txt'
```

because my text file was correctly stored in the `texts` folder, which itself is one level up from the `code` folder.

After the `except` block, simply use something similar to the following to retrieve the lines from the file and store them in a list

```
lines = file_handle.readlines()
```

Once we have the lines, we're done with the file and can close it like this:

```
file_handle.close()
```

To make the output more useful, and for you to learn an additional useful function, we next use `enumerate` to produce line numbers, so that we can later output the lines including a message that shows these line numbers, too. However, as the highly useful `enumerate` function, just as all indexes for sequences in Python, starts at 0, when we create the message, we need to add 1 to each number returned by `enumerate`, making the loop something like this:

```
for (num, line) in enumerate(lines):
    line = line.strip()
    print(f'line number {num+1}: {line}')
```

Note that I didn't have to cast the number to a string here because I used an f-string, but if I'd used multiple arguments to `print` instead, I would have had to write something like

```
print('line number', str(num+1)+':', line)
```

The `enumerate` function can be used whenever you need to provide any indication as to which line a particular phenomenon has occurred/been found inside a file. In other programming languages, such as Java, C, C++, or Perl, we would normally use a loop counter for this, but since Python doesn't have loops with counters, we can use this function instead whenever we want to generate a number associated with a line in a file or element of a list, etc., which is why I introduced it at this point.

Of course, adding `1` here wasn't described in the exercise text, so this is one of the things I wanted you to observe in the output, and deal with independently. The other thing I didn't describe is that `readlines` actually returns the list of lines in their original form, i.e. including the trailing newlines, so that we need to strip these because otherwise we end up with two lines at the end of each line of output, one that was part of the line and one generated by the `print` function. I've deliberately used a separate line of code preceding the `print` statement in my sample code to illustrate this more clearly, but of course you could also have applied the `strip` method to the `line` variable during output, saving yourself one line.

Discussion 29   Reading from a File (b)

As we're essentially performing more or less the same tasks here, much of the file will remain the same, and we'll just discuss the differences. The main difference while opening the file is in the `try` block shown below:

```
try:
    with open(fileName, 'r', encoding='utf-8') as inFile:
        fileContents = inFile.read()
```

Here, because we're using the context manager, the file contents need to be read while the file is still in context, so both opening and reading need to be carried out inside the `try` block because otherwise the file would no longer be in context after the block. By contrast, in the previous exercise, we only needed to do the opening operation in the `try` block, and were then able to access the contents afterwards.

In addition, we're also using `read()` here instead of `readlines()`, initially storing the whole file in a single string. This also forces us to find a different way of retrieving the lines from the string inside the loop because we still want to number them, and of course because I wanted you to also practise using the `splitlines` method of the string object. The `for` loop would then look like this:

```
for (num,line) in enumerate(fileContents.splitlines()):
    print(f'line number {num+1:>2d}: {line}')
```

Note that we don't need to use the `strip` method any longer because `splitlines` automatically discards all newlines when splitting a string by default, so that we save ourselves the extra line. The formatting for the number will hopefully be self-explanatory, but if not, go back Section 4.6.4 to refresh your memory.

Discussion 30   Reading from a File (c)

Because we're now working on the file directly, essentially all the processing on it needs to happen inside the `try` block, including the `for` loop. The latter would now need to look as follows:

```
for (num, line) in enumerate(inFile):
    print(f'line number {num+1:>2d}: {line.strip()}')
```

Note that we need to use the strip method again because, just like with `readlines`, we're dealing with a list of lines here that have not yet been stripped of their trailing newlines.

Discussion 31   Copying a File

In order to be able to get command line arguments for the input and output files, we first need to import the `sys` module again in the first step. Storing these in appropriate variables can be achieved efficiently via a tuple like this:

```
(inputFile, outputFile) = sys.argv[1:]
```

Here, we simply take everything apart from the program name out of the `argv` list, but only assign the two arguments we want to a two-element tuple. If there were more than two arguments provided, the remaining ones would simply be ignored.

Writing the `with` statement may be more of a challenge because we haven't seen it used in this way before, but if you followed my instructions closely, you should have come up with something like the following:

```
with open(inputFile,'r', encoding='utf-8') as inFile,
         open(outputFile,'w',encoding='utf8') as outFile:
```

Iterating over the lines of the input file is something we just practised in the previous exercise, only that we don't use `enumerate` this time. Also, because we want to create an exact copy of the original file, we can simply output all the lines exactly as they are without needing to worry about the line endings.

While testing the program, you'll hopefully have noticed that if you 'accidentally' provide the same file path, you end up with an empty input file. The reason for this is that, although you've only opened the file for reading in the first call to open, as soon as you use the file path again in the second call to open that specifies opening the file for writing, an empty file is created using the same file path. This hopefully shows you that you need to be extremely careful when using the opening mode options in order to prevent any loss of data. Incidentally, this is also the reason why the default mode for opening is set to read access only. To prevent any errors like this from happening, whenever you copy or manipulate files, the best practice in non-destructive file handling is therefore always to create your output files in a different folder, which we'll soon practise some more using more advanced path-handling techniques.

Discussion 32   Reading from a Folder

To be able to use `scandir`, we of course need to import the `os` module at the very top of the program. If you forget to do so, the interpreter will throw a `NameError` once it reaches your first for loop when it tries to execute the program. Setting up the two lists should really not be a problem anymore, and you probably ought to name them `files` and `folders`, respectively.

The loop to iterate over the folder contents should again be straightforward, provided you call `scandir` correctly and test for whether the respective elements are either files or folders using the appropriate methods.

```
for element in os.scandir():
    if element.is_file():
        files.append(element)
    elif element.is_dir():
        folders.append(element)
```

Instead of `elif` for the second alternative, you might have tried to use `else` instead, assuming that this would then only find folders. However, what I haven't told you yet is that there is also a third type of object that may be found, which is a symbolic link. As we really only want to identify files and folders, though, we'll ignore this type of object.

When you write the parts for outputting the list contents, there's one snag that you need to be aware of, which is that there may not actually be any (sub-)folders present in the current folder. In this case you'd of course not want to print the 'header' message appearing before the (empty) folder list, but instead provide an indication to the user that no folders were found. In order to test for the presence of folders in the list, you can use the length of the folders list as a criterion, as in the following code:

```
if len(folders) != 0:
    print('folders:', end='\n\n')
    for element in folders:
        print(element.name)
else:
    print('No folders found!')
```

To be able to print the name of each file or folder, you use the `name` property as shown above. Note that the property is referred to without any trailing round brackets because it's not a method.

For the list of files, we don't need to run a test first because we know that we have at least one present, which is our program. However, if you wanted to make this program usable with any folder, including those that may not have any files inside them, you'd need to adjust it in an appropriate manner.

Discussion 33 Copying to a Backup Folder

As we want to copy a file provided as an argument on the command line, we of course need to import the `sys` module alongside the `Path` object, which we achieve using the syntax described in Section 5.7.2. Getting the input file from `sys.argv` is something we've now practised repeatedly, so we don't need to discuss it again here, bearing in mind that we simply need to get a file name of a file in the same folder now. Obtaining the program path can be done quite easily via

```
path = Path.cwd()
```

and creating the backup folder path like this:

```
backupDir = path / 'backup'
```

In the same way, we can just as easily create the full path for the output file using

```
outputFile = backupDir / inputFile
```

Next, we test for the existence of the backup folder using a simple `if` statement, then try to create the backup folder if necessary, and print out a corresponding success message, or an indication that it already exists, all within the same `if...else` structure:

```
if not backupDir.exists():
    try:
        Path.mkdir(backupDir)
        print('New folder', str(backupDir), 'created')
    except OSError as err:
        sys.exit(str(err))
else:
    print(str(bkDir), 'already exists.')
```

Although we would assume that we have write access to the location where our file to be backed up resides, and therefore ought to have permission to create our backup folder as well, an error could still occur, for instance if the disk were already too full. Hence, we use the `try` block to prevent our program from terminating unexpectedly and without an appropriate error message. If you look closely at the two `print` statements, you'll hopefully see that I've converted the path objects for the backup folder to strings. The same goes for using the path for the output file in copying, but otherwise the code for the copy operation remains the same.

6

Recognising and Working with Language Patterns

In this chapter, we want to learn how to recognise and work with language patterns through the use of so-called ***regular expressions***, or ***regexes***, for short. We'll start by introducing the re module that provides various methods for identifying, extracting, and manipulating simple to complex patterns, and learn about the general syntax for matching patterns and working with them. We then go on to learn about different regex concepts step-by-step until you've developed a solid understanding of both basic and advanced aspects relevant to identifying and manipulating language patterns, including the specific options for error handling the re module offers.

6.1 The re Module

Regexes offer options for defining and searching far more complex patterns than the ones we've been able to identify using the basic string methods. These options also go far beyond the means we've so far discussed for cleaning up or otherwise processing data through substitutions of matched patterns. Regexes can be used via the built-in re module, and are defined as regex objects that provide access to their search results via different methods, most of which are listed in Table 6.1.

Table 6.1 Regex methods and functions.

Method	Functionality
search(pattern, string)	Searches for occurrence of pattern in string
match(pattern, string)	Searches for pattern at the beginning of a string
findall(pattern, string)	Returns all results as list of strings
finditer(pattern, string)	Returns an iterator over all match objects found
sub(pattern, replacement, string)	Replaces all instances of pattern in string
split(pattern, string)	Returns list, similar to equally named string method, but much more flexible through patterns

Python Programming for Linguistics and Digital Humanities: Applications for Text-Focused Fields,
First Edition. Martin Weisser.
© 2024 John Wiley & Sons, Inc. Published 2024 by John Wiley & Sons, Inc.
Companion website: https://www.wiley.com/go/weisser/pythonprogling

Many of these methods/functions allow additional arguments to the ones presented in the table, e.g. for limiting the number of results to be found, but we won't discuss these here because we don't use them in our programs.

Now that you know what kinds of operations the re module allows you to perform, we can do a short exercise to reflect on the potential uses of these methods in working with language patterns.

Exercise 34   Brainstorming Patterns in Language

Think about what kinds of patterns exist in language, and how you might be able to work with them using the methods described above.

In doing so, not only apply your linguistic knowledge, but also try to draw on the experience you've gained so far in working with strings and files.

Also try to imagine what kinds of options might need to be provided by the module for accessing or extracting specific bits of data.

6.2   General Syntax

To use re objects, we have two options, either to apply the module directly, which we often do if the pattern is only needed once, or to pre-compile patterns, especially if they're to be used repeatedly. I'll illustrate the general syntax using the search method/function, which is probably the one we'll use most often. For the first option, it is:

```
result = re.search(pattern, target, [compilation flags])
```

Here, we call the search function directly on the re module, specifying a pattern and string to search in, and assign the resulting match object, described below, to a variable. The optional compilation flags allow us to modify the options in various ways, and will be described in more detail in Section 6.10.

The syntax for the second option requires two steps:

```
pattern = re.compile(pattern, [compilation flags])
result = pattern.search(target)
```

In the first step, we compile an re object based on a pattern and optional flags, and assign this to a variable. The second step then involves calling the method on the object with a target string, and again assigning the result to a variable. In both cases, if the search is successful, a match object is returned, else a Boolean value of None. The latter makes it possible to run a simple test for a match via

```
if result:
```

The difference between the module's functions and methods will be discussed in the next chapter, once you have a better understanding of modularity.

6.3   Understanding and Working with the Match Object

The match object that is returned when a successful matching operation is achieved (theoretically) contains a list of match groups, discussed in Section 6.8 once we've learnt how to specify general patterns. The complete match can always be found at index 0 of that group list, which is set as a default for the different access methods. Any possible subgroups then start from index position 1, but subgroups can also be accessed via names, if these have been defined. To understand how this works, though, we again need to gain more knowledge of groups first, so I'll defer the explanation until Section 6.8.

The match object provides different methods for accessing information about a match, which are listed in Table 6.2.

Table 6.2 Methods of the re match object.

Method	Functionality
group(index/name)	Returns the match or a specific subgroup
start(index/name)	Returns the start index of the match/group
end(index/name)	Returns the end index of the match/group
span(index/name)	Returns a tuple containing both start and end

Let's put our newly gained knowledge about the re and match objects into practice. This time, though, I won't describe all the steps in the program one by one, but assume that you'll know how to perform some of the basic operations, and only provide instructions for things that are new to you.

Exercise 35   Searching, Extracting, and Highlighting Results

Write a new program (17_simple_patterns.py) that searches for a string, provided as a program argument, in the file sample_sentences.txt, finds all lines that contain that string, and outputs them with all of its instances marked.

While iterating over the lines, check each line to see whether the string can be found on the line.

If so, use the span method to first identify the relevant index positions and store them in two suitable variables.

Then write a print statement in which you

- first output the contents of the line before the match, '[', the match, ']' and the contents of the line after the match (tip: use slicing);
- then, to supress the line breaks in the output, use the keyword argument end with an empty string.

Test the program with the strings in, the, and you. What can you observe?
What kind of a program did you produce in its simplest form?

We now know the basics of how to work with search results for simple strings, so it's time for us to explore our options for expressing more and more complex and variable patterns step-by-step in the following sections. The regex concepts we'll be discussing initially, until we've achieved a better understanding of how the different aspects of specifying patterns work together, will perhaps not make too much sense to you initially, but as we continue learning about them and putting them together, they'll hopefully increasingly start making sense, and will eventually provide you with an in-depth understanding of how regexes can help us to execute highly complex pattern matching and manipulation operations.

6.4 Character Classes

Character classes represent the lowest level in defining patterns. They only allow us to specify simple alternation of single characters within a string. To give you an example from morphology, this difference may represent the distinction between the two allomorphs {able} and {ible}, where the adjectival suffix may be realised with either an <a> or <i> as its first character. To become more useful, character classes require quantification, which will be discussed in the next section.

To create a character class, you normally list the possible alternatives in square brackets ([. . .]). For instance, searching for the character class [ae] finds all words/strings that either contain the lowercase characters <a> or <e>, or both, e.g. *y*e*s*, *a*n, *ea*r, *d*ea*ctiv*a*t*e, or kn*a*v*e*. You can already try this out using the program we wrote in the previous exercise, bearing in mind that the program in its current form will only ever find the very first occurrence of either character on a line. If your file contains adjectives ending in either {able} or {ible}, you can also search for those by specifying the pattern

```
[ai]ble
```

Again, you can try this out by adding such words to your sample file. In addition to the basic notation where you list each individual character in a row, classes can be expressed as ***ranges***, marked by hyphen(s), where e.g. [0-9] finds all strings containing digits/numbers. A special type of such ranges are ***shorthand character classes***, which represent predefined classes comprising specific sets of characters, and are usually indicated via a backslash followed by a letter. For example, \w finds all word characters, \W all non-word characters, \s all forms of whitespace (including tabulators and newlines), and . any character whatsoever, apart from a newline. However, the definition of \w is somewhat sub-optimal from a linguistic point of view, as it doesn't include hyphens, which we'd normally want to accept as parts of words – at least if they're surrounded by letters and not spaces –, but instead also finds underscores (_), which we'd normally not want to regard as word characters.

Character classes can also be negated by adding a caret behind the opening bracket, so [^0-9] finds everything that's not a digit. Beware, though, that negations may not always mean the opposite of what you might naively expect. Hence, if you negate the class [A-Z], i.e. all English uppercase characters, using [^A-Z], and expect to get all lowercase characters instead, then you'll be in for a surprise. You can see why once we've completed our next exercise and use this negated character class as an argument.

This next program will be rather more complex than any we've written before, so do take your time in developing it, and try not to get frustrated if you can't get it to work immediately. I'd also suggest you comment your code copiously so as not to lose track of what happens where.

Exercise 36   Testing for Valid Character Classes

Write the program 18_test_character_classes.py that will allow you to do what the filename says. Note that we won't do any error handling for incorrectly formulated regexes in this program yet.

To ensure that only proper character classes can occur as search terms, first write a try block in which you

- first store the search term in a variable
- then use an `if` statement in conjunction with the `not` operator and `re.search` with the character class `[.\ [\\\]` – which will be explained later – to test if the search term does not contain any valid character classes. If so, end the program with an appropriate message.

In the `except` block, if you trap an `IndexError`, also end the program with a suitable message, as this means that no argument has been passed to the program.

In the main part of the program, again using error handling, iterate over the file line-by-line and first test – using `re.search` on the line – if the search term has been found at all.

If so, set up an empty string variable for the marked-up line contents, and a numerical variable for the start position of the hit, which we'll later use to assemble the results.

Next, use the `finditer` method to run a loop over all matches found on this line.

Inside the loop, again determine the start and end positions of the matches and store these in suitable variables.

Then add everything from the current start position up to the beginning of the match, an opening square bracket, the match and a closing square bracket to the new string.

Assign the end position of the match to the start variable, as this will become the new starting point.

Finally, output the newly assembled line with the markings and the rest of the original line from the last end position, but excluding the line break.

Take a deep breath and test the program without arguments, using the patterns `[Ii]t`, `[Yy]ou`, `[^\w]`, as well as other examples of your own choosing.

I already pointed out above that character classes are really more useful once we can say how frequently they should occur, so how to express this will be the subject of the next section.

6.5   Quantification

Quantifiers make it possible to specify that a character, character class, or group of characters (see Section 6.8), should be optional, e.g. in British English *colo*u*r* vs. American English *color*, or that it has to occur at least a given number of times, e.g. in *s*ee. They're ideally used with boundary markers or anchors (see Section 6.8) to allow us to specify where exactly these quantified constructs should occur. For quantifying, different quantifier symbols and brackets are used.

An asterisk (`*`) means that whatever directly precedes it is optional or may occur 'up to' an unlimited number of times. In natural language, we could express this as 'none to infinitely many occurrences'. Hence, for instance `e\w*` finds the character e on its own, or `<e>` followed by an unlimited amount of word characters (e.g. in *s*eason, *tr*eason) or none (e.g. in *th*e).

A question mark (`?`) signifies that what precedes is optional or can occur maximally once, so is the natural language equivalent of 'possibly (no) to (maximally) one occurrence', so e.g. `t?here` finds *here* or *t*here.

The plus symbol (`+`) marks the prior construct as having to occur at least once, but up to an unlimited number of times, hence meaning '(minimally) once to infinitely many occurrences'. Thus, e.g. `state\w+` finds *state*s or *state*ment, but not *state* without any word characters following.

To achieve greater precision in specifying numerical ranges, we can use a notation involving curly brackets (`{...}`), where commas, if present, separate the upper and lower bounds of the range. Hence

- \w{5} means exactly 5 word characters,
- \w{5,} at least 5 word characters,
- \w{5,10} between 5 and 10 word characters, and
- \w{0,5} (between) none and 5 word characters.

To really find all potential words, though, including longer, hyphenated ones, you'd ideally need to change the word character definition to [\w-], though.

The quantifiers + and * try to match as many characters as possible, i.e. are what's technically called **greedy**. This may cause problems in setting limits in cleanup operations involving the re.sub method, e.g. while attempting to remove HTML tags (explained in more detail in Section 10.2). For example, if we naively formulate an expression re.sub('<.+>', '', 'bold text'), apply this to the HTML snippet provided as the target argument, and assume that it will only remove the tags in angle brackets, we end up with no more text at all because .+ will start to match immediately after the opening bracket and then consume all characters before reaching the second closing angle bracket that represents the end of the string, only seeing the pattern finished at that bracket, and then replace the whole string. This is definitely not what we want, so we need to find a way to constrain this greedy matching operation. The solution to this issue is really quite simple and consists in us constraining the quantifier through another quantifier symbol, the ?, changing its function in this case. Thus, our non-greedy expression would be re.sub('<.+?>', '', 'bold text'), which would indeed only leave the text between the tags after the replacement operation. This is because the ? following a quantifier effectively tells the regex to stop matching once it finds the first occurrence of the character that follows it.

6.6   Masking and Using Special Characters

We've already seen that 'punctuation' characters sometimes have special meanings in regexes, e.g. the ? as a quantifier, the . as any character (except normally newlines), and the hyphen (-) as a range indicator in character classes. To use any of these literally, you can either mask/escape them by preceding them with a backslash, so that e.g. \. now actually means 'full stop', or put them in character classes, e.g. [.?]. However, as hyphens normally indicate ranges, they need to be put into positions within character classes where they cannot do so, i.e. either at the beginning or end, e.g. [\w-]+ to really find all word characters. Because the \ can also be used in regular strings to mask characters such as quotation marks, it needs to be masked itself (see [\[\\] in Exercise 36). To avoid this, the string can be marked as raw, so that the example from Exercise 36 would then become r'[\[\\]', as now only the backslash as a possible component of an abbreviation, as well as the opening bracket, need to be masked. Using raw strings in regexes is therefore always advisable to save typing and increase the legibility of our patterns.

6.7   Regex Error Handling

I already pointed out in Discussion 36 that regexes throw their own type of error. This produces an re.error object, which can be stored in the same way as the other error objects we're already familiar with. However, to do something useful with this error object, it's usually best not to simply convert it to a string to pass to sys.exit, but instead create a more meaningful error message by accessing the attributes of this object. The three most useful of these attributes are:

- `msg`: a message stating which error has occurred;
- `pattern`: the pattern in which error occurred;
- `pos`: the position of the error.

Unfortunately, the `position` attribute doesn't always allow us to identify the source of the error straightforwardly, as for instance for an unclosed character class, the position of opening bracket is reported as the error position! Hence, error interpretation often requires jointly interpreting the position and the corresponding error message. Let's practise using the `re.error` object and its attributes in another exercise now.

Exercise 37   Writing a General Regex Tester and Simple Concordancer

Our previous program was a little too restrictive by requiring character classes as input, so we want to rewrite it as `19_test_regexes.py` in such a way that you can not only test all well-formed regexes, but also trap any potential regex errors in addition to index errors.

In order to handle regex errors, add another exception for an `re.error` behind the one we used for the program argument. In this, end the program with a message combining error message, pattern and position of the error object to inform users of the regex error. To ensure that the regex error can be triggered, use `re.compile` on the command line argument before assigning it to the search term variable.

Test your knowledge of quantification by trying out a few of the examples from the previous sections – as well as some of your own – using the program you just completed. Also make some deliberate errors in creating your arguments, so that you get to test the regex error handling. Try especially to find words of a specific length. However, while doing so, still bear in mind the limitations of our program, as well as any that the 'mere' quantification imposes on us. Due to the latter, what are we still unable to achieve?

As you've seen in this exercise, although we can already achieve many more useful things now using quantified regex patterns, our results are still sub-optimal, so let's see how we can improve them further by learning a few more regex concepts in the following section.

6.8   Anchors, Groups and Alternation

Anchors allow us to specify more precisely where a pattern should match. For language analysis purposes, perhaps the most useful anchor is `\b`, the word ***boundary marker***. This special regex character, depending on where you place it, either allows you to say that what occurs to its right is a word character or whatever appears on the left, allowing you to mark the beginnings and ends of words by 'bracketing' them with word boundaries. Hence, e.g. `\b[\w-]{5}\b` will indeed find words that are exactly five characters long, no matter whether these are bounded by spaces, occur at the beginning or end of a line, or preceding punctuation.

Other, occasionally useful, options for anchors are:

- `^` (beginning of a line) and `$` (end of a line)
- `\A` (beginning of a string), `\Z` (end of a string)

Of course, it's important to remember that we now know two different functions of the caret symbol (`^`) in regexes, as a negation marker in character classes and as the anchor shown above.

In strings that contain multiple lines, the caret and dollar symbols by default function in the same way as \A and \Z. This behaviour can be changed, though, by adding a compilation flag we'll discuss in Section 6.10.

While anchors allow us to specify the positions where patterns can match, groups permit us to match – and, more importantly, quantify – sequences of characters instead of only single ones. Grouping is achieved through bracketing the characters you want to be treated as a group using round brackets ((...)), e.g. (ed)? or (en)?, to mark potential past perfect suffixes in English, where of course both are marked as optional.

A side-effect of the bracketing is that the matched contents in brackets are normally captured for extraction or use as/in so-called **backreferences**, explained below. To save memory, though, capturing can be suppressed by using ?: after the opening round bracket whenever you only need to test for a pattern, but not actually work with anything that can be captured.

Groups can also be named for easier identification using the syntax

```
?P<groupnname>
```

e.g. (?P<past_part_suffix>en) to refer to one of the options for past participle suffixes shown above. To access individual groups, we then either use

```
match.group(number)
```

for regular grouping or

```
match.group(name)
```

for named grouping.

A backreference, i.e. making reference to the captured contents of a group, can be made by using a backslash followed by the name of the group, e.g. \1 or \2, etc., or (P=name), for instance in simple substitutions with re.sub or to match repeated content.

There are two additional methods for groups we want to introduce here:

- groups() returns a tuple of all matched groupings as strings, and
- groupdict() returns a dictionary of named groupings.

To specify multiple alternative character sequences within a group, we can use the separator |, e.g. (ed|en)?. The latter makes it possible to specify more complex patterns in a very efficient manner, such as all forms of a verb paradigm like (go(es|ne)?|went). Yet, one important thing to bear in mind while constructing such patterns is that you always have to use the right ordering for the alternatives, especially when similar patterns of different lengths may occur. In such cases, it's always the pattern occurring first inside the grouping that will be matched, and any later, potentially longer and more specific one, will be ignored because the regex engine has already found a suitable hit.

Knowing how to specify longer, more complex patterns – as well as how to quantify and anchor them – already takes us quite a bit further again in our ability to match specific linguistic constructs. However, as with word boundaries, we sometimes want to constrain the context of our matches, but not actually include this context in our match. How to achieve this will be the topic of the next section.

6.9 Constraining Results Further

To constrain the context of our matches further, we can use so-called **lookaround** options. This essentially means that we either specify constructs that the regex engine is supposed to look at or identify in what either follows (**lookahead**) or precedes (**lookbehind**) a potential match, and only matches if these conditions are given, but without actually including the lookaround pattern in the match. In a sense, the lookaround options thus serve as potential anchors of the match. The two terms lookahead and lookbehind may be a little confusing, but if you think of a sequence of characters, 'ahead' always means 'further on' in the sequence, and 'behind', in contrast, 'earlier on'. If you find it easier to remember this, you can also use arrows to picture this, a right-pointing one (→) for lookahead, and a left-pointing one (←) for lookbehind. Just as in groups, the patterns for lookaround are surrounded by round brackets, but without capturing anything, and marked by special mnemonic two-symbol combinations following the opening bracket.

For both forms of lookaround, there are always two options, a positive and a negative one, where positive means 'must be present', and negative 'mustn't be present'. Positive lookahead is marked as (?=...), while its negative counterpart is indicated through (?!...). For both positive options, variable patterns are permitted, while only fixed length patterns may be used with lookbehind, where the positive option is denoted by (?<=...), whereas the negative one is marked as (?<!...). To get around the fixed length restriction for lookbehind, a little-known trick is to use different brackets in a row, even if this makes the regex less elegant and readable.

Exercise 38   Testing Your Understanding of Regex Concepts

Test your knowledge of the regex options just described by searching for words in the example file using the last program you wrote.
Search for words with

- a definite, precise, and variable length,
- different pre- or suffix groups, or
- in specific positions.

Using a backreference, also test to see if you can find any 'duplicated' words, both via regular and named grouping.

As a final option in defining and controlling regex patterns, we now want to discuss compilation flags in the next section.

6.10 Compilation Flags

Compilation flags, as their name implies, can influence the behaviour of regexes when they're compiled, and before they're executed. They modify the regular properties of regex expressions in different ways, and can be combined with each other via a |, only that, unlike in groups, where the pipe symbol is used to separate alternatives, here the modifying effects co-exist. The four most useful flags in Python 3 are re.I, re.X, re.M, and re.S, but if you ever encounter any Python 2 code, their more explicit equivalents are re.IGNORECASE, re.VERBOSE, re.MULTILINE, and re.DOTALL, respectively.

The re.I flag makes the pattern case-insensitive, so that all potential upper- and lowercase permutations will be found. Hence re.compile(r'this', re.I) will not only find *this*, *This*, *THIS*, but also the unlikely *tHiS*.

The verbose flag `re.X` can be used for commenting complex regexes or improving readability. As with normal Python code, here everything to the right of # is a comment, and all whitespace, including newlines, is ignored, so that to use whitespace in your pattern, it needs to be made explicit via \s.

The multiline flag `re.M` changes the behaviour of the line anchors ^ and $. Whereas in a multiline string without this flag, ^ would only anchor the match at the start of the very first line in the string, i.e. the beginning of the string, and $, conversely, at the very end, using `re.M`, patterns are matched at the beginning of the string and every other line start, as well as the end of the string and every other line end, respectively.

While the normal behaviour of the . is to match all characters apart from a newline, with `re.S`, it also matches line ends. This may be important in programs that ignore line breaks and treat the whole text as a stream of characters, as most concordancers do. In this way, it becomes possible to match constructs of variable length across line breaks, especially if these may be spurious, anyway, as in data that has been extracted from PDFs.

In this chapter, you've learnt about one of the most important, and very advanced, ways of specifying patterns – regexes –, which will allow you to create highly sophisticated language processing applications that go far beyond what would normally be possible using ordinary string processing. Because regexes are very complicated, though, even if you'll probably be using them in almost all of your programs, don't expect to be an expert in their use after this chapter as – just like with programming in general – it takes years of practise for you to really master them. And even once you've become something of an expert, you'll still end up making the occasional mistake. This is why, as I pointed out before, it's best to test any slightly more complex regex you're using – apart from perhaps the simplest ones you use all the time – thoroughly before relying on them. With this level of sophistication in your basic programming skills, we can now move on to discussing ways of making your programs more efficient and reusable in the next chapter.

6.11   Discussions

Discussion 34   Brainstorming patterns in language

Patterns abound in language, ranging from morphological forms, via variable phrases, to fixed idiomatic expressions. We've already seen basic ways of handling affixes in Chapter 4, but also noted there that there are limitations in doing morphology, as well as cleaning up strings, using the basic string methods.

A basic search – using the `search` method of the string object – will normally only allow us to find a specific pattern, for instance to determine whether it exists at all in a string representing a word, sentence, paragraph, or book, or to perform some form of processing on it if it does. However, what we'll obviously need in order to work with a variable pattern once it's been found is some way of determining where exactly it applies because we can't simply use slicing if we don't know how long the matched expression will actually be. In other words, we need to be able to determine where it starts and ends, so this is certainly information the module will need to provide on each *hit* – which is the technical term for each occurrence found – we obtain. In contrast to the `search` method, `match` will only find patterns at the beginning of a string, so essentially it's the equivalent of the `startswith` method of the string object, only that the patterns we can specify are far more complex. As `match` only needs to check the beginning of the string, it should theoretically be faster if your pattern really does occur there.

However, if you're trying to find something that occurs anywhere within a longer string, or if there could be any leading spaces you were unaware of, then it simply won't work, so in most cases, you'll probably end up using search. You may now have noticed that, although match is the re counterpart to startswith, there seems to be no such counterpart to the endswith method of the string object, so that the re module at first glance seems to offer no option for handling suffix patterns. This, however, is not really the case, as we'll soon see when we'll discuss regex anchoring in Section 6.8.

Finding single occurrences of a pattern may be something we use to determine if a condition applies, but for many linguistic applications, such as creating concordances or word (frequency) lists, we really want to be able to find and/or extract either all potential examples, or at least a substantial part of them. This is where findall and finditer come in. The former is useful if all you're really interested in are the individual occurrences of your pattern, but as soon as you need to have more control over what exactly happens with your hits, you need to switch to using the latter. For instance, while it may be useful to create a list of hits and then count the different sub-patterns that have been matched, as e.g. for all forms of a lemma to determine which form may be most frequent, for a concordance display that should also list some context, as in a KWIC (key-word in context) concordance, we need to be able to extract more than just the hits themselves, and also ideally be able to highlight the hit we display in context in some way, which is actually something we'll soon learn to do.

As we've seen in Chapter 4, we may frequently need to clean up our data in various ways. There, we only dealt with very simple examples on short strings, but when we work with actual data, there are many different things we might potentially need to clean up for different tasks, such as removing punctuation or quotation marks if we want to create word lists, etc. Of course, we could easily define a set of different statements where we use the replace method of the string object, but this is a rather cumbersome way of achieving a task that can easily be solved by creating a suitable regex pattern for use with the sub method, where of course *sub* is short for *substitute*. The sub method also allows us to perform far more complex replacements, even involving our own functions, or based on parts of the patterns we identify, at least some of which we'll discuss in due course.

Something similar goes for split, where we've already used the method by the same name of the string object. However, the former only allows us to specify a single character for splitting, which may not allow us to split in all the places we might want to split at. For instance, again in creating word lists, we may wish to treat both spaces and apostrophes as word separators, which is not possible while using the string method, but easily so using the re one.

Discussion 35   Searching, Extracting, and Highlighting Results

Retrieving the string from the command line and storing it in a suitable variable – ideally called something like pattern –, opening the file using appropriate error handling, and iterating over the lines of the file is something we've now practised repeatedly, so I won't describe this anymore. To check if the line contains a match, we can of course use the search method in almost the same way as described in the syntax above, only replacing the target slot with the variable representing our line like this:

```
result = re.search(pattern, line)
```

We can then easily check to see if there is a hit, again in the way described above, i.e.

```
if result:
```

Extracting the start and end position via the span method can be achieved by assigning the result to a two-value tuple where the two elements can mnemonically be named start and end, yielding

```
(start,end) = result.span()
```

Once we have these positions, it becomes very easy to use a print statement with an f-string as argument in which we combine

- a slice starting at the end of the line string and running up to the start of the match, but excluding it,
- an opening square bracket to mark the beginning of the hit,
- the hit itself,
- a closing square bracket to mark the end of the hit,
- and finally another slice ranging from the end of the hit to the very end of the line,

thus making our print statement:

```
print(f'{line[:start]}[{result.group()}]{line[end:]}', end='')
```

As the hit is stored in result.group(0), but the default is set to 0 for the group method, anyway, we can use the shortened expression above. As usual, though, it's important that you include all slices and method calls in curly brackets inside the f-string.

You may still be wondering why we set the keyword argument end to an empty string here, but there's a simple explanation. Because we didn't strip the newline markers off the original lines, if we used the print function unmodified, we'd end up getting two line breaks in the output, one from the original line, and one that print automatically appends.

When you test the program using the strings I asked you to use, you should observe that, depending on the exact nature of your text, these strings will not always be found as whole words only, which is due to the fact that the grapheme combinations that make them up may well appear as parts of longer words, especially if they're really short strings. Hence, when you look for the, you may also find *they, there,* or *their,* for *you* also *your,* and for *in* also *within, into,* but also any verbs that may occur in their -ing forms, as well as many other words that just happen to contain the grapheme sequence <in>. You'll also not be able to match any of the words discussed above when they occur at the beginning of a sentence, as regexes are by default case-sensitive, unless we instruct them not to be, which we'll learn about in Section 6.10. Furthermore, the hits you'll have found may well not represent a full list of all the occurrences of these strings on each line because we're actually only ever finding the very first one.

Regarding the question as to what kind of program we produced here, of course this is a very simple – and yet imperfect – version of a concordancer. To improve on this, we'd at least want to be able to find and highlight all potential forms of the strings we're looking for, as well as – in case no hit at all should have been found inside the file – indicate this to the user. It would also be nice to have a count of all hits found, if any are present. How to achieve the first of these improvements is something we'll soon practise, but, based on what you've already learnt, you should already have some ideas as to how you can make the second and third improvements, bearing in mind that you somehow need to keep track of whether any hit has been found at all, not just on any given line the program may currently be processing. This makes modifying the program a little more difficult, but you should still be able to do this as an advanced exercise.

Discussion 36   Testing for Valid Character Classes

As pointed out before providing the instructions to this exercise, this program is rather complex compared to the ones we've written previously. Essentially, the first thing to realise is that there are two parts to this program, one where we test to see if we have any valid input at all, i.e. whether the user has provided a valid regex – which we do in the `try` block – and handle the exception that might occur if the user hasn't provided any argument. The other consists of looping over the input file, identifying whether any hit occurs on each line, and if so, extracting the relevant parts of the line and highlighting all hits before finally printing out the line we assemble from these parts. Before we begin writing the two main components, we shouldn't forget to import the relevant modules, though.

The first main part of the program starts with the first `try` block, where initially we attempt to retrieve the search term from the command line, and immediately run our test to see if any valid character class may be present.

```
try:
    search_term = sys.argv[1]
    if not re.search('[.\[\\\]', search_term):
        sys.exit('No character class defined in search_term!')
```

The character class we use for the test needs to contain all possible symbols that can form part of a character class, either one that contains brackets, a shorthand, or the dot that matches any character. We use a negated test because we only want our condition to apply if the search doesn't return the expected result. The reason for why we have so many backslashes in our character class above will be explained in Section 6.6. If the user hasn't provided a string containing any valid character class, the remainder of the program would be useless, so we can use `sys.exit` with our own message as an argument to terminate the program. If no argument has been provided at all on the command line, we can catch this as an index error because then `sys.argv[1]` will not exist, and again terminate the program, this time telling the user that they haven't provided a necessary argument.

```
except IndexError:
    sys.exit('No search term defined!')
```

Although we could obviously use `sys.argv[1]` directly in our test, it makes sense to store it in a dedicated, and more explicitly named, variable because we need to use the search term repeatedly in our program.

Opening the file and iterating over the lines – including the error handling – is essentially the same as in our earlier program, so I won't discuss this part here again. Instead, we'll only talk about identifying the term on the line, and what needs to be done if at least one occurrence has been found. Identifying whether we have a match on the line inside our condition doesn't require us to store the result of our `search`, so we can simply write:

```
if re.search(search_term, line):
```

If the condition yields `True`, we set up the empty string for assembling the results and the variable to hold each start position for the slices we'll require like this:

```
lineNew = ''
start = 0
```

The start position is here set to 0 because our first slice in fact starts at the beginning of the line. Next, we need to iterate over the hits, extract the start and end positions for each hit, similarly to how we did this before, extract the relevant part from the line, mark, and append them to the line variable, making our loop

```
for hit in re.finditer(search_term,line):
    (startPos,end) = hit.span()
    lineNew += f'{line[start:startPos]}[{hit.group()}]'
    start = end
```

Inside the loop, because I already used the variable `start` to refer to the position on the line to extract from, I now use `startPos` to refer to the starting position of the current hit. Whenever we've found the first hit on a line, `start` – as it's initially set to 0 – will retrieve everything from the beginning of the line up to, but – as before – excluding, the `startPos` of the hit, then insert the marker, the hit, and the final marker, into the f-string that represents the beginning of the newly assembled line. However, if we have a second hit, because we assigned the end position of the hit to `start`, we'll now get a slice starting where the first hit ended, and up to the beginning of the next, plus the next hit, and so forth for any other hits found on the line, thereby gradually adding each hit to the line. To illustrate this more graphically, let's take a look at the line 'It normally depends on whether it's high season or not'. from 'sample_sentences.txt' and match the pattern [Ii] t to it. When we first encounter the pattern at the beginning of that line, the start position for the match will be 0, and the end 2, so we extract the hit, wrap these in square brackets, and append

```
[It]
```

to the newly created string. The initial slice that would normally have been appended before the hit is empty, due to the hit occurring at the beginning of line, so nothing is included before the marked hit. The second time we find a hit, the end position 2 has then become new the starting point for the next slice up to – but excluding – the next starting position of the second match it, which starts at position 31 and ends at position 33. We can therefore extract the string "normally depends on whether " from the line and append it to the string holding the modified line, together with the current hit, making the newly assembled line now

```
[It] normally depends on whether [it]
```

The next end position of the hit, 33 now becomes the starting position for the next slice to be extracted. The next time around the loop, no more match is found, and `finditer` has completed, so we can simply take a slice starting at the current end position and ending before the final newline character, and append that to the string containing the newly assembled line, making the final output

```
[It] normally depends on whether [it]'s high season or not.
```

This makes the final line in the second `try` block, where the newly assembled line and the end of the line are effectively concatenated inside the f-string

```
print(f'{lineNew}{line[end:-1]}')
```

Although the program itself wasn't too long, understanding what needed to be done was probably a little difficult, even if we'd practised working with iterations and slices repeatedly.

The fact that we had to use different types of error handling for different purposes probably didn't help, either, but the more you use the techniques we've discussed so far, the more you should start feeling comfortable and accepting them as a necessity. And sooner or later, using conditional test and exceptions will probably become second nature to you.

Once you've managed to make the program work in the way it ought to, and have tested it using the expressions I suggested, you'll hopefully have realised that this program is already much more useful as a concordance program than our previous one because now all instances of a search term will in fact be identified and highlighted on each line. However, there will still be spurious results because we haven't been able to eliminate the issue of short 'words' being parts of longer ones. One other thing that you'll only have noticed if you've made a mistake in writing one of the character classes is that we still haven't learnt how to deal with malformed regexes, which is something we'll discuss in Section 6.7. Until we can trap such re errors, though, your program will unfortunately still crash with an error message if you use a malformed character class in your argument.

Discussion 37 Writing a General Regex Tester and Simple Concordancer

Essentially, in order to re-write the program, we only need to change three things in the very first part of the program. The first is to use re.compile directly when we retrieve the program argument and assign it to search_term, yielding

```
search_term = re.compile(sys.argv[1])
```

Since we're now no longer testing for valid character classes, we can then simply delete the conditional statement and associated block and add the additional exception directly after the one for the index errors, thus changing the single exception to two in the following way:

```
except IndexError:
    sys.exit('No search term defined!')
except re.error as e:
    sys.exit(f'Regex error="{e.msg}" in pattern: '
             f'"{e.pattern}" at position {e.pos}')
```

Although we now have regex error handling implemented, this doesn't actually mean that the regexes you specify will always be correct because the regex error object can in fact only detect syntax errors like missing brackets. What it will not be able to catch are logical errors related to the way you construct your regex. Hence, whenever it's crucial that a regex you're trying to use for a particular task should actually work the way you expect it, you always ought to test it thoroughly. However, this is really something the program we just completed will help you with because all you need to do is include examples of what you're hoping to identify through a regex in your sample file and then see if your regex will match them.

When you try out a few patterns that contain character classes and quantification, especially in attempting to find words of a specific length, you may be in for a surprise. Even using precise quantification, e.g. \w{3}, you won't only find words that are exactly as long as you expected them to be. Instead, they may contain additional word characters or multiple sequences of the number of characters you specified. So why doesn't this work? The reason for this is quite simple: we haven't actually specified where our sequence of characters of a given length should start and end, and that it should actually constitute a whole word at all, because we simply don't know how to do so. Hence, what the regex does is look for so many word characters in a row anywhere it might find them, which isn't really good enough for finding words. A naïve way of optimising our strategy here would be to say that a word is anything that is bounded by spaces, so we could e.g. use ␣\w{3}␣ instead, where ␣ symbolises a space. However, of course this'll only find those 3-letter words that are actually bounded by spaces, but not ones that may occur at the beginning of the line or be followed by punctuation, also making our hit five characters long, as you'll see in the output if you try this. In addition, as finding and highlighting words in a concordance may not be the only goal we might have when searching for words of a specified length, this method is clearly not optimal. To be able to actually achieve our aim of finding words of a specific length, we still need to learn how to anchor our sequences in a suitable way, which we'll do in the next section. As an additional exercise here, though, you could create a version of your program that doesn't send the results to the command line, but instead writes them to a file that you can specify as an additional argument on the command line.

Discussion 38   Testing Your Understanding of Regex Concepts

Which words or suffixes you'll find of course depends on the exact nature of the sample file and which suffixes you choose, so I cannot really make any predictions as to what exactly you'll find through your searches, even though I've of course added a few interesting options. However, to be able to find hyphenated words in the text, you obviously shouldn't forget to 'redefine' the word character class to [\w-]. Unfortunately, given the implementation of the re module, there's no way for us to exclude the underscore from that definition. This would be possible using a more advanced regex engine like the one that's implemented in the regex module, which, however, you'd need to download and install once we've learnt how to do so in the next chapter.

Finding any duplicated words, or rather word forms, to be more precise, which are indeed rare in well-formed text, you could either use the basic grouped form

```
(\b\w+\b) \1
```

or, for named grouping, something like

```
(?P<redup>\b\w+\b) (?P=redup)
```

One of those rare well-formed 'reduplications' in English, for instance, would be *that that*, where of course the first word form represents a conjunction and the second a demonstrative determiner. An example of this combination is in fact included in the sample file. However, in spoken language, it's also not uncommon for words to be repeated as a form of dysfluency or emphasis.

7

Developing Modular Programs

In this chapter, we want to discuss how you can make your programs more efficient by designing modular components that will help you to structure your programs better and make the components re-usable for different tasks, or even 'plug them together'. We'll begin with a brief discussion of modularity in general. Then we'll explore dictionaries, which form an important part of modular designs, in some more detail. And finally, I'll introduce the different levels of modularity and their applicability to different language analysis tasks, step-by-step.

7.1 Modularity

Designing your programs in a modular fashion makes it possible to render the program flow more obvious by splitting program into smaller logical steps, and re-use frequently needed program components by extracting and storing them in different files, thereby also avoiding redundancy. There are essentially three different levels of modularity.

Functions – both built-in and user-defined ones – encapsulate smaller program steps and generally allow us to manipulate smaller pieces of data or perform actions that may be performed repeatedly. The data that is processed by a function is, as we've already seen in the built-in functions we've used, normally passed to the functions as one or more arguments. Modules are basically containers that group together, and store frequently used functions and variables that can then be imported into other programs without having to re-write these components. At the highest level of modularity, we find classes, which enable us to create new data types as objects with their own methods and import them into our programs in the same way as module components.

7.2 Dictionaries

As stated above, dictionaries play an important role in designing modular components, especially objects, but also represent a highly useful data container for language-related analysis in general. They allow us to store key–value pairs together, where every key is unique – as in sets –, only that it has to be of an immutable type and needs to have a value associated with it, even if this value may only be an empty string. In practice, in most cases, the key will be a

Python Programming for Linguistics and Digital Humanities: Applications for Text-Focused Fields,
First Edition. Martin Weisser.

meaningful string, though, such as a word type that can have a counter associated with it as its value or a property of a verb, such as its number or person. The ability to associate keys with values linked to them makes them ideal for storing simple to complex lexica or frequency lists for words or longer expressions, generally referred to as ***n-grams***, where *n* stands for 'any number'.

To set up an empty dictionary, as usual, we have two ways, either by using the `dict` function like this

```
dict_name = dict()
```

or directly by using a set of empty curly brackets

```
dict_name = {}
```

If we already have some key–value pairs to initialise the dictionary with, we can use these inside the curly brackets as comma-separated 'lists' in which each pair is linked via a colon (`:`), e.g.

```
lexicon = {'ein': 'a', 'das': 'the', 'die': 'the'}
```

to set up a simple German to English dictionary. To make the individual key–value pairs more recognisable, we could also write it like this:

```
lexicon = {
    'ein': 'a',
    'das': 'the',
    'die': 'the'}
```

In general, though, we tend not to create dictionaries like this manually, but instead read them in from appropriately structured files. As dictionaries are mutable, we can also add new keys and values to them, or change any values already associated with keys, e.g.

```
lexicon['eine'] = 'a'
```

which would, in this case, add a new key plus value to the dictionary we just set up above. However, if the key `eine` already existed inside `lexicon`, its value would be changed to a. To access a key in order to retrieve its value, you use the same notation as can be seen on the left-hand side of the expression in the previous example, so, to `print` the value associated with a given key, you'd write

```
print(dict_name['key_name'])
```

Beware, though, because if you try to access a non-existent key in this way, this will throw a `KeyError`, so it's best to ensure that the key exists, which we'll soon learn about. One highly important feature of dictionaries is that they are by default unsorted, i.e. the order of the keys inside the dictionary initially corresponds to the order in which the keys have originally been added. It is, however, possible to create a sorted version of a dictionary (see Chapter 8) where the order of keys will then also be stable. Table 7.1 lists a number of useful dictionary methods.

Table 7.1 Useful dictionary methods.

Method	Functionality
keys()	Returns all keys
values()	Returns all values
items()	Returns a list of key–value tuples
setdefault(key, value)	Returns current value of key, if it exists, and sets default for value if key doesn't exist yet
del(key)	Removes an existing key; otherwise throws KeyError
clear()	Empties the dictionary

The setdefault method is especially useful if the key name needs to be generated dynamically inside a program and a counter for its value set up because setting up or accessing an uninitialised key would otherwise throw an error. We'll especially need this option when we start creating frequency lists in the next chapter.

The in operator can be used in two different ways with dictionaries, either to check if a given key exists, thereby potentially avoiding a KeyError, or to iterate over all keys or values in a loop using the respective method calls.

7.3 User-defined Functions

User-defined functions, just like the built-in ones such as print, input, len, or open we've already used, usually take one or more arguments, and also return values or change program internal data. The only difference is that you write them yourself, so you decide how many arguments they take and which tasks they should perform. The basic syntax for a function definition, with optional elements indicated in square brackets, is:

```
def functionname([argument(s)]):
        [statement(s)]
        [return variable/expression]
```

As you can see, any user-defined function starts with the keyword def, followed by the name of the function, a set of round brackets (that may or may not contain arguments), and a colon that signals a block. Inside the function block, you can have one or more statements, the last of which is usually a statement starting with the keyword return, which causes the function to return a variable or the result of an expression. A variable returned may be of a simple or complex data type, so you can also return tuples, lists, or dictionaries in addition to strings or numbers. If the return statement is missing, e.g. if the function simply creates some output through a print statement, a value of None is automatically returned.

Again, just like built-in functions, user-defined ones are called via

```
functionname([argument(s)])
```

There are two more very important things to know about user-defined functions. The first is that any variables defined inside these functions are purely **local**, even if they may have the same names as global program variables, and are hence different from them. Thus, if you're trying to modify a variable defined outside your function from within the function, this will not work, unless we use a special technique we'll learn about in Section 10.7. You can, however, of course take the current value of that variable, use it as an argument to the function, compute a new value and assign that to the original one. The advantage of being able to use the variable name in local scope, though, is that you can use the same variable name for similar types of data in two different places. Hence, if you have a variable that refers to a `word`, `sentence`, or other linguistic construct in different places inside your program, you don't always need to come up with a new telling variable name.

The other important fact related to user-defined functions is that they need to be defined in the program prior to being called! If you forget to do so, this will lead to a `NameError`, which is a very common error when you start defining your own functions. Hence, you can expect to see this quite frequently until you get used to it.

7.4 Understanding Modules

Modules are in essence containers for collections of frequently used functions or classes, and usually also contain their own variables. Simple modules are basic Python files, and can be imported like internal modules, simply leaving off the extension. More complex modules may consist of multiple files and folders, which can frequently be installed as **packages**, e.g. using the Python package installer (pip or pip3). We don't cover creating more complex modules here, but will only discuss simple ones.

Module names are by convention written in all lowercase, but may contain underscores to improve legibility. Frequently, only specific functions are imported via

```
from modulename import functionlist
```

where the 'list' may also only consist of a single item. Although everything at once may be imported via

```
from modulename import *
```

this is generally discouraged, as it may lead to conflicts if functions, methods, or variables by the same name are imported from different modules. Hence, we should only use this if we're relatively sure that this problem won't occur or if there are really too many things from a module that need to be imported to write out a list. We can also import whole modules, such as `re`, via

```
import modulename
```

and then access their functions via

```
modulename.functionname
```

if the module is not object-oriented, or generally

```
modulename.methodname
```

for object-oriented modules.

The `re` module is special in the sense that, despite being object-oriented, it provides both functions and methods that have the same name. If, for instance, `search` is called on the module directly with a pattern and a string as arguments, as in the first syntax example in Section 6.2, we're using it as a function that first implicitly compiles an `re` object and then calls its `search` method. If we pre-compile the pattern and then call `search` on it with a string as its argument, we're in fact calling the method.

If we explicitly use the module name and the name of the function, method, or variable, we avoid accidentally using the wrong item from a different module. When importing whole modules, it's also possible to use an alias for the module name via

```
import modulename as alias
```

particularly if the module name or path is very long. Now that you have a basic understanding of modules, let's try creating a simple one ourselves. This module will allow us to attach word-class – i.e. part-of-speech (PoS) – information to the each of the words read in from any file we specify. To be able to do so, our module should provide a number of user-defined functions that offer the different types of functionality we want to make available through the module:

a) one function that reads in word–tag pairs from a lexicon file provided as an argument, which we'll store inside a dictionary that is then returned by the function;

b) another to read in sentences that we want to tag from a file, and which is returned as a list of sentences;

c) a third one that will take the lexicon and a sentence as arguments, and return a tagged version of it;

d) finally, a function that allows us to output a tagged sentence in some form we can specify in a flexible manner, even though we'll initially only produce a very simple output.

To be able to test the module – given our current state of knowledge –, we'll need to create another program that will import the different functions, as well as a lexicon file and one containing our sentences.

Exercise 39   Writing a Basic Part-of-Speech (PoS) Tagger (a)

Write the module `tagger.py`, through which you can add word-class (PoS) tags to a number of simple sentences, using multiple functions you design, a lexicon, and a list of sentences.

Start by creating the UTF-8 encoded `lexicon.txt` file, and store it in your texts folder. This should include the entries `this:DET, is:VB, are:VB, a:DET, here:RB, clever:JJ, have:VB, sentence:NN, book:NN, flower:NN, newspaper:NN, Jane:NP, woman:NN, man:NN, I:PRP, you:PRP, .:PUN`, in your texts folder. Each entry should here be listed on a separate line.

Next, create the file `sentences.txt` – also in your texts folder –, containing the following simple declarative sentences, again one per line: *You have a book. Jane is a clever woman. This is a person. I have a newspaper. This is another sentence. Here is a flower. This is a house. This is not a joke.* Note that these also include a few items that don't exist in our lexicon, and that the second and seventh sentences contain erroneous spaces before the noun and after the determiner, respectively.

Now define the function `read_lexicon` inside the module. This is supposed to take a lexicon file as its single argument, process this file line-by-line, split each line into a word and PoS tag at the colon, and store them in a dictionary as key–value-pairs. Once the lexicon dictionary has been constructed, it should be returned via a `return` statement.

Now write the function `read_sentences`, which should read in a sentence file and return a list of sentences.

Pay attention to appropriate error handling. If an incorrect file name is provided to either the function generating the lexicon or the one producing the list of sentences, the program that will later use the module should be terminated.

Create the file `20_tag_sentences.py`, in which you start by importing both functions from the module explicitly.

Next, use the two functions to create a lexicon and the list of sentences from the two files, respectively.

To test if they work, use `print` statements for intermediate debugging that will allow you to see if the files have been read in correctly and the dictionary or list created correctly. Once the module is complete, we'll no longer need those, though, and can either delete or comment them out.

We've now seen how we can create our own module and use the functions defined in it in another program in the most rudimentary fashion. However, obviously, the functions we've written so far only represent helper routines, but don't produce anything of value yet, so, in the next exercise, we want to add the actual tagging and output functionality.

Exercise 40   Writing a Basic Part-of-Speech (PoS) Tagger (b)

Add a function `tag_sentence`, which takes a lexicon and a sentence as arguments and returns a tagged version of the input sentence where words and their tags are joined by an underscore.

In this function, first set up an empty list to later store the tagged words, and modify the sentence passed as argument in such a way that the first letter is downcased and the punctuation mark will be separated from the last word via a space.

Split the sentence on spaces, accounting for the fact that sometimes electronic texts may erroneously contain extra ones, and iterate over the words.

Inside the loop, first check to see if the current word exists inside the lexicon.

If so, add it and its tag, joined by an underscore, to the tagged word list using the `append` method. Otherwise,

- if the capitalised word exists in the dictionary, add it and the tag, in the way described above.
- if neither of the above applies, add the word and `_???` to indicate words not occurring in the lexicon in your output.

Return the list, now joined by spaces, capitalising the first word.

Write the function `output_tagged`, which simply outputs a tagged sentence passed to it as an argument.

Add the remaining function imports to `20_tag_sentences.py`, and write a loop in which you output all tagged sentences.

When you write a longer module, and later want to use functions defined in it in other programs, you may not always remember all the arguments, etc., the function takes, and don't want to have to open the module itself all the time in order to look up this information. Likewise, you don't want any potential other users of the module to have to do this, just in order to be able to use it. To make it easier to understand what kind of functionality your module offers, you can document your code in a more advanced form of documentation than the one we discussed in Section 2.6. How such documentation can be created and used in different ways will be the topic of the next section.

7.5 Documenting Your Module

To create documentation for your code that can automatically be extracted and shown in various ways, you can include triple-quoted docstrings that describe the code in relevant places, such as the top of a module or function. This type of documentation can get quite extensive and be formatted using advanced options, but we'll only discuss the basics here again.

To provide a brief summary of the functionality of a module itself, you can add a docstring immediately at the top of your program, before any potential imports. Here, you normally at least provide a brief description of its purpose, your name as author, etc. Your main documentation effort, though, will usually be spent on documenting any functions you create, to show the users which arguments are required, and which order these need to appear in. The docstrings for this should be written on the line immediately after each function head, and be followed by a blank line before the main body of the function. For instance, the documentation for the `tag_sentence` function could look like this:

```
def tag_sentence(lexicon, sentence):
    '''Using a lexicon and sentence as arguments,
    tag the sentence with PoS tags from the lexicon
    and return the tagged sentence.

    arguments:

    :lexicon: a dictionary containing word:PoS pairs
    :sentence: a string containing a sentence '''
```

The extra line breaks in the docstring above ensure visual separation in all the output formats we'll discuss below, and the cola before the arguments in the final two lines make the arguments appear in boldface if we view the documentation in the WingIDE, which is one of the ways of making use of it.

To view the documentation that can automatically be generated from the docstrings, we have a number of different options, some of which we'll discuss here. The most basic one would be to display the information in the Python Shell by importing the module and using the command `help(tagger)`. However, to be able to do this, you have to have started the Shell from the folder in which you've created the module because otherwise it may not be found. To achieve this in the built-in Shell in WingIDE, you need to ensure that the editor window containing the module is active and choose the 'Evaluate tagger.py' option form the Shell's 'Options' menu before importing the module.

Another option for viewing – and keeping – the documentation is to create a web page from it using the built-in `pydoc` module like this on the command line

```
python -m pydoc -w tagger
```

again ensuring that you're in the right folder. This will create a basic HTML page containing the documentation for your module, which you can then open in a web browser or even distribute to potential users.

However, the most useful option for accessing the documentation while writing a program that uses your module is usually provided by your IDE. In order to make use of this, you don't even have to have your module open in the IDE, but only have imported the relevant functions, which, of course, you'd need to know exist beforehand. As soon as these functions will have been imported, once you click on a function name in the importing program, WingIDE will show you the relevant documentation in the 'Source Assistant' tab in the pane on the right-hand side of the window. In other IDEs, it might not even be necessary to have a tab like this or click on the function, but you may get the information directly as a tooltip when you hover over the function name. This way – just as for built-in functions – you'll always be able to find out new information about function arguments or refresh your memory quickly.

We now have a better understanding of what modules are and how they work, so we can move on to finding out how to install additional modules that don't form a part of the standard Python installation.

7.6 Installing External Modules

Although, as we've seen, Python already has a number of highly useful modules pre-installed, we can increase its standard functionality not only by developing our own modules, but also drawing on external modules that we collect and install from repositories. Although such modules can also be downloaded and installed manually, the easiest way to integrate them into your existing Python configuration is to install them via the Python package installer (***pip***) from the ***Python Package Index*** (***PyPI***; https://pypi.org) using the command line. If you only have version 3 installed on your system, this is referred to simply as `pip` when you run it, but for parallel installations of versions 2 and 3, you'd need to write `pip3`.

The exact syntax you use for installing module packages via pip depends on the level of permission you have on the computer you're working on. If you have full permissions, you can use

```
pip(3) install modulepackage
```

and if you're using the command line in administrator mode, the external module will normally be installed for all users as well. However, if you're a standard user on an administrated system, you won't be able to install the module for all users, but instead will have to use

```
pip(3) install --user modulepackage
```

which will install the package only for your own use. For more details, e.g. the installation of already downloaded modules, see https://packaging.python.org/tutorials/installing-packages/#installing-from-pypi. To practise installing external packages, let's now install one that we'll use later as another exercise.

Exercise 41   Installing PyQt

Go to the PyPI page, https://pypi.org, and search for 'PyQt5'.

Follow the link to the package referring to "Python bindings for the Qt cross platform UI and application toolkit".

Read the description and look for a suitable pip command for installation.

Copy it and use the command line to install the package, if necessary only as standard user.

We'll later make use of PyQt for creating graphical user interfaces (GUIs).

During the time of writing, PyQt6 also became available. However, as the differences between the two version are relatively small, we'll still stick to version 5 here.

What we've discussed above in creating our own modules are really only non-object-oriented modules that provide simple functions, but of course many module packages, such as the one you've just installed via pip, are object-oriented, so now's an appropriate time for developing a deeper understanding of objects and object-orientation as the next level of modularity. This is what we'll do in the following section.

7.7   Classes and Objects

Objects are essentially containers for data that contain their own variables and provide their own methods for processing this data they encapsulate. The methods of an object represent the interface for the user, who shouldn't necessarily need to know anything regarding the internal data structure and how this is processed, only what is done by the methods. Objects are defined as *classes* in Python, which constitute their blueprint, and are only *instantiated* as concrete objects when they are created. New objects, as for the built-in data types, are created via

```
objectvariablename = Objectname([argument(s)])
```

Class names, by convention, usually start with capitals, unlike functions or modules, so that they can easily be distinguished from the former. Basic class definitions start with keyword `class`, followed by the class name, a pair of round brackets, and a colon, starting, as usual, a block. Inside this block, all variables and methods of the class are defined.

The variables associated with a class can be of two different types, *class variables*, which apply to all objects of class jointly, and *instance variables*, which only belong to the individual object itself. The former can e.g. be used to keep a record of how many objects have been created based on the class blueprint, and are defined like ordinary variables, only inside the class definition, while the latter need to be prefixed by self, i.e. declared as

```
self.variablename
```

where `self` is a reference to the class, and needs to be used in this way inside the methods of the class as well. Once a class has been instantiated as an object, both types of variables can be accessed in the same way, though, as

```
objectname.variablename
```

Variables that belong to a class are used to hold the properties of an object. For instance, a class for a word object could have an instance variable `self.word_type` that could be set to any word class it might represent. Class definitions are simply stored in module files, but one file can actually hold multiple class definitions, making it possible to group similar classes together conveniently, and then only import them from one module.

7.7.1 Methods

Methods – just like normal functions – are defined using the keyword `def`, followed by the method name, a colon, and a following block. The first argument in a method definition always has to be a reference to the class, i.e. `self`. When the method is called on an object though, `self` is always implicit, so it should not be listed as an argument!

The first method defined inside a class definition is generally its initialisation method, or **constructor**,

```
__init__(self[, argument(s)])
```

Any keyword arguments passed at object instantiation are usually used to initialise instance variables of same name, so you'll often see declarations like

```
self.argumentvariable = argumentvariable
```

inside the constructor, where the value of the keyword argument is transferred to the instance variable. This is also useful if default values are set via

```
argumentvariable=value
```

when the arguments are passed because then the default can simply be copied over unless a different value is provided when the object is created. Now that we know how variables and methods are defined for classes, I'll provide a short summary of what a class schema looks like in the following brief section.

7.7.2 Class Schema

The general class schema, including instance variable declarations, looks like this:

```
classname([parent_class(es)]):
    def __init__(self[, argument(s)]):
        self.variableX = argumentX
        self.variableY = argumentY
        ...

    def method1(self[, argument(s)]):
        method definition

    def method2(self[, argument(s)]):
        ...
```

If you've paid close attention, you'll have noticed that I've added an optional slot inside the round brackets in the head of the class definition. This optional slot can hold a list of potential parent classes that the current class may be derived from. We'll learn more about this in Chapter 9, where we'll derive new objects from existing PyQt elements.

7.8 Testing Modules

So far, we've always included modules, or parts thereof, in other programs via `import` statements, but modules can also be executed themselves as standalone programs if we add a short section to their end. This is particularly useful for testing, where we don't need to write an additional program to try out the functionality as we did with our `tagger` module. To do this, we only need to add a conditional block at the end of the program that tests if the module is executed as an independent program – referred to as __main__ –, and which takes the form

```
if __name__ == '__main__':
    block for testing
```

Inside this block, you can initialise any objects you want to work with or test and functions or methods defined in your module. To try this out, and gain some experience in creating and working with objects, let's now create a module for modelling one of the most common objects we encounter in language, a word. In this module, we'll implement objects for a small number of word classes. However, even if this may sound like a very simple task, it will require a fair degree of understanding of morpho-phonological processes from you, and you'll need to be able to test for a number of complex options, so that developing this module will most likely take you a fairly long time, as well as many refinement steps.

Exercise 42 Creating a Word Object

Create a new file `word.py`, in which you'll set up a rudimentary verb class that only produces tense forms for regular verbs, as well as a noun class that allows you to create plurals for regular nouns. First import the `re` module, which we'll need later.

Next, set up the class `Verb` using an `__init__` method.

Inside this constructor, keyword arguments for base form, person, number, tense, and type (regular/irregular) should be passable, with appropriate defaults. Hint: `type` is a reserved word in Python, so you'll need to use a different name for this argument. In addition, the argument for the non-optional base form needs to have a suitable value that we can test for, so that we can do some basic error handling that will allow us to `raise a NameError`.

Next, still inside the constructor, initialise the corresponding instance variables via the arguments.

Implement methods for generating the present participle and past tense/participle. If the type is set to anything but 'regular', make sure an appropriate message is generated, alerting the user that handling irregular forms hasn't been implemented yet.

Add a test block at the end of the module and test your object, using the methods already implemented, as well as a number of different regular verbs with different endings.

Next, model the generation of verbs in the present tense, and also add a method that generates any of the implemented tense forms, given the tense form as its argument or using the tense form set when the object was instantiated.

Test the new functionality.

Now implement a noun object with a plural method, following a similar approach, and also test it.

As you've hopefully observed in this exercise, being able to create our own objects with their own properties and methods, as well as integrated error handling, is a highly useful thing. And even if the process of creating useful objects may have been rather time-consuming, you'll soon hopefully come to appreciate its benefits. What we've covered here in terms of object orientation still only covers the basics, though, and objects can get far more complex than our still relatively simple word objects when you delve deeper into the subject. For instance, as our two word classes sometimes shared similar properties, such as number and type, we could have started by creating a basic class `Word`, and then derived our specific (sub-)types from this, allowing them to inherit some of the features of the parent class, as well as implementing or over-riding others by redefining them. We'll see how this works in Chapter 9, only still without going too much into the theory behind it. Before doing so, though, we want to make use of our newly-gained expertise in employing object orientation by implementing objects that allow us to create frequency lists, which represent a highly important means of quantifying different properties of language.

7.9 Discussions

Discussion 39 Writing a Basic Part-of-Speech (PoS) Tagger (a)

Creating the lexicon and sentence files should present no problem to you. The first function, `read_lexicon`, essentially does most of the things we've been doing with files all along in terms of opening and iteration when we've processed them before. The only thing that's really new here is that we now first create an empty dictionary, then fill it by splitting each line in turn, creating the key plus associated tag value, and then assigning the tag to a key inside the dictionary in the next step. To split the line – which we first need to clean of its trailing line break –, we use the `str.split` method with a colon as argument to create a tuple of word and tag. This makes the body of the `for` loop something like this:

```
line = line.strip()
if line:
    word, tag = line.split(':')
    lexicon[word] = tag
```

As we also want to use error handling with the file, the empty lexicon needs to be set up before opening the file and once the file reading operation and error handling are complete, the lexicon can simply be `return`ed saying

```
return lexicon
```

Hence, our complete function could look like this:

```
def read_lexicon(lexicon_file):
    lexicon = {}
    try:
        with open(lexicon_file, 'r', encoding='utf-8') as lex:
            for line in lex:
                line = line.strip()
                if line:
                    word, tag = line.split(':')
                    lexicon[word] = tag
    except OSError as err:
        sys.exit(str(err))
    return lexicon
```

To be maximally useful here, the complete path to the lexicon file should be provided by the calling program, so that we can use lexica that may be stored anywhere on our computer, and not only in the same folder as our program.

The function `read_sentences` would be almost identical in structure to the preceding one, only that it should accept a path to the sentence file as argument, and return a list, so that the creation of the list inside the loop doesn't require any work apart from stripping the line break and using `append` to add the line to the sentence list.

For both functions, the exception handlers also use `sys.exit` with any errors that may have been thrown. We do this for simplicity's sake here because, for any program that may use the module, if the relevant files cannot be used as input, it would make no sense to keep them running, anyway. However, if the module were to be used in a larger application where more different processing steps could occur and perhaps the users could be presented with different options for choosing the files, it would be better to only report the error to the calling program, which is something we'll learn about later. Note that, in the complete version listed in the Appendix, I've also included docstrings to document the whole module, which we'll discuss in the next section of this chapter.

Unfortunately, at this point, given what we know about modules, we have no way of testing the functions directly because we have no calling program that would actually use them, so we now need to write the test program `20_tag_sentences.py`, which will initially be incomplete since we haven't added the tagging functionality yet. The import statement with the existing functions should look as follows:

```
from tagger import read_lexicon, read_sentences
```

and the lines that use the functions and display the debugging output like this:

```
lex = read_lexicon('../texts/lexicon.txt')
print(lex)
sentences = read_sentences('../texts/sentences.txt')
print(sentences)
```

Discussion 40   Writing a Basic Part-of-Speech (PoS) Tagger (b)

Writing the `tag_sentence` function is a little more difficult than creating the two earlier functions, `read_lexicon` and `read_sentences`, because it's necessary to modify the original sentence in different ways before it can be re-assembled – including the tags –, and returned. As the sentences normally all start with an initial capital, in the first step, we need to create a version of the sentence where the first letter is lowercased, and the trailing punctuation mark is detached from the word it occurs after, which we can achieve by putting together a new f-string like this:

```
sentence = f'{sentence[0:1].lower()}{sentence[1:-1]} {sentence[-1:]}'
```

Here, we slice off the first letter, apply the lower method to it, then add another slice ranging from the second to the penultimate letter, a space, and another slice containing the final letter, i.e. the punctuation mark. As all our sentences are declaratives, we could of course simply have added a space and a dot instead of the third slice, but the way we're doing it here would also allow us to handle non-declarative sentences, provided that we add the other punctuation marks to the lexicon, too. Note that sentence-internal commas are not handled here, but then again, we only wanted to work with simple declaratives by means of illustration. As an additional exercise, though, you might want to think about how you could use regex replacements to handle all punctuation at once in an additional step.

For the loop over the elements of the sentence, I added an extra catch, as you'll hopefully have noticed. In order to be able to handle all the sentences, including the ones that contain erroneous spaces, you cannot simply use the `str.split` method, but instead need to make use of `re.split` with `r'\s+'` as the pattern argument, which naturally only works if you've imported the `re` module at the top of your program.

Despite our having 'decapitalised' the first letter of the sentence, the conditional block still needs to test for three options. The first, and simplest, is if the word – in the form that has been found by the program – occurs in the lexicon, and hence has a tag associated with it. The second is whether a capitalised form of the word occurs in the dictionary. This, for instance, is the case for the pronoun *I* and any proper names that may be listed there. Even if these may have been lowercased in the program, we still want to preserve their original form and be able to look them up. The third option is our fallback, just in case the dictionary lookup failed to find any corresponding words, which is a common issue, even with large-scale dictionaries. Thus, our conditional block could look like this:

```
if word in lexicon:
    tagged.append(f'{word}_{lexicon[word]}')
elif word.capitalize() in lexicon:
    tagged.append(f'{word.capitalize()}'
        f'_{lexicon[word.capitalize()]}')
else:
    tagged.append(f'{word}_???')
```

Of course, in a proper tagger, we wouldn't just want to depend on a lexicon, but would instead add a component for morphological analysis that may allow us to identify the word class. This component would then be run prior to triggering the fallback option.

Once we've tagged all our words in this way, we can put the sentence together and then only need to apply the final correction, which is to re-capitalise the first word, which we can achieve like this:

```
tagged_sent = ' '.join(tagged)
tagged_sent = tagged_sent[0].capitalize() + tagged_sent[1:]
```

And, as our final step in this function, we still need to return the finished product:

```
return tagged_sent
```

The function for creating the output is really overkill here because we could just as easily use a simple `print` statement in the calling program. However, a more complex module may still enrich the output in other ways, so having a specific function for achieving this, as well as allowing us to change the appearance of the output if needs be, and without the user of the module needing to be aware of this change. All they'd need to know is that to create an output, they ought to call this function.

Once you've finished implementing this function, you can write the remaining one, add the two new functions to your list of imports in the calling program, and add a loop like this there:

```
for sentence in sentences:
    output_tagged(tag_sentence(lex, sentence))
```

which will now output all your tagged sentences, provided of course you haven't got an error elsewhere in your program.

When you test the program, you should note that, because we hadn't defined all the word–tag combinations in our dictionary, there will be some words tagged _??? in the output. If this doesn't occur too often when you use your tagger, you can simply ignore it, but if your intention is to improve your lexicon coverage, you'd probably want to have a way of easily identifying all such unknown words, so that you can add them to the lexicon. I'll leave it up to you as an additional exercise to add some functionality to your module that will provide a list of unknown words to your user in some form.

Discussion 41   Installing PyQt

Essentially, this exercise shouldn't present any problems, provided that you have a relatively stable internet connection, and have used the syntax relevant for your level of permissions, either as administrator,

```
pip(3) install PyQt5
```

or as a simple user

```
pip(3) install -user PyQt5
```

In case you receive an error stating the pip wasn't found, you should try to follow the steps described in Chapter 1 for troubleshooting Python path issues, and try again.

Discussion 42   Creating a Word Object

Creating the file and importing the `re` module should present no problems, so we won't discuss these further. As this is going to be a slightly more complex module, though, you may want to add some docstrings describing its functionality before the `import` statement. I won't do this here to save space.

The first difficulty will arise when you create the first class for a verb, where of course you shouldn't forget that, by convention, the class name should have an initial capital. Here, again, it would make sense to add some documentation, so the first part of the class definition could look like this:

```
class Verb():
    """Class for modelling verbs

    base -- base form: non-optional
    person -- person: default '1'
    number -- number: default 'singular'
    tense_form -- tense form: default 'present';
        options: present, past, present participle
    v_type -- verb type: default 'r' für regular,
        otherwise i (or anything else ;-))"""
```

As you can already see, to get around the limitation of the reserved word `type`, I've chosen to use `v_type` because we're dealing with a verb here. The description already shows you to some extent which default values make sense to use in the following constructor, which would then look like this, where, to save space, I've not added the indentation that would be necessary because the method definition obviously occurs inside the block for the class definition:

```python
def __init__(self,
    base=None,
    person='1',
    number='singular',
    tense_form='present',
    v_type='r'):
    """Constructor"""

    if not base:
        raise NameError('No base form provided!')
    self.base = base
    self.person = person
    self.number = number
    self.tense_form = tense_form
    self.v_type = v_type
```

As you can see, since the base form is non-optional, I've set its initial value to None. This is because we need to be able to check on whether it's present or not, and if not, pass the potential NameError on to the calling program via `raise`, so that it can be handled there. We do this via the simple test

```python
if not base:
```

which will return True if the default value of None has not been changed to any valid string that could be used as a base form. Please note, though, that we have no way of being sure that the user of the class doesn't later provide a nonsense base form that will be used to generate a 'valid' result. In some cases, of course, this is exactly what we might want to do, though, for instance in an experiment where nonsense words are inflected in some form to fit into a particular context, and the test participants might then be asked to guess the meaning, etc.

If no argument for the base form is provided, the calling program will be responsible for handling the error in some form that is appropriate for processing in the relevant context. In other words, whenever a module user wants to create a verb object, they should use try/except blocks to ensure that valid objects are created. We don't need to test for any other values here because we already set valid defaults in the method head, so our constructor would automatically generate a suitable object, provided that a base form has been passed.

Because we're only handling regular verb forms, writing the two methods to create the present participle and past (participle) tense form is fairly easy. All we need to do initially is test if the verb is supposed to be a regular one, and if not, output a message saying that irregular ones haven't been implemented yet. If the verb is a regular one, we need to distinguish between two options each time, whether the base form already ends in an <e>, in which case we only need to add a <d> to the end to create the past form, or to slice it off if we want to create the present participle before adding the {ing} suffix. In all other cases, we first need to check and see if the base form ends in plosive (including nasal) or liquid consonants, which would force us to handle reduplication. For the past form, we also need to consider verbs ending in <y>, but isn't preceded by <a>, <o>, or <u>, which needs to be 'converted to' <i> before adding the relevant suffix. In all other cases, we simply add the suffixes {ed} or {ing}, respectively, making these two methods:

```
def past(self):
        if self.v_type=='r':
            if re.search(r'e$', self.base):
                return self.base + 'd'
            else:
                redup = re.search(r'([dlmnprt]])$', self.base)
                if redup:
                    return self.base + redup.group(1) + 'ed'
                elif re.search(r'(?<![aou])y$', self.base):
                    return self.base[0:-1] + 'ied'
                else:
                    return self.base + 'ed'
        else:
            return 'Irregular verb. Not yet implemented.'
```

and

```
def pres_part(self):
        if self.v_type=='r':
            if re.search(r'e$', self.base):
                return self.base[0:-1] + 'ing'
            else:
                redup = re.search(r'([dlmnprt])$', self.base)
                if redup:
                    return self.base + redup.group(1) + 'ing'
                else:
                    return self.base + 'ing'
        else:
            return 'Irregular verb. Not yet implemented.'
```

Most of the lines in these two methods will probably be relatively straightforward to understand, but handling the reduplication may still be a little difficult to comprehend. Here, we first test for the occurrence of the types of consonants listed above at the end of the base form, at the same time using the bracketing to allow us to store the matched form for reduplicating it. If such a consonant occurs, the value of `redup`, which of course stands for 'reduplication', will be `True` because we have a match object. We can then simply access the bracketed element via

`redup.group(1)`

and use it like a backreference to insert it in between the base form and the suffix before returning the reduplicated and inflected form.

Writing the method to generate the present form works in a similar way, only that this time, apart from testing for irregular verbs, we need to make a basic initial distinction between 3rd person singular forms and the rest of the options, which simply correspond to the base form. Within the 3rd person singular option, we again need to distinguish a number of cases, forms where the base ends in a sibilant, where we need to add <es>, where the base ends in <y>, again not preceded by <a>, <o>, or <u>, where the final letter needs to be sliced off and <ies> appended, and the rest, where a basic {s} suffix can be added, making the method definition:

```python
def present(self):
    if self.v_type=='r':
        if self.number=='singular' and self.person=='3':
            if re.search(r'[cs]h$', self.base):
                return self.base + 'es'
            elif re.search(r'(?<![aou])y$', self.base):
                return self.base[0:-1] + 'ies'
            else:
                return self.base + 's'
        else:
                return self.base
    else:
        return 'Irregular verb. Not yet implemented.'
```

As you'll have seen above, implementing a verb form generator of this type, which is of course an important part of any system for natural language generation, but can obviously equally be used for teaching morphology or other purposes, is by no means an easy task. When you test the functionality, you should also ensure that all potentially occurring cases are covered. However, coming up with a suitable number of examples in itself isn't an easy task, which is why it makes sense to implement your test strategy in the form of a loop that iterates over a list of verb forms and produces all the different forms we might want to generate. If we spot an error in the development process, or discover new options, we can then amend the rules in a circular fashion, each time iterating over the list of words again to see if the newly added parts work as expected and do not accidentally break any of the previously implemented ones. Of course, you could equally well add an option to test different words via the command line, but then you'd end up testing only one case at a time, and may well overlook any issues that could arise with other word forms, so the approach using a loop is generally preferable.

Modelling the Noun class is in fact very similar, only that the number of properties is obviously reduced to two, number and n_type, where the former should have the default singular and the latter, again, r for 'regular'. The definition is simpler than for verbs, though, as – apart from the constructor – we only need to write one method, plural(). In this method, because we're again only handling regular forms, we just need to model four different forms, the default case where only the {s} morpheme is attached, the case where the base ends in one of the sibilants we encountered above, where we again add <es>, and another special one where it ends in a different sibilant, <f>, in which case we again need to strip off the final letter and add <ves>, or again a final <y> not preceded by the vowels shown above, where we again slice off the final letter and append <ies> making the method:

```
def plural(self):
    if self.n_type == 'r':
        if re.search(r'(ch|sh?)$', self.base):
            return self.base + 'es'
        elif re.search(r'(?<!f)f$', self.base):
            return self.base[0:-1] + 'ves'
        elif re.search(r'(?<![aou])y$', self.base):
            return self.base[0:-1] + 'ies'
        else:
            return self.base + 's'
    else:
        return 'Irregular noun. Not yet implemented.'
```

When handling the final <f>, you'll hopefully have noticed that I've used lookbehind to ensure that there's only one final <f> present because otherwise the rule wouldn't apply.

As devising suitable lists for tests may have been a little difficult for you, I'll here show you my test block for reference:

```
if __name__ == '__main__':
    for v_base in ['star', 'stare', 'brim', 'stun', 'gaze',
        'rot', 'compel', 'top', 'pop', 'bed', 'cry', 'bay']:
        try:
            verb = Verb(base=v_base,
                person='3', number='singular', v_type='r')
            print(f'Base form: {verb.base}; present for person '
                f'{verb.person}: {verb.present()}')
            print(f'Present participle: {verb.pres_part()}; '
                f'past participle: {verb.past()}')
            gen_arg = 'past'
            print(f'Current verb form for "{gen_arg}" '
                f'via generator method: '
                f'{verb.generate_tense_form(gen_arg)}\n')
        except NameError as e:
            print(str(e))
    for n_form in ['cow', 'calf', 'puff', 'match',
        'house', 'baby', 'bay']:
        try:
            noun = Noun(n_form)
            print(f'The plural of the noun {noun.base} is: '
                f'{noun.plural()}')
        except NameError as e:
            print(str(e))
```

8

Word Lists, Frequencies and Ordering

So far in this book, we've seen different ways for identifying, manipulating, and presenting language data, as well as storing our analysis results. However, while being able to simply show the wealth of information that exists in such data, this only constitutes one part of the analysis spectrum, essentially the qualitative one. Yet, in order to fully understand linguistic data, we equally need to take into account the quantitative side. Being able to say whether a certain phenomenon is frequent or rare is an important means of gaining insights, establishing theories about language, or making use of our findings in a more applied way, e.g. in finding ways to improve the communication skills of language learners or professionals. Done properly, it's also a means of identifying pertinent topics in performing a distant reading of texts. Hence, in this chapter, we want to learn about ways and means for summarising and quantifying language patterns through word and frequency lists, as well as how to display such quantitative results in meaningful ways in the form of simple tables.

8.1 Introduction to Word and Frequency Lists

Word or frequency lists form an essential component of lexicographical, corpus linguistic and computational linguistics work. Before we'll discuss how to create and work with them, though, let's spend a little time again thinking about what their uses may be.

Exercise 43   Brainstorming the Use of Word and Frequency Lists

Think about how word lists or lists of other language patterns may be useful in dealing with different aspects of language.

Once you've identified a few potential uses, also reflect on which forms they might need to take to be most useful and how we may be able to get them into such shapes.

Now that you've spent a short while thinking about the usefulness of different types of lists, it's time to discuss how they can be created.

8.2 Generating Word Lists

The general approach to creating a word list is quite simple. We first split our text(s) into individual words, n-grams, or other units of analysis, creating a list of **tokens**, i.e. all individual forms that occur. This process is referred to as **segmentation** or **tokenisation**. We already performed some

Python Programming for Linguistics and Digital Humanities: Applications for Text-Focused Fields,
First Edition. Martin Weisser.
© 2024 John Wiley & Sons, Inc. Published 2024 by John Wiley & Sons, Inc.
Companion website: https://www.wiley.com/go/weisser/pythonprogling

form of segmentation earlier when we split strings into words or sentences, creating lists thereof. Before we can perform the splitting, though, we might initially need to carry out some cleanup operations, such as removing punctuation or quotation marks, etc., essentially anything that doesn't constitute a part of the patterns we want to identify.

After tokenisation, we of course end up with an unsorted list that contains duplicates because most tokens will occur more than once, and in an order that is only meaningful from a textual point of view. Our next step therefore involves identifying all unique forms, referred to as *types*, by removing duplicates, which is normally achieved through comparing and sorting the list elements. Python offers efficient ways of sorting via the `sort` method for lists and the `sorted` function for all iterables, where the former modifies the original list, while the latter creates a sorted copy. Reducing a list of tokens to types can just as easily be achieved by using the `set` function, though. The final step then consists in outputting the sorted list.

8.3 Sorting Basics

As already pointed out above, Python offers two different options for sorting, the `sort` method of the `list` object, and the `sorted` function. Both provide two optional keyword arguments, `reverse`, and `key`. The `reverse` argument is Boolean, so it can take on either `False` or `True`, defaulting to `False`. When set to `True`, the order of the elements to be sorted is – as the name says – reversed, so that strings are sorted from z-A, due to case distinctions, and numbers from n-1, i.e. from highest to lowest. As all sorting is based on a comparison between values, using the `key` argument, we can provide a function or method for generating a *sort key*. This is a special way of telling Python how exactly the comparison should be carried out. For instance, using the `str.lower` method as a key, we can use downcased copies of the original strings during comparison, allowing us to ignore case distinctions and produce a dictionary sorting where words starting in upper- and lowercase are sorted next to each other, rather than all words starting with capital letters coming first. Note, though, that we're essentially providing the name of the method as an argument here, rather than calling it directly, so that the round brackets that usually form a part of calling methods are omitted!

It's also possible to use more complex options for generating sort keys, which we'll discuss in Section 8.5. For now, though, we first want to start creating simple word lists sorted in dictionary order.

Exercise 44   Creating a Word List

Write the program `21_word_list.py`, in which you create a word list from Mary Shelley's *Frankenstein* using the file `frankenstein.txt`, which you should already have downloaded from http://www.wiley.com/go/weisser/pythonprogling along with the sample text file, and which should, again, be stored in your `texts` folder.

First import the `sys` and `re` modules.

Next, set up a variable for the word list, then another variable for the input file, using the relative path to its folder.

Generate an output file path for the word list from the input file path. To do so, use the file name as a suitable basis, and add an indication as to the nature of file we're producing. To achieve this end, use `os.path.split` to split the file path into the original path and the file name, first making the file path absolute using `os.path.abspath`. Then, split the base path once more, so that we end up one level above the `texts` folder and can use this new base path to generate the final file path to the `output` folder and with the new file name. If necessary, refresh your memory about how to handle file paths by going through Section 5.7 once more.

Next – with appropriate error handling – open the input file and iterate over the lines.

Use regexes to clean the line. First, after performing a cursory examination by scrolling through the file, replace all special characters or constructs you can identify in the file by spaces, then substitute at least two occurrences of spaces in a row by single ones.

Use the `strip` method on the line to remove any potential leading or trailing whitespaces.

As the cleanup operation may have resulted in empty lines, test if the line is empty using the `not` operator. Hint: an empty string is always `False`. If the condition is fulfilled, use a `continue` statement to skip the line and continue the loop with the next one.

If the line isn't empty, extend the word list by using `re.split` to split the line at spaces and add the resulting list to the end.

Open the output file, again using suitable error handling.

Iterate over the word list, first removing duplicates through the `set` function and sorting the elements using the `sorted` function with `str.lower` as key in the iteration.

Inside the loop, write the current word and a line break to the output file.

Check the result in the output file.

As you've just seen, generating a simple sorted word list is possible without ever needing to worry about how to identify the types or to do the comparison for putting them in the right order. However, as useful as this list may already be, as pointed out earlier, for most purposes, having a frequency list is much more useful, so we'll look into how to produce one next.

8.4 Generating Basic Word Frequency Lists

The procedure for creating word frequency lists is very similar to generating word lists, only that the words we find are set up as keys in a dictionary with an associated counter. Since the keys in a dictionary are unique, anyway, we no longer need to use the `set` function, either, but only increment the counter for each type each time we encounter a new token of it. However, as Python doesn't allow dictionary keys to be created without a corresponding value, when we identify a new type, a default value of 0 first needs to be set via the `setdefault` method before we can increment a counter at each occurrence of a token.

Because the word types we encounter while creating the frequency dictionary will obviously not occur in alphabetical order, but the order the words appear in the book, it's important to sort the keys using the relevant order when we create the output. However, given our current knowledge, we can still only do this with alphabetically ascending or descending sorting, where we don't need to use the `reverse` keyword argument for the former, but set it to `True` for the latter. Armed with this knowledge, let's now modify the previous program to produce a frequency list instead of the original word list.

Exercise 45 Creating a Word Frequency List

Save the previous program as `22_frequency_list.py` and adjust it, so that it generates a frequency list in an aptly named file.

Instead of the empty list, set up an empty dictionary, as well as a variable that can store the length of the longest word, so that we can later produce a suitable tabular output.

Where you previously appended the results of the `re.split` method to the list, now iterate over the results instead, and add the current word as key, each time assigning an incremented counter to this key via `dictionaryname.setdefault(key, 0) + 1`.

In addition, set up a test to see if the current word is longer than the previously longest one, and change the value accordingly if necessary.

For the output, this time you need to iterate over the sorted keys of the dictionary, using the appropriate technique. Inside the loop, output the current word, left aligned and formatted to the length of the longest word, a tab, the value of the word, and a line break.

Run the program again on the same file as before and check the result.

As we've just seen, frequency lists can already be more informative and useful than mere word lists, even in the limited form we are able to produce so far. Nevertheless, their usefulness for us is still restricted because we'd really like to be able to sort according to the frequencies, which the standard, simple sorting options using basic Python functions don't allow us to do. To learn how to perform more complex types of sorting, we first need to find out about a special type of function Python offers for this and other purposes, which we'll do in the following section.

8.5 Lambda Functions

Anonymous functions in Python are called *lambda functions* or *lambda expressions*. They're called anonymous because they can be defined ad hoc inside your code, and used directly without having to give them a name or using the keyword `def`. They're extremely useful for filtering operations or generating sort keys, e.g. to sort frequency lists by values, with the negation of the values triggering reverse sorting. The basic syntax is:

```
lambda variable: expression
```

or

```
lambda variable: (tuple)
```

For example, we can use the lambda function on the right-hand side of the assignment operator as an argument to the `key` keyword like this

```
key = lambda x: words[x]
```

which then fetches the value of word x – i.e. its frequency – as sort key from the dictionary `words`, thereby creating a list that is sorted according to ascending frequencies. In other words, we're creating a frequency list starting from a frequency of 1 and going up to the most frequent types. To reverse this sorting, we can simply add a negative prefix, hence writing

```
key = lambda x: -words[x]
```

which in effect is the numerical counterpart to using the `reverse` keyword in alphabetical sorting. To add a secondary sort key after achieving the numerical sorting, we need to use a tuple where we specify the primary key – in the above case the descending frequency – as the first element, and then a secondary key as the second element inside the tuple. When creating numerically sorted frequency lists, the secondary key is normally the alphabetical order, so that, effectively, the word types are first sorted by frequency, but then – because different types may of course occur with the same frequency – by their alphabetical order, too. Hence, to generate a list that is first sorted by descending frequency and then case-insensitively in dictionary order, we would simply write

```
key = lambda x: (-words[x], x.lower())
```

Please note, too, that whereas we had to specify the call to the `lower` method of the `str` object in our earlier example without the round brackets when we specified the key argument, we now have to add the round brackets. This is because we're now applying this directly to a string, rather than in a sense stating that this method should be applied to all strings in general. In some cases, it may also even be useful to have a tertiary sort key, as you'll hopefully realise while doing the next exercise.

Exercise 46   Implementing a Frequency List Object

Write the new module `frequencies_a.py`, in which you implement the frequency list as a `Frequency_list` class.

This class should take the input file, the output file and the sort order as arguments to its constructor, with the default for sorting being `'n-1'`, i.e. by descending frequency. To refresh your memory on how to create a constructor, you can turn back to Section 7.7.1 if necessary.

Inside the constructor, you should first set up empty instance variables for your frequency list, as well as a list to later contain the sorted keys only, and then test to see if the input file name was provided, just as we did for the objects in Exercise 42. If not, raise a `NameError` again, and if no error occurs, generate the output filename here directly, but only if it hasn't been specified, using the same safe option for generating the file path as before.

Next, write a method to first produce the list in memory, with suitable error handling and passing a potential `OSError` to the calling program. Inside this method, you should also determine how long the longest word and longest counter are, and store these in instance variables of the class, so that these can later be used for formatting the output. Hint: To identify the length of a number, it first needs to be cast to a string. Before you start the list generation, though, you first need to empty any potentially existing frequency list because the object may have been used before with a different input file that may or may not contain the same words.

Now write a method `make_sorted_list` that will create a list of sorted keys from the frequency list dictionary, given a sort order that is retrieved from the relevant instance variable of the object. The sorting options you should implement are alphabetical (`a-z`) and reverse alphabetical (`z-a`), descending (`n-1`) and ascending numerical (`1-n`), by word length (`w_length`), and by endings (`reverse`). Bear in mind that you'll need to use lambda functions with tuples in the sort key for all but the alphabetical sorting options, where usually the second option is a case-insensitive comparison, but even a third key may be possible.

Next, add a method `output_list` to generate the output, in which you – again with suitable error handling – open the output file and write the frequency list out by iterating over the list of sorted keys, and outputting each key and its associated value that you fetch from the original frequency list dictionary.

Finally, also implement a test block, again adding suitable error handling options for errors that may be reported by the class, and test the various options for sorted output.

So far, all the frequencies we've looked at were absolute, raw ones, but of course we can also calculate relative frequencies, and should especially do so if we want to make comparisons between files or even whole corpora. We'll learn how to do this in Chapter 11, when we'll create an illustrative graph that allows us to make such a comparison visually. We also haven't discussed how to create frequencies of other linguistic features, but as these often simply involve extracting the relevant information, such as PoS tags, from annotated data, I'll leave this up to you to think about you can best achieve this. As another part of this exercise, you could also think about how it may be possible to extract n-grams, and perhaps even implement an n-gram frequency counter by revising your frequency object in a suitable manner.

8.6 Discussions

Discussion 43   Brainstorming the Use of Word and Frequency Lists

If you think about pure word lists, i.e. those that don't contain any frequency information, the first use that perhaps comes to mind is to create a vocabulary list from one or more files that represent a new topic to either be discussed in class (for teachers) or to be learnt (for students). However, lists of words aren't the only thing that could be of interest in analysing language. We can also create lists for other language patterns, such as multi-word units, more commonly referred to as *n-grams*, where 'n' stands for 'any number', or – on the shorter side – lists of phonemes, graphemes, PoS tags, etc., which may represent various aspects of language. On a grander scale, such lists may help us in identifying the whole lexicon of a language, provided, of course, that we have a large enough *corpus* of data from as many domains or genres as possible, thereby covering – as far as only possible – all semantic or lexicographic aspects of language. N-gram lists, even for smaller corpora, may allow us to discover phraseological units or idiomatic structures, and also give us hints about the topics under discussion.

However, pure lists are generally less informative than those that also provide an indication as to the frequency of words or patterns. This is because high frequencies point towards common language functions that may represent generally accepted usages, while low ones can imply rather idiosyncratic usage that could either constitute a deviation from a norm or standard variety, or deliberate attempts at 'playing with language', i.e. some form of stylistic device, for instance in poetry. Frequency lists are hence more informative and representative, and also more comparable to other lists because especially through comparisons, we can identify key functions or topics more easily.

Just how informative word and frequency lists can be of course depends on how they are structured. For a vocabulary list, having the words ordered by frequency, even if the frequencies aren't shown, will allow teachers and students to identify which words may be more relevant for a given purpose, i.e. whether they may be more common or specific, while for looking words up in a dictionary, it is not only common, but also obviously more useful, to be able to look them up in alphabetical order. The same essentially goes for identifying patterns using frequencies. Here, we'll normally prefer an ordering according to descending frequency to be able to view the most common words or patterns first, only switching to the opposite ordering if we're interested in identifying rare items. If we're looking for very specific patterns, though, that may start or end in the same characters, we might prefer an alphabetically or even reverse alphabetically sorted list, at the same time retaining the frequency information to be able to ascertain which of the sub-patterns are more frequent.

   To create such lists, we can use different means. Pure word lists can theoretically be generated as simple lists, but in general, it's still more useful to use dictionaries where the key represents the word or pattern we want to quantify, and the value its associated frequency. To be able to generate the types of meaningful output discussed in Sections 8.3 and 8.4, we obviously need to have a way of sorting the data.

Discussion 44   Creating a Word List

Importing the `sys` and `re` modules should have become second nature to you because we use them in almost all of our programs now, but of course you also shouldn't forget to import the `os.path` module at the top of your program, so that you can use it to safely extract the file name from the whole path and create a new one by joining the path elements together again. Of course the word list should initially be set up as an empty list because we don't require any frequency information yet, making the first few lines after imports something like this:

```
words = []
input_file = '../texts/frankenstein.txt'
pathName, fileName = os.path.split(os.path.abspath(input_file))
basePath, _ = os.path.split(pathName)
outputFile = os.path.join(basePath, 'output', 'wordlist_' +
fileName)
```

Note that we need to use `os.path.split` twice here, first to extract the original file path, which still points to the `texts` folder, though. We then split this again, this time discarding the final folder name assigning it to a dummy variable – because we don't need the folder name anymore, but the function returns a two-element tuple. Once we have successfully extracted the base path, we then use this again as the first argument to `os.path.join`, the name of the output folder as the second, and then concatenating the original file name into a new, meaningful one that we use as the third argument, ending up with the complete output file path again. Note that we here don't need to test for whether the output folder exists because we know that we've created it earlier. For a more general program that may take any arbitrary combination of input and output paths, we'd need to test for the existence of the output path and, if necessary, create it before we attempt to write the output file.

   Opening the input file and setting up the `for` loop that iterates over the lines is nothing new, so we'll only discuss what needs to happen inside this loop here. The special characters that you need to remove essentially comprise punctuation and quotation marks, as well as brackets, hyphens, and underscores, which you can easily define as a character class. The reason why we initially want to convert these to spaces is because the file contains double hyphens to mimic dashes that aren't surrounded by spaces, so that by simply removing them, we'd end up with concatenated words. To illustrate this, let's take a look at the part where this occurs for the first time inside the text:

   There--for with your leave, my sister, I will put
   some trust in preceding navigators--there snow and frost are banished

As you can see, here, the narrator first starts a sentence, but then inserts a parenthetical aside marked through the double hyphens, before picking up the original train of thought, repeating the first word. Now, if we were to simply delete the hyphens, we'd end up with the two 'words' *Therefor*, which could of course easily be confused with the actual word *therefore*, and *navigatorsthere*, which obviously doesn't even resemble any valid word in the English language. By replacing these characters by a space, and collapsing all repeated spaces into single ones, though, we effectively isolate the original words and make it possible to split on whitespace only. Hence, the whole cleanup operation for the line could look like this:

```
line = re.sub(r'[".,;!?:()\[\]`_-]',' ', line)
line = re.sub(r'\s{2,}', ' ', line)
line = line.strip()
```

Of course, `strip` not only removes leading or trailing actual spaces, but as we learnt before, also the trailing line break that would otherwise end up becoming a part of the final word once we split the line on whitespace later. The test for whether there's any actual content on the line, including skipping over the line in case it's empty, would simply be

```
if not line:
    continue
```

Splitting the line into words and adding these words to the existing lists can easily be achieved in one line like this:

```
words.extend(re.split(r'\s', line))
```

The reason why we need to use the `extend` method here, which I'd already hinted at in the instructions by using the word *extend*, is that if we used `append` instead, we'd be adding a list object to the existing list, rather than appending the individual words. If you remember, I already alerted you to this issue in Section 3.2 while discussing the methods of the list object. The last line concludes the iteration over the lines, so, if nothing else has gone wrong, you should now have a list of – as yet duplicate – words, and we can proceed towards creating the output. Here, again, we can skip the part where you open the file with error handling in our discussion, and only talk about how you can efficiently arrive at outputting the sorted list of types. You can do so by creating a `for` loop to iterate over all unique words from the word list, produced via the `set` function, in turn using this as the first argument to the `sorted` function, while lowercasing the words for comparison, like this:

```
for word in sorted(set(words), key=str.lower):
```

All that remains to do then is to write each word to the output file, which should present no problem to you. As we've seen before, the only drawback here is that we end up with a trailing newline at the end of the file. However, in terms of the results, when you open the file, you can see that the alphabetical order we've achieved through the sorting initially shows you rather uninteresting 'words', i.e. an apostrophe and numbers, which aren't really very meaningful. Even the first 'real' word, *a*, which should occur on line 38 in your file, isn't really very interesting from a semantic point of view. However, soon afterwards, you should be able to spot word forms that are more interesting, especially as many of them are negatively connotated, which already gives us a first subtle hint about the nature of the whole text. In addition, you should be able to spot that – unlike in a dictionary – the entries in your list don't only constitute base forms, but are often inflected, and that we've really achieved a dictionary sort order where capitalised and lowercased versions of word forms occur next to each other.

Discussion 45   Creating a Word Frequency List

Setting up the empty dictionary and a variable for storing the length of the longest word should present no problem, and you'll probably have written something like this:

```
words = {}
longest_word = 0
```

Iterating over the words of course necessitates a `for` loop where we can access each word in turn and either add it to the dictionary or increment the counter if the relevant key exists. Luckily, though, the `setdefault` method allows us to either get the current value of an existing key or create one if it doesn't, so we only need one line to achieve this, making our loop:

```
for word in re.split(r'\s', line):
    words[word] = words.setdefault(word, 0) + 1
    if len(word) > longest_word:
        longest_word = len(word)
```

In case you still have difficulties understanding the assignment in the second line above, the `setdefault` method is here applied to our dictionary `words`, and first checks to see if the key is present in this dictionary. If so, it returns its current value, which we can simply increase by 1 and then assign this new value to the key again. If the key doesn't exist, the method uses the second argument to create and initialise it, so that we then have an original value of 0 that we can increase to 1 and assign it to the key.

The `if` statement checks to see if the length of the current word is longer than any previously recorded length, and if it is, uses this as the new value of `longest_word`. When we process the first word in the text, this will obviously be longer because we initialised the variable to 0, but with each new word, there will be two options, either that it's longer or not.

To iterate over the keys in the dictionary in alphabetical order, we simply use the `keys` method as the first argument to the `sorted` function, ensuring again that case distinctions are ignored through the keyword argument `key`:

```
for word in sorted(words.keys(), key=str.lower):
    outFile.write(f'{word:{longest_word}}\t{words[word]}\n')
```

When you run the program and view the output, you should immediately be able to see the obvious difference to the previous list in that – despite the words still appearing in the same order – the presentation has changed to now incorporate the frequencies, and that these are neatly arranged in tabular form. However, the informativeness is still not optimal, due to the fact that we retain the alphabetical order, even if the frequencies already do provide more information. For instance, we can see that the indefinite determiner occurs with a much higher frequency than the other words listed around it, and that some of the negatively connotated forms, despite being much rarer, are still in a range that distinguishes them from the rarest ones, especially if we add the frequencies for the lemma *abhor* and its nominal and adjectival forms together.

You may have noted that we haven't actually made use of the `reverse` option in sorting yet. If you really want to try this out, you can simply add it to your code in the relevant place or even modify the program to accept the Boolean value as a command-line argument as an additional exercise.

Discussion 46   Implementing a Frequency List Object

Because we don't actually terminate the program when we report errors, we don't need to import the `sys` module, but only `re` and `os.path`. As many of the elements in the constructor are similar to the ones we used in Exercise 42, I won't discuss them here in detail, but simply show you the constructor and then explain some of its parts.

```
def __init__(self,
        input_file=None,
        output_file=None,
        sort_order='n-1'):
    self.sort_order = sort_order
    self.words = {}
    self.sorted_list = []
    if not input_file:
        raise NameError('No filename provided! '
            'Unable to create frequency list...')
    else:
        self.input_file = input_file
        pathName, fileName=os.path.split(os.path.
            abspath(input_file))'
        basePath, _ = os.path.split(pathName)
    if not output_file:
        self.output_file = os.path.join(basePath, 'output',
            'frequency_list_' + fileName)
    else:
        self.output_file = output_file
```

Here, the keyword arguments for the input and the output files should both be set to None as defaults. For the input file, this is because, without an input path, we also cannot generate an output path, and hence no frequency list at all. However, for the output file path, it's slightly different, since it can either be provided as an argument or – if not – generated from the input file name. If it's been provided as a keyword argument, it can simply be transferred to the instance variable `self.outputfile` from its keyword argument. Because the default has been set for the sort order, we can again copy it into the instance variable `self.sort_order` from the keyword argument, and only need to specify it as an argument if we really want to use a different option. The two variables for the frequency dictionary and key list also need to be defined as instance variables because they have to be accessible by the methods of the class.

The method for creating the list, suitably called `create_list`, is very similar to the way we generated the list in the previous, non-object-oriented, version, only that, as stated in the instructions, you need to empty any previously existing frequency list. If you don't do this, the keys (and values) for words that don't exist in the current input file may be preserved and inadvertently end up in your output, thus falsifying your results. The variable to hold the length of the longest word again needs to be defined as an instance variable, again to allow you to access it from anywhere inside the class. In addition, you now also need to add another instance variable for the longest number because we later want to align the numbers in the output, too. As the only part of the method that differs from our previous implementation is the loop, I'll only show and briefly discuss this here.

```
for word in re.split(r'\s', line):
    if len(word) > self.longest_word:
        self.longest_word = len(word)
    self.words[word] = self.words.setdefault(word, 0) + 1
    if len(str(self.words[word])) > self.max_len_number:
        self.max_len_number = len(str(self.words[word]))
```

As you can see, the variables that record the lengths are both used as instance variables, and also need to be initialised to 0 before the list is created, even if this isn't shown in the code above. This is also the reason why we declare and initialise them inside this method, rather than in the constructor. In the final two lines of code above, we need to use the `str` function twice while accessing the value associated with the current key. This is because the `len` function doesn't work for integers, so we first need to cast the numbers to strings to determine how long they are as strings because this is really what we'll later need to use for the alignment in the output method.

The `make_sorted_list` method essentially consists of a series of conditional expressions where we test for which sort key has been defined when the object was created. Hence, it needs to test against the value of the instance variable `self.sort_order`, making the complete method something like this:

```
def make_sorted_list(self):
    if self.sort_order=='a-z':
        self.sorted_list = sorted(
            self.words.keys(),
            key=str.casefold)
    elif self.sort_order=='z-a':
        self.sorted_list = sorted(
            self.words.keys(),
            key=str.casefold, reverse=True)
    elif self.sort_order=='n-1':
        self.sorted_list = sorted(
            self.words.keys(),
            key=lambda word: (-self.words[word],word.casefold()))
    elif self.sort_order=='1-n':
        self.sorted_list = sorted(
            self.words.keys(),
            key=lambda word: (self.words[word],word.casefold()))
    elif self.sort_order=='w_length':
        self.sorted_list = sorted(
            self.words.keys(),
            key=lambda word: (-len(word),-self.words[word],
                word.casefold()))
```

```
    elif self.sort_order=='reverse':
        self.sorted_list = sorted(
            self.words.keys(),
            key=lambda word: (word[::-1],len(word)))
```

Although we could do the sorting directly in the output, using a list of keys that can later control the retrieval of values from the frequency list allows us to define this in a compact way that will also make it easier to add different sort keys later. As the first argument to the `sorted` method, we iterate over keys of our frequency list in each case, but of course the procedure regarding the use of keys and/or reverse option then differs. The simplest case is the alphabetical order (`a-z`) we already employed before, but where – instead of using `str.lower` – we use `str.casefold` with the keyword argument `key` to also cater for languages that may require a special sort order along with the lowercasing. Reversing the order is only slightly more complicated because all we have to do is to add the keyword argument `reverse` with a value of `True`. The remainder of the options all require the use of lambda functions with tuples containing either two or three sort keys.

Achieving the descending numerical option, which is the most useful one for many analysis purposes, first requires us to access the value of the current key – where reversing the order is done by using a negative prefix – as the primary sorting criterion. However, as multiple words with the same frequency may occur in the data, it makes sense to then also sort these alphabetically using a caseless comparison. Please note here that simply providing the name of the method without the round brackets doesn't work because the lambda function actually needs to call the method directly. If you omit the brackets, your program will fail with a `TypeError`. To generate the opposite sort order (`1-n`), all we then need to do is leave out the negative prefix.

The most complex of our sort operations in terms of keys is `w_length`. Here, we normally want to see longer words first because they're more likely to contain compound morphemes or suffixes, so we sort by descending length of the word itself, then by descending frequency because more frequent constructions tend to be more interesting, and finally by the word itself, again using caseless comparison.

The reverse-sorted list of keys can be created using the slice syntax with negative step value I already showed you in Section 4.3.2, only that I've added a secondary sort by length, again to be able to see common suffixes better.

Writing the output method should present no obstacle to you. The only thing that may be unusual for you here is that we use the sorted list of keys as a way to retrieve the keys from the frequency dictionary, somewhat like an index the dictionary itself doesn't have. To format the output, we use the instance variables of the object containing the lengths of the longest string and number we determined when we created the original frequency list.

```
def output_list(self):
    try:
        with open(self.output_file, 'w',
                encoding='utf-8') as outFile:
            for word in self.sorted_list:
                outFile.write(f'{word:{self.longest_word}}\t'
                f'{self.words[word]:>{self.max_len_number}d}\n')
    except OSError as err:
        raise OSError(err)
```

How exactly you write the test block is up to you, but in it, you should follow all necessary steps to create and output a frequency list, which first involves creating the object, and then calling the relevant methods, `create_list`, `make_sorted_list`, and `output_list` on it. All these steps should occur in a `try` block, and the exception should catch any errors that might occur at object creation, input or output time, which of course means that you don't only need to trap `OSErrors` that get reported if either input or output file cannot be opened, but also the `NameError` that we `raised` if no input file was specified. Hence your `except` blocks could look like this:

```
except OSError as f1:
    print('Wrong input or output file provided!',
        str(f1).split(' ')[-1])
except NameError as f2:
    print(str(f2))
```

To allow me to make the information for the potential `OSError` more compact and informative, as either the input or the output file may throw this error, and to add my own special message at the beginning, I've here only extracted the final part of the original error message, which is the name of the file that caused the error.

9

Interacting with Data and Users Through GUIs

In this chapter, we'll learn how to facilitate our interaction with data and users by exploring basic graphical user interfaces. We'll start by discussing what they are and also to some extent how they work, then move on to finding out about PyQt, the GUI module we'll be using for this book – which you already installed in Exercise 41 in Chapter 7 – and how to use the window elements, called **widgets**, it puts at our disposal in order to create simple, yet powerful, interactive applications.

9.1 Graphical User Interfaces

Graphical User Interfaces, often abbreviated to *GUIs* and pronounced /guʷiːz/, simplify our interaction with data and/or users. For instance, they allow us to choose program options that would otherwise need to be provided as arguments at program start, such as files to process, different display options for data (sorting options, formatting, etc.). This makes it possible to process our data more interactively than has been possible using the programs we've designed so far. To provide this functionality, GUI programs usually display an initial interface, and then wait for user actions or other types of events in a so-called **event loop**. These events may be mouse clicks for starting actions or selecting options, choosing/opening files or folders, typing text in editor or input windows, outputting results, etc.

Before we take a look at how we can design such GUIs in PyQt, let's first spend some time thinking about the usefulness of such an approach for our particular purposes.

Exercise 47   Brainstorming the Potential of GUIs

Take a few minutes to reflect on how we could have made use of GUIs for the programs we've written so far, in terms of input or output options, making other choices, or displaying and working with data in general. If you already have experience in working with language analysis programs, feel free to draw on this, but otherwise perhaps rely on your knowledge of word processors, spreadsheets, etc.

Python Programming for Linguistics and Digital Humanities: Applications for Text-Focused Fields, First Edition. Martin Weisser.
© 2024 John Wiley & Sons, Inc. Published 2024 by John Wiley & Sons, Inc.
Companion website: https://www.wiley.com/go/weisser/pythonprogling

9.2 PyQt Basics

GUI toolkits, such as PyQt, provide facilities for creating a number of widgets, i.e. windows or graphical objects that offer different types of functionality for various purposes, some of which I've already referred to in the discussion of the previous exercise. We'll explore the most useful widgets in the following sections, but for now want to discuss only the two main types of interface windows for designing programs that PyQt offers, those that provide the basis for creating or deriving new applications.

The first – more basic – type is the *dialog window* (QDialog), which is useful for creating simple programs with limited functionality and simple layout. Dialog-based programs generally have no menus or status bars, either, and only consist of a few essential widgets.

The window type that allows us to develop more complex programs similar to the ones you're using on your computer every day is the *main window* (QMainWindow). Main window-based applications generally have menus, optionally also tool bars, status bars, or even dockable bars that can be positioned in different places. They always require one widget to be set as their *central widget*. This may be an editor window or a frame or layout that holds other components.

Both types of window need to run as part of an application (QApplication) that sets up and handles the event loop, as well as providing access to some system information related to display size, etc. As you may already have noticed, all components in PyQt start with a Q and use camel case for the component names. The communication between widgets and the program runs via *signals*, e.g. mouse clicks, that are linked to *slots* that represent functions or methods to be executed when a signal occurs. When we design PyQt applications, we generally require imports from three different sub-modules.

The PyQt5.QtCore sub-module offers basic functionality and objects required for interaction, such as signals and slots, coordinates (QPoint), sizes (QSize), and in/output (*I/O*) methods and operations. PyQt5.QtGui brings in basic functionality for widgets, such as for setting or getting their colours (QColor) and fonts (QFont), keyboard shortcuts (QKeySequence), mouse or cursor positions (QCursor), as well as text properties and operations. Finally, PyQt5.QtWidgets offers functionality for creating programs via QApplication, main windows (QMainWindow) and dialogs (QDialog), various layout options, many types of specialised widgets, menus, and actions (QAction). The latter allow us to create abstract events that can then be linked to slots, and mapped onto multiple different widgets like menus, buttons, or keyboard shortcuts at the same time. For imports from both PyQt5.QtCore and PyQt5.QtGui, using from module import * is suitable, but for PyQt5.QtWidgets, more selective options are advisable to save memory.

9.2.1 The General Approach to Designing GUI-based Programs

The general approach to designing GUI programs always involves a similar number of steps. We first need to make a choice regarding the initial option of a dialog-versus a main window-based approach. If we opt for a dialog-based approach, we can directly create the dialog and add a few widgets to it, generally using a fixed layout where we manually position the elements. However, for most of our analysis purposes, we tend to require more complex programs comprising a multitude of widgets, such as buttons, drop-down lists, text fields, etc., so that we'll predominantly be working with main windows, and the following discussion will focus on those.

Here, again we have the option to make direct use of QMainWindow class if our programs are small and relatively simple. To be truly flexible and give us the ability to design customised components for our applications, it makes more sense, though, to derive classes from the main window class via its __init__ method, and customise them in a suitable manner. We'll learn how to do this in Section 9.2.4.

The next step consists in making a selection of layout options and the setting up and configuration of the individual GUI elements required for our specific purposes. Setting up and arranging these options is often done via a user-defined `initUI` or similarly named method during derivation, which improves the separation between graphical interface and program routines and logic.

Once the layout for the program has been created, the final step consists in tying actions and methods to widgets using `QActions` or user-defined methods linked to signals.

9.2.2   Useful PyQt Widgets

PyQt offers a large variety of widgets ranging from simple buttons to fully fledged web browsers or multimedia components, so that we certainly won't be able to cover all of these here. Before we start getting to know more about the ones that will initially be most useful for us, let's first do another exercise to give you an overview of what these may be in an exploratory fashion.

Exercise 48   Familiarising Yourself with Some Useful PyQt Widgets

Download the file `widget_demo_en.zip` from
https://martinweisser.org/tools/zips/widget_demo_en.zip.
Unpack it, start the program `widget_demo.py`, and familiarise yourself a little with the different types of widgets, initially without looking closely at the associated descriptions.
Think about for which purposes the different types could be useful in our work.
Which widgets would you use to write a program for demonstrating the syntactic inversion of simple declarative sentences?
Draw a layout for this and briefly reflect on how the individual elements should be linked to different events, and which potential errors would need to be handled.

To get some real, yet still fairly basic, hands-on experience in developing GUI programs, we'll develop this program step-by-step from here, each time implementing the things you'll learn from now on.

Although you've already seen examples of many widgets that may be useful for our analysis purposes in the previous exercise, Table 9.1 presents a compact overview of these, including brief descriptions, and adds a few that weren't shown there, partly because they may not always be visible. This list will still be complemented by further widgets as they become relevant for layouting and other purposes.

Table 9.1   Some useful widgets.

Widget type	Brief description
QWidget	Base class for all widgets
QFrame	Frequently invisible container for layouts (more on this later)
QLabel	Non-editable text field for displaying information or messages
QLineEdit	Single-line, editable text field for inputting arguments or outputting copyable results
QTextEdit	Multi-line text field for working with texts
QPushButton	Button for triggering actions
QListWidget	List field listing entries line-by-line
QComboBox	Editable dropdown list
QSpinBox	Field for setting number values via buttons that can in- or decrease values

(Continued)

Table 9.1 (Continued)

Widget type	Brief description
QCheckBox	Field for selecting/unselecting options
QRadioButton	Toggle button (generally in QButtonGroup)
QMenuBar	Menu bar
QToolBar	Container for QPushButtons
QStatusBar	Status bar for displaying settings, options, etc.
QFileDialog	Dialog for selecting files or folders

Armed with some knowledge about which widgets you might end up using most frequently, we can now start looking into what the setup for a minimal GUI program looks like before delving further into creating more complex ones.

9.2.3 A Minimal PyQt Program

To be able to understand better how GUI programs are set up and run, let's first take a quick look at a minimal program that can display some text to the user. Unlike most of the other GUI programs you're likely to design, though, this program will also accept an argument from the command line to make it slightly more interesting. Figure 9.1 shows what this minimal program will look like, and where the text displayed in the box has been provided as the command-line argument.

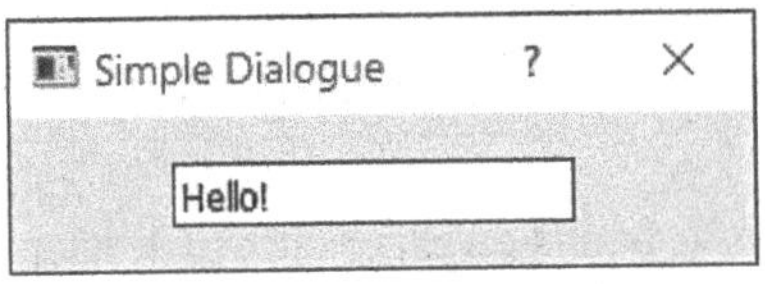

Figure 9.1 A minimal GUI program.

In order to be able to accept command line arguments, as well as terminate the program in a graceful manner should something go wrong, we first need to import the sys module again, and then a few additional widgets. Since this is only a very simple program, we'll be using a dialog-based approach. Because all PyQt programs minimally require the program to be defined as a QApplication, we also import this, the QDialog widget, and a QLineEdit widget that will allow us to display the text provided as the command-line argument, making the import section this:

```
import sys
from PyQt5.QtWidgets import QApplication, QDialog, QLineEdit
```

This is all we need to create a program, which is then set up in a __main__ block, as we did for testing our previous programs. Inside this block, we first have to create the application, which is done by instantiating a QApplication object with the sys.argv list as an argument, so that we'll have access to the command line:

```
app = QApplication(sys.argv)
```

The variable name app is frequently used to create such application objects, but you're obviously free to choose your own name. In the next step, we need to create a dialog window as the main interface to the program:

```
window = QDialog()
```

Once we've set up this window, we first want to configure some of its display properties:

```
window.setGeometry(100,100,250,50)
window.setWindowTitle('Simple dialogue')
```

In the first line, we use the `setGeometry` method to define where the window will be placed once the program is actually running and is displayed, as well as its dimensions. The first two arguments represent coordinates on the x- and y-axes with respect to the output screen, so our dialog will be shown 100 pixels from the left and down from the top left-hand corner of the screen. Arranging it to show up in the top left-hand corner, as it would otherwise do, simply wouldn't look nice.

Arguments three and four allow us to define the width and height of the window. If we simply set them to 0 each, PyQt would automatically handle the size of the window, which may end up looking sub-optimal, so we define sensible sizes in pixels. Placing and sizing windows and widgets in this way involves some trial and error, which makes it rather cumbersome. Luckily, though, working with layouts later will greatly simplify these issues. Once we've created the primary interface for our application, we can add the output field to it like this:

```
output_field = QLineEdit(window)
```

Note that the only argument we've here provided for the 'label' is a reference to its parent window, but no text yet, because we want to get this from the command line. The reference to the parent object is required here, though, because otherwise the application wouldn't 'know' which program window the text should be placed in. Once we start working with layouts, however, we'll generally be able to omit this because then widgets will be directly added to those, automatically making them their parent. To be able to assign the value of the command line argument to the output field, we call its `setText` method with `sys.argv[1]` as the argument:

```
output_field.setText(sys.argv[1])
```

This step has now allowed us to set up the output field and populate it with some text, but would leave the field to be aligned with the left-hand side of the application window. That doesn't look very neat, either, so it's better to position it somewhere near the centre of the dialog widget, which we do by calling its `move` method:

```
output_field.move(55,15)
```

All that's left to do now is to actually tell the window to display itself once the program's running, and start the program itself. Doing so requires us to use the following two lines:

```
window.show()
sys.exit(app.exec_())
```

If we were to omit the call to `show`, the program would in fact run, but simply not show up on screen, so it's essential not to forget this. Executing the program is essentially achieved via the `exec_` method of the application object, but we use this as an argument to `sys.exit` here so that Python can clean up memory once the user clicks on the close button, the 'x' in the top right-hand corner on Windows or Linux, and the little red ball on the Mac. Of course, we could also have added another button to our application to close the program, but then it would no longer be as minimalistic as I'd promised you.

To get a better feel for how to work with window and widget geometry, I'd suggest that you copy this program into a file called `minimal_gui.py` and play around with it a little, changing sizes and positions, also testing out what happens if you comment out some parts of the program. Always ensure, though, that you actually provide a command-line argument when you run the program because we didn't add any error handling, so that the program will crash if the `argv` list is too short. I'll leave it up to you as an additional exercise to figure out how this could be achieved. However, as I stated previously that dialog-based programs aren't very useful for most of our purposes, let's now turn towards creating your very own customised main windows.

9.2.4 Deriving from a Main Window

When we discussed object orientation previously, we more or less only talked about creating completely new classes from scratch. However, both Python and PyQt allow us to use parent classes as blueprints for child classes derived from them. These derived classes then modify existing functionality or add to it. It's even possible to derive new classes from multiple original ones, thereby combining their features, but this is something we won't do here.

Following all necessary imports, new main window widget classes are created via definition of a class with `QMainWindow` as its argument. As usual, we then write the initialisation method `__init__`, where the first step is to call the initialisation method of the superordinate class via `super().__init__`, and `super` is a function that retrieves a reference to the parent class. Once this has been done, other potential arguments can be handled and, the application window configured via a dedicated method (here called `initUI`), which we'll discuss step-by-step next while we develop our GUI-based version of the syntactic inversion program as a multi-part exercise.

Exercise 49   Designing a GUI Syntax Inverter (a)

Create a new program called `syn_inversion_GUI.py`.
Import the modules `sys` and `re`.
Also import `QApplication`, `QMainWindow`, `QHBoxLayout`, `QVBoxLayout`, `QLabel`, `QLineEdit`, `QPushButton`, `QFrame`, and `QMessageBox` from `PyQt5.QtWidgets`, and `QFont` from `PyQt5.QtGui`.
Set up a new class `Inverter`, derived from `QMainWindow`.
Now define the `__init__` method as just described and add the following two lines:

```
self.setFont(QFont("Courier", 12))
self.initUI()
```

Define the `initUI` method, but only include the keyword `pass` inside the method block.
Now, write the main block in which you initialise the program, setting its title to *Simple syntactic inversion* and the geometry to `15,35,750,100`, and run the program.

We'll flesh out the `initUI` method next in order to create the layout and widgets of the program. Before we can write the next parts, though, we first need to learn about how to manage the layout of widgets on the screen in a more efficient manner than placing them manually.

9.2.5 Working with Layouts

Layouts allow us to group and arrange widgets in such a way that the program windows can also be re-sized flexibly without needing to reposition the elements manually. There are four types of layouts that may be relevant to us. Table 9.2 lists these, along with a brief description.

Table 9.2 PyQT layout options.

Layout	Description
QVBoxLayout	Allows vertical positioning of widgets in a column
QHBoxLayout	Allows horizontal positioning of widgets in a row
QGridLayout	Allows positioning of widgets in a grid with fixed positions or areas spanning multiple columns or rows
QFormLayout	Used to lay out tabular forms, e.g. labels and associated text boxes, in rows

Layouts are often nested to facilitate creating more complex arrangements and group elements with similar or related functionality together. And even if we could – in theory – use a QFormLayout to achieve our objective, as rows containing only a single widget will span both parts, this would be more difficult to achieve because we couldn't easily align the button in the middle. Hence, what we want to do here – also to give you more practice in using nested layouts – is to use multiple layouts arranged inside a container, for which we'll use a QFrame. The QFrame is often the most suitable central widget and container for layouts in main windows, and to be able to add layouts to it, it must be created first, e.g. like:

```
container = QFrame()
```

This container then needs to be set as the central widget of our class:

```
self.setCentralWidget(container)
```

Once we've done so, we can start defining main and sub-layouts to be nested within each other. For instance, for our GUI inverter, we need to have a vertical layout to hold three horizontal ones, so we can define this layout like this:

```
main_layout = QVBoxLayout()
```

then create the other three layouts, and add each to the main layout in turn, e.g.:

```
main_layout.addLayout(decl_layout)
```

to add a layout we've created to accommodate a label and entry field for the declarative sentence. Once we've added all sub-layouts to the main one, we finally need to assign this to the container by setting it:

```
container.setLayout(main_layout)
```

Let's try this as the next part of our exercise.

Exercise 50   Designing a GUI Syntax Inverter (b)

Define the initUI method further.
Add, as just described, one container, one main layout, and three sub-layouts.
Here, the first sub-layout should later contain the elements for displaying an editable declarative sentence, the second for outputting the (copyable) interrogative counterpart, and the third for holding a button to trigger the inversion.

We'll add the widgets in the next step.

9.2.6 Defining Widgets and Assigning Layouts

Widgets are created just like any other object. However, those that need to be accessible to the whole program have to be defined as instance variables of the derived main window class, for instance if their properties need to be readable or editable. Hence, to be able to later access the contents of the input field for the declarative sentence from within other methods of the class, we need to write something like this:

```
self.decl_input = QLineEdit('This is a declarative sentence.')
```

As the element text needs to be editable by the user, but we only require a relatively short piece of text, the `QLineEdit` widget is our best option here. If we wanted to be able to invert multiple sentences, though, we could also use a `QTextEdit` widget, so that the user could provide multiple lines of text containing one sentence each, and the inverted sentences could then be output to another `QTextEdit` widget in order to be able to save the results or copy them elsewhere. Other widgets, especially labels or buttons whose properties don't need to be accessible in this way, can simply be created like this:

```
convert = QPushButton('Convert')
```

For labels that need to be accessible to change their text programmatically, of course again an instance variable needs to be used. This should never be necessary for buttons, though, because they can always be connected to slots using their `clicked` signal within the same method, as we'll see later on in the exercise. Adding a widget that is assigned to a variable inside a layout is achieved via the `addWidget` method of the layout, using the variable as an argument. Simple widgets without editable properties or functions can also be set up directly like this while adding to the layout:

```
decl_layout.addWidget(QLabel('Declarative sentence:\t'))
```

This makes the code more compact because no extra variables and lines are required.

As pointed out before, in general, all widgets, apart from the main program window, need to be assigned to a container, with the name of the container explicitly being passed via `parent=X` as the last element during instantiation. However, if we use layouts, the layout automatically becomes the container, so that it doesn't need to be stated. Explicitly naming the container may potentially be important for elements such as message dialogues, though, that are only displayed temporarily, at least if they should be shown over a specific part of the program. Otherwise, the parent will automatically default to the program itself, which may not be optimal, even if it will work in most cases.

9.2.7 Widget Properties, Methods and Signals

Widgets have different properties, that may – depending on their purpose – be controllable to a greater or lesser extent, e.g.

- text/values/ranges, that can be set or read;
- display or selection lists;
- options that can be toggled on or off.

Some of these can be initialised via (keyword-)arguments on creation, others only via special methods. Sadly, though, the implementation of these properties is rather inconsistent, and the documentation that's available online at https://doc.qt.io/qtforpython-5/index.html[1] isn't always

---

1 This documentation is meant for the slightly different PySide2 module, but generally applies to PyQt, too.

very helpful, either, so that sometimes identifying how to configure a particular widget may not always be easy. This is why I created the widget demo program you used earlier, to give you at least an overview of the most common properties, methods, and signals of the widgets you're most likely to use frequently. When you'll later create your own GUI programs, you can always try to use this as your first port of call in terms of reference before embarking on any web searches. There are also whole books on designing GUIs using PyQt, but unfortunately I cannot really wholeheartedly recommend any of them, as they often either just describe individual characteristics of widgets, or present the information through highly specific projects that make it difficult to find the relevant details easily.

In terms of events, some widgets (generally) react to

- clicks/double clicks (buttons);
- changes in input text (editors);
- selection or change of options (selection lists/buttons); and
- toggling of states (toggle buttons).

These events can be assigned to a widget either via predefined signals of the widget or using the `mousePressEvent` for clicks if no suitable signal is available, so that the general syntax for calling functions or methods without arguments would be:

```
widgetvariable.signalname.connect(function/method)
```

or

```
widgetvariable.mousePressEvent = function/method
```

Calling functions or methods with arguments requires the use of lambda expressions

```
widgetvariable.signalname.connect(
        lambda x:[classename.]function/method(argument(s)))
```

or

```
widgetvariable.mousePressEvent =
        lambda x:[classname.]function/method(argument(s))
```

To get a general overview of the properties of the widgets discussed so far, let's take another look at the demo, this time exploring the widgets a little further.

Exercise 51 · Designing a GUI Syntax Inverter (c)

Start the program `widget_demo.py` again.
Click or double-click on the respective widget types, or select an option, so that its associated information appears inside the `QTextEdit` window on the left.
Familiarise yourself as much as possible with the properties, methods, and most useful signals of the individual types, especially those that we'll need for our current program.

Once you feel familiar enough with the features for the widgets relevant for our purpose, move on to the next part of the exercise.

Exercise 52   Designing a GUI Syntax Inverter (d)

Now set up the widgets required for our program. These are:

- some descriptive text for our entry widget for the declarative sentence,
- the entry widget containing the initial text *This is a declarative sentence.*,
- some descriptive text for the output,
- an output field, and
- a button to trigger the conversion.

Add these to the respective layouts, and run the program again.

In order to make our program fully functional, we still need to implement a method for converting declaratives to interrogatives, and then link this to the button. We'll discuss how to connect signals to slots to achieve this in the next section.

9.2.8   Adding Interactive Functionality

As I explained before, the events that occur in our PyQt applications, such as mouse clicks, can be captured as signals and connected to methods or functions via slots. Our `QPushButton` has a default signal `clicked`, which we can link to the `invert` method we define inside our `Inverter` class via the `connect` method. Within this method, which will later be passed as an argument to `connect`, we can access the text of the input field, transform it within the method, and then assign it to the output field. Let's do this in the next part of our exercise.

Exercise 53   Designing a GUI Syntax Inverter (e)

Implement the `invert` method.

In it, extract the current text from the input field using the appropriate method, then use a regex search with a suitable number of groups to store the first word, the second word and the rest of the text, apart from the punctuation mark, in a fitting variable.

Then test to see if the input field contained a string at all, and the regex search has been successful.

If so, assemble the individual parts you found via the grouping, plus a question mark, paying attention to correct capitalisation, and assign the result to the output field via the relevant method.

If not, display the following error message using the pre-defined message dialog box:

```
QMessageBox(
    text='Please input a complete simple declarative!!',
    windowTitle='Input error',
    icon=QMessageBox.Critical).exec_()
```

Now connect the `clicked` signal of the inverter button – back in `initUI` – to the newly created slot.

Test the program, also deliberately introducing some errors.

Although the program we've just developed is already much more complex and useful than the minimalistic GUI example we looked at earlier, it is still a fairly simple example of the type of program we might want to create for proper analysis purposes, so let's try and develop a GUI interface for our word frequency lists while we learn about some more useful PyQt features in the next sections.

9.3 Designing More Advanced GUIs

More advanced GUIs derived from `QMainWindow` contain more complex interface components than the simple labels, input fields, and button we used for our last program. They often also have menus or tool bars that provide access to file saving or selection options, and where specific actions can often be triggered in multiple ways to make them more user-friendly.

9.3.1 Actions

Actions are frequently used items of functionality that may appear in different places inside the program, and can also be triggered in different ways, such as via menus, buttons, keyboard shortcuts, or possibly even other events, such as selecting items from a drop-down list. They are set up via

```
QAction([QIcon(Icon),] 'menu text', parent, [,
shortcut='Ctrl+X'][, statusTip ='description for status
bar'][, tooltip='description as tooltip'])
```

and then assigned to menus or tool bars via `addAction` or `addActions`, and linked to the functions or methods they call via the signal `triggered`. If they're used on tool bars, either the menu text or the tooltip description will be used as tooltip, depending on whether the latter has been defined or not. The menu text and tooltip should be kept short, but if a description to display in the status bar is present, this can also be longer, provided there is enough space there to display it.

If a keyboard shortcut has been defined as part of an action, pressing this will automatically activate the action once it's been connected to a slot. This will happen even if the action hasn't been assigned to a menu or tool bar yet, but of course the user may then not be aware that the action exists because the shortcut won't be displayed anywhere. Once the action has been assigned to any menu item, it will be indicated on it next to the menu text, as can be seen in Figure 9.2.

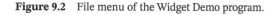

Figure 9.2 File menu of the Widget Demo program.

9.3.2 Creating Menus, Tool and Status Bars

Menus, tool bars, and status bars, because they always have fixed positions inside the main window layout, are created without adding them to any (sub-)layouts or the central widget. Most programs generally only have a single menu bar, which is created via

```
menubar=mainwindow.menuBar()
```

More complex applications composed of multiple widgets that are derived from main windows can also contain multiple menus, one for every sub-component. As macOS normally displays the menu bar at the top of the screen, and not as part of the application window, if you want to ensure that your programs look more or less the same on all platforms, you can use

```
menubar.setNativeMenuBar(False)
```

to force MacOS to display the menu inside the application window. Once a menu bar has been set up, both top-level menus and their sub-menus are created via

```
menu=menu(bar).addMenu('&text')
```

e.g.

```
fileMenu = mainMenu.addMenu('&File')
```

If the menu text contains an ampersand (&), as in the above example, the letter it precedes will be underlined when the top-level menu is opened, and then pressing that letter will trigger the associated action. Top-level menus can normally be accessed on Windows or Linux by holding down the Alt key and pressing the letter defined for accessing it, which will automatically be highlighted. Once a top-level menu is active, you can also navigate to it or between them by using the arrow keys on your keyboard. On the Mac, at least if you use native menus, i.e. the ones that get displayed in the macOS menu bar at the top of the screen once the application is active, this menu bar can be accessed by pressing Ctrl + F2, and you then need to use the arrow keys to navigate to the relevant menu entry.

Tool bars are created using

```
toolbar=mainwindow.addToolBar(name)
```

Apart from actions, they can also be assigned other widgets via addWidget, which can then be linked to functions or methods via the signal actionTriggered, unless they have their own signals, anyway, such as QPushbuttons do. If you want to have multiple tool bars below each other, you can add breaks between them using

```
mainwindow.addToolBarBreak()
```

If no breaks are added manually, and the tool bars are relatively short, these will be fitted side-by-side as long as there is space, giving the appearance of a single tool bar, which may not be what you want.

In analogy to menus, status bars are created via

```
statusbar=mainwindow.statusBar()
```

They either display status information for actions, can be instructed to show messages via showMessage, or house permanent widgets that can be created using

```
statusbar.addPermanentWidget()
```

Such permanent widgets can be highly useful for displaying genuine status information, such as which file or folder has been loaded, or whether a specific program mode has been switched on. We'll see an example of the former soon when we do our next exercise, but first, we want to discuss how to perform file and folder operations in PyQt.

9.3.3 Working with Files and Folder in PyQt

To allow users to select file or folder names, or create them when we want to save new files, the QFileDialog widget can be employed with different methods and options. For obtaining a path for a single file, we use

```
fileName,_ = QFileDialog.getOpenFileName(self, 'Open file',
directory='folder path', filter='*.extension;;*.extension' ,
initialFilter='*.extension')
```

For choosing a path for saving, or creating, file, we write

```
fileName,_ = QFileDialog.getSaveFileName(self, 'Save file',
directory='folder path', filter='*.extension;;*.extension',
initialFilter='*.extension')
```

If you've looked at the syntax above carefully, you'll have noticed that both of the above methods actually return two values, a file name and the selected filter, which is essentially the extension you've picked. Because we usually don't need the latter, we simply assign it to the dummy variable _ we then discard. The first argument is a parent (keyword: parent), which will normally be the derived widget. This is followed by a caption you can provide for the dialog's title bar (keyword: caption), a filter for an initial folder path to search in (keyword: directory), a list of potential extensions (keyword: filter), and an option for pre-selecting a default extension (keyword: initialFilter). If you use the arguments in the right order, you can also omit the keywords, but using them makes things more explicit and therefore easier to read, so I'd recommend doing so. As the argument names for the final two arguments here suggest, providing lists of extensions allows you to filter the contents of whichever folder gets displayed inside the dialog. There are some further options that may be provided as additional arguments here, but as we usually don't need them, I'll ignore them here.

For allowing us – or our users – to choose multiple files, we can use the following syntax

```
fileNames,_ = QFileDialog.getOpenFileNames(self, 'Open file(s)',
directory='folder path', filter='*.extension;;*.extension',
initialFilter='*.extension')
```

which, as the name of the method implies, returns a list of file paths instead of a single file name. To make a selection, the user here has to use the general selection mechanisms for choosing files, i.e. clicking on a single file and then pressing Shift and clicking on another to make a contiguous selection ranging from first to last clicked, or clicking on multiple non-contiguous file names while keeping the Ctrl key pressed, before clicking on OK to get the file names. Of course, when using this method, it's also possible to select only a single path so that only a one-item list is returned. For choosing folders, we can use

```
folderName = QFileDialog.getExistingDirectory(self, 'Load
folder', directory='folder path', QFileDialog.ShowDirsOnly)
```

where the final argument is used to suppress any files from being shown inside the dialog in addition to the folders. As soon as file or folder paths are stored in simple variables or lists, you can use the standard file and folder operations on them that we discussed in Chapter 5.

If the selected files should not be opened directly for processing, but be available for performing different analysis tasks on them, it's advisable to list them in QListWidget for further selection or processing, whereby, in using folders, these generally need to be read and possibly filtered before adding items to the input file list.

Now that we know how to add these advanced components to our programs, let's embark on the final, fairly extensive, exercise in this chapter, designing our GUI frequency list editor.

Exercise 54   Creating a Frequency List Editor (a)

Create a GUI interface for our frequency analysis module called frequency_GUI.py, in which you'll be able to load a file via a menu and display the file name on the status bar, select a sorting order, run an analysis, display the results in a QTextEdit window, and save them from there. In addition, the user should be alerted in an appropriate manner if no input file has been specified when the analysis is triggered, or if no output file can be generated. As in our previous program, we'll also want to set a larger font.

Before you start writing the program, first think about all the widgets and PyQt components you may need, so that you'll be able to import them, along with any other modules or module elements. Figure 9.3 illustrates what the final program should look like.

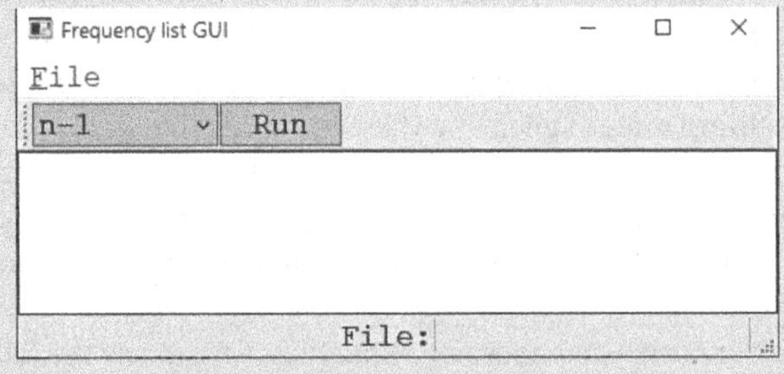

Figure 9.3   The frequency list GUI.

Import all relevant components, adding QAction to your imports from QtWidgets, and QTextCursor to those from QtGui.

Once you've imported all, define a class GUI_frequencies, set the font size and window title, and use an appropriate geometry setting to determine the size and placement of the window, this time inside the constructor. Also add two instance variables, one to hold the complete path for the file to be loaded, and one for the base folder, which you initialise to the current folder (.). The initial geometry setting doesn't have to be optimal, since you can always play with this later.

Define the methods `initUI`, `load_file`, `analyse`, and `save_file`, initially only using `pass` in the method block because we'll implement these step-by-step-later.
Add a call to `initUI` to the constructor.
Set up a test block in which you create an instance of our derived class and run it.

In the next part, we'll set up the GUI interface, adding the menu bar, the actions, a tool bar, the status bar, as well as the editor window as our central widget.

Exercise 55 Creating a Frequency List Editor (b)

Add a main menu, and make it behave the same on all OSes as described in Section 9.3.2.
Now add a `File` menu to the menu bar, then create two `QActions`, `loadAction` and `saveAction` with appropriate menu texts and the shortcuts `Ctrl + o` and `Ctrl + s`, respectively. We'll here omit the other possible descriptive texts.
Once you've set up the actions, connect them to the relevant slots, and add both actions to the `File` menu.
Next, add a tool bar, and first place a combo box in it to which – in turn – you add the sort options we defined in the frequency analyser object before putting it on the tool bar.
Also add a button labelled `Run` to the tool bar and connect this to the appropriate slot.
Set up a status bar, adding two labels as permanent widgets to it, where the first indicates that the second widget will display the file name of the file to be analysed, once loaded. Before adding the second label, use the method `setMinimumWidth` to give it a minimal size of 200 pixels, which should ensure that most file names can be shown in their entirety.
All that is left to do now to complete the GUI setup is to add the edit widget and make it the central widget.

We've now completed setting up the GUI interface again, and all the GUI functionality should be available if you haven't forgotten to remove the `pass` statement from `initUI` before you run the program again. However, obviously, because all our other methods still haven't been implemented, selecting things or clicking on any buttons still won't do what it's supposed to, so let's move on to fleshing out the remaining methods in the following parts of the exercise. We'll begin by implementing the `load_file` method.

Exercise 56 Creating a Frequency List Editor (c)

Remove the `pass` statement from the `load_file` method, or comment it out.
Use the appropriate method of the `QFileDialog` to retrieve a file path, and store it in the relevant instance variable of our class. Inside the method, set the `directory` keyword-argument using a relative path to the `texts` folder, and the `filter` to `'*.txt;;*.*'`.
Next, test to see if the instance variable has actually been initialised to a file path.
If so, use `os.path.split` to extract the path for the base folder and the file name, and set the so far empty label text in the status bar to the file name. Store the path for the base folder inside another instance variable of the class.
If no file name has been provided, due to the user having cancelled out of the file dialog, set the label text to an empty string.

If you test the program at this stage, you'll be able to select a file (path) and have its name displayed in the status bar, but of course still not be able to carry out any analysis. So far, the file path will only be made available for processing and stored in the class, so now we need to implement the analysis method.

Exercise 57   Creating a Frequency List Editor (d)

Implement the `analyse` method, first again testing to see whether we have a valid file path. If so, create a `Frequency_list` object, initialising it using the selected file as an input file and with the current value of the sort-order combo box for the `sort_order` keyword argument. Call the relevant methods of the object to create the list and produce a sorted list of keys for controlling the output.

Make sure that the output window is emptied before running the analysis, then iterate over the sorted list and add each word and associated frequency to the editor window. Hint: You only need to modify the code from the frequency list object's `output_list` method so that it will be suitable for writing to the editor window.

Once you've generated the output, call the methods `moveCursor` and `setFocus` on the output window, using `QTextCursor.Start` as an argument for the first, and no argument for the second one.

If no valid file path exists, use a message box to display an appropriate error message to the user and `return` from the method.

If you run the program now, you'll be able to select a text to be analysed, as well as run the analysis and have the output written to the editor window. The only thing that's still missing is our method for saving the output to a file, which we'll flesh out as the final part of our exercise.

Exercise 58   Creating a Frequency List Editor (e)

To get a file path for the output path, use the appropriate method of the `QFileDialog` again, using the same filter as before.

Test again to see if we have a valid file path.

If so, open the output file for writing, using appropriate error handling, and write the text contained in the output window to the file using the appropriate method for retrieving the window content. If any I/O error occurs, present a suitable message to the user and `return` to the program.

If no valid file path exists, simply `return` to the GUI.

Test the program again.

If everything went well, you should now have a fully functional GUI version of our word frequency analysis program. Analysis programs that handle single files aren't as useful as they could be, though, because we normally want to be able to handle data from multiple files or even whole corpora. I leave it up to you as an additional exercise to develop the existing two objects further to allow us to do so.

In this chapter, I've provided you with an overview of the most useful widgets and approaches in designing GUIs using PyQt. Hopefully, even through our limited number of exercises, you'll have seen how much easier interacting with our data becomes for ourselves and any potential users, but also that, even if some of the processes, such as selecting files, do become considerably easier, we still need to pay close attention to any potential errors that may arise.

By now, we've already covered how to work and even interact with locally stored data in fairly sophisticated ways, but the next challenge that we're going to tackle lies in learning how to obtain data from the internet and deal with the special types of annotation formats it may come in, or ought to be converted to, in order to increase its usefulness for language analysis purposes, as well as further distribution. This will be the topic of the next chapter.

9.4 Discussions

Discussion 47   Brainstorming the Potential of GUIs

For the very first few simple programs, it probably wouldn't really have made any sense to write a GUI because they were so basic and we didn't really do anything that required much interaction, although of course getting user input is something that would be achieved much more easily via an input field and a button to trigger an action once the input was completed. Hence, for instance, our collocate collector, especially the open-ended version I suggested as an additional exercise, could have allowed the user to type their collocates into a multi-line text field from where they could either be saved to a file or database, with the number of entries submitted being checked by testing for the number of lines in the text field. This would also allow the user to verify and possibly edit the words they wanted to submit prior to doing so, for example to see whether they may have repeated a word in a longer list. An illustrative text above the text field could provide more or less detailed information as to what was required. To save results to a file would require being able to enter or select a file path, probably via a menu entry or icon, while submission in some other form would require a button to click on for triggering the submission.

Our prefix stripper could become more interactive by providing input fields for both prefixes and words, and an output field for the results, from where, again, results could possibly be saved as illustrative examples in the way described above. Triggering the stripping process and saving results would of course require buttons, too, and again illustrative descriptions could be added to the relevant fields and for instruction.

Copying a file would again require an option for creating or selecting input and output paths, but being able to choose folders would of course minimise any errors related to mis-typing such file paths, and input or output errors could be signalled to the user, allowing them to choose different file names or locations without first terminating the program. In addition, this would also make it possible to work with different files while the program was running, rather than having to restart it for each operation. A further option would also be to add line numbers to the output file if a check box were ticked, but otherwise simply copy the file. The general design approach would also make it possible to write converters that would allow us to select one or more files, choose an output folder, and then have each file processed in a way that would include some form of annotation, something we'll learn about in the next chapter. Likewise, it would also be possible to remove such annotations, for instance to convert web pages to plain text or some other format.

The regex tester we wrote in Chapter 6 could either be extended into a proper tester that would allow us to provide different or multiple input texts and see the effects of regexes typed into a multi-line text field. However, more importantly for language analysis purposes, we could in fact turn it into a concordancer that would allow us to view, edit, annotate, and store analysis results along with perhaps information about where the individual hits were found. In addition – for such a program – it should also be possible to set or change the context display, as well as ideally jump to where a hit was found inside a file to get the full context.

Last, but not least, we could of course also write a useful GUI for creating different types of word, word frequency, or n-gram lists, where the lists wouldn't immediately be stored in a file, but could be displayed in a multi-line text window again and manipulated in different ways before storing the results, e.g. by changing the output format from lists of possible sorting options in dropdown fields, etc. Additionally, it would become possible to filter the lists to be displayed in different ways, e.g. by using regexes to only show specific patterns or set thresholds for frequencies above which items should be shown only.

Discussion 48   Familiarising Yourself with Some Useful PyQt Widgets

Starting from the top, you should be able to notice a menu (QMenuBar) and a tool bar (QToolBar), which are linked to the same actions (QAction), so that they can be triggered using either a menu entry or button on the tool bar. When you open the single menu, you should be able to see the actions there, along with the keyboard shortcuts that have been defined for them. When you hover over the buttons in the tool bar, you should not only get to see some tooltips, but when you look towards the bottom of the program window, also that there should be an informative message displayed in the status bar, which can also house some permanent widgets that may display different types of information about things that go on in your program.

Moving down along the left-hand side of the program window, you can first observe that labels are useful for displaying longer descriptive texts, but may of course also be used to describe associated widgets, as is the case for some of the widget types on the right-hand side, where short descriptions sometimes accompany the widget names formatted in blue. The two widgets for handling text represent options for either dealing with short bits of text suitable for providing textual input (QLineEdit), or longer, editable text, such as language data we may want to annotate, or some output from a program that has been directed there for further scrutiny and/or processing (QTextEdit).

Starting again from the top, this time on the right-hand side, we first see a button, which of course is supposed trigger an action when clicked, only that, in our case, this action is not what is says on the button's label, but rather places the relevant information about the QPushButton widget in the multi-line QTextEdit editor window. The QListWidget below the button is here used to display a simple word frequency list. In a sense, this widget is also like a multi-line text widget, only that the text contained in it cannot normally be edited, but it's only used to output information in list format. The combo box below it (QComboBox) is similar to the list widget in that it contains a vertical listing of elements, only that their text can be edited (if configured to allow this), and the general function of such a box is to provide a list of options to choose from in a compact, space-saving format. Setting this widget to be editable also makes it possible to add choices that were not part of the original specification. In our case here, we could e.g. add another option for *.html to allow us to filter a folder for web pages. The spin box (QSpinBox) below the combo box is, in a sense, its numerical counterpart, only that it provides a range of numbers to choose from. This can e.g. be used for setting specific thresholds for frequency ranges, etc.

The remaining two options, check boxes (QCheckBox) and radio buttons (QRadioButton), essentially represent toggle switches, where the former constitutes a single, binary, choice, and the latter usually appear as groups of mutually exclusive choices where the number of options is low, so that no list or combo box is necessary. Radio buttons don't need to be exclusive, though, but it's also possible to use them for small groups of options where more than one option can be switched on at the same time.

To be able to write the GUI inversion program, you'd minimally need two QLineEdit fields to input and display the declarative and interrogative sentences, and one QPushButton to trigger the inversion process. Of course, the output field could also be a QLabel, but then the interface might look less consistent, and users would also not be able to copy the results as a bonus because labels can normally only be changed programmatically, but aren't accessible to the user to work with. However, this simplistic design would leave the users without any kind of information regarding the nature of the program, so they'd have to guess its purpose from the button text. A better solution would therefore be to add some descriptive labels to the input fields, making the layout something like what can be seen in Figure 9.4.

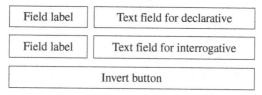

Field label	Text field for declarative
Field label	Text field for interrogative
Invert button	

Figure 9.4 Layout for GUI inversion.

Upon clicking the button, the text from the declarative field needs to be retrieved, processed, and the result assigned to the interrogative field. The errors that could occur here are essentially that the user could leave the declarative field empty or input something that is not formally a declarative, i.e. doesn't end in a full stop. These ought to be trapped by the program and flagged to the user via a means that is appropriate for a GUI program, which is normally a pop-up dialog the user can acknowledge and close before inputting a correct sentence. Thus, the program doesn't need to be terminated when an error occurs, but only closed once the user wishes to do so.

Discussion 49   Designing a GUI Syntax Inverter (a)

As for any PyQt GUI, our first import should be the QApplication because it's always required. And because we want to derive from a main window, we obviously need to include this, too. The QFont class is already needed for this initial part of the exercise, but all other imports will only be required in later steps.

Setting up the new class with its __init__ method should not present a problem, and could look like this:

```
class Inverter(QMainWindow):
    """GUI for illustrating syntactic inversion"""

    def __init__(self):
        # call constructor of parent/super class
        super().__init__()
        self.setFont(QFont("Courier", 12))
        self.initUI()
```

Note that I've included a brief Docstring describing what the program does, as well as a comment that reminds us where the `__init__` method of the parent class is called to include all the functionality and properties that the `QMainWindow` class normally provides or has. The first line after calling the constructor of the parent class adds a suitable font setting to the window because, as you'll probably have noticed looking at the minimal GUI program, the default font is way too small.

We used `pass` in order to allow us to set up the `initUI` method and call it from the class constructor, so that we'll already be able to start the program without any errors. Of course, we could simply have left out the method and call to it altogether, but because we knew that we were going to need it later, anyway, this is a cleaner way of writing the program because the method can simply be called at program startup, but without doing anything. When you design larger programs, thinking about which methods you may need first and implementing skeletons for them in this way is always a good strategy because it then becomes easier to see the logic of your program and how the individual components will be tied together.

The main block that allows us to run the program independently, including some comments, should then look as follows:

```
if __name__ == '__main__':
    # instantiate the program
    app = QApplication(sys.argv)
    # set up window object
    inverter = Inverter()
    inverter.setWindowTitle('Simple syntactic inversion')
    inverter.setGeometry(15,35,750,100)
    # show window
    inverter.show()
    # start program
    sys.exit(app.exec_())
```

This block ought to be fairly self-explanatory since the general approach is the same as for the minimal GUI program, only that, in this case, we didn't use a pre-defined PyQt class, but instead our derived version of a main window – and with a different geometry. Obviously, though, when you run the program, it will be only displayed with this geometry and a window title that shows in the title bar, but because we haven't added any widgets yet, there won't be anything to see but the bare window.

Discussion 50   Designing a GUI Syntax Inverter (b)

If you've successfully set up the layout as instructed in the exercise part, and start the program again, you'll still get an empty window because – apart from giving the program an internal layout – we haven't set up any widgets yet. However, you'd still get the same effect if you forgot to comment out or remove the `pass` statement, so make sure you do so, making the initial part of the method block something like this, again including some descriptive comments:

```
# set up container for layouts
container = QFrame()
# set container as central widget
```

```
self.setCentralWidget(container)
# define main & sub-layouts
main_layout = QVBoxLayout()
decl_layout = QHBoxLayout()
interr_layout = QHBoxLayout()
conv_layout = QHBoxLayout()
# add sub-layouts to main layout
main_layout.addLayout(decl_layout)
main_layout.addLayout(interr_layout)
main_layout.addLayout(conv_layout)
# set layout of container as main layout
container.setLayout(main_layout)
```

Discussion 51   Designing a GUI Syntax Inverter (c)

As this part of the exercise is exploratory, there really isn't much I can say here, other than that you'll hopefully have noticed that the QLabel, QLineEdit, and QTextedit widgets share the same method for changing their text programmatically, i.e. setText. Furthermore, the QListWidget and the QCombobox, essentially both being containers for lists, share the addItem and addItems methods. And, finally, that the QCheckBox and QRadioGroup share the method checkedId. In addition, some of the widgets share a clear method to empty their contents. Otherwise, most widgets have their own specific properties and methods that reflect their purposes.

Discussion 52   Designing a GUI Syntax Inverter (d)

Creating and adding the relevant widgets shouldn't have proved too difficult if you've followed the descriptions I provided earlier. Hence, the next part of the initUI method should look more or less like this:

```
# define widgets
self.decl_input = QLineEdit('This is a declarative sentence.')
self.interr_output = QLineEdit()
invertBtn = QPushButton('Invert sentence')

# add widgets to layouts
decl_layout.addWidget(QLabel('Declarative sentence:\t'))
decl_layout.addWidget(self.decl_input)
interr_layout.addWidget(QLabel('Interrogative sentence: '))
interr_layout.addWidget(self.interr_output)
conv_layout.addWidget(invertBtn)
```

In order to make their functions clearer, I've here opted to separate the creation of the widgets that are involved in any events – i.e. the two input fields and the button – from the steps for adding them to the layout. We could obviously also combine these steps to create and add everything in one sequence, but using this approach also illustrates more clearly how some pre-created widgets are simply added to the layout, while some widgets can be added and created using one single statement. Note also that I've named the button `invertBtn`, where the 'suffix' `Btn` signals the nature of the widget, whereas I've opted for using a slightly different naming format to label the input and output widgets indicating their purposes, mixing the two formats for naming variables in a suitable manner.

This time, when you run the program, you'll get to see all the widgets, and the input and output fields will even already be editable. However, when you click the button, you'll immediately notice that we still don't have a fully functional program because we haven't actually implemented the essential part yet, which is of course our inversion method.

Discussion 53   Designing a GUI Syntax Inverter (e)

To extract the text from the input field, we need to employ its `text` method, which we can use as the second argument to our regex in the second step. Should you have forgotten to declare the input field as an instance variable of the class, though, you'll get a `NameError` here causing your program to fail.

As we're extracting different parts of a declarative sentence, my idea of a fitting name for the match object we're using to capture these via `re.search` would simply be `parts`. For grabbing the three parts we're interested in, we need three groups, where the first needs to capture a word that is anchored at the beginning of the line and is followed by a space not to be included, then the second word, and everything up to the final full stop that should occur at the end of the input string. However, as it's always possible that the user may type spaces at the beginning or end of the input, just to be on the safe side, we can incorporate these as optionally occurring in our complete match, still allowing us to extract the relevant parts. Hence, our method could look like this:

```
parts = re.search(r'^\s*([\w-]+\b)\s(\b[\w-]+\b)(.+?)\.\s*$',
        self.decl_input.text())
if self.decl_input.text() and parts:
    self.interr_output.setText(
        f'{parts.group(2).capitalize()} '
        f'{parts.group(1).lower()}{parts.group(3)}?')
else:
    QMessageBox(
        text='Please input a complete simple declarative!!',
        windowTitle='Input Error',
        icon=QMessageBox.Critical).exec_()
```

Because we may also have hyphenated words as subjects and, less likely, also as verbs, I've here defined words as a repeated character class that is either anchored and/or bounded appropriately, and where I've also included the hyphen because Python's regex definition doesn't usually see this as a word character, while we definitely want to treat it as such. The final dot, which should be behind the third group that captures everything up to it non-greedily, obviously needs to be escaped.

In the next step, we need to test for two conditions at the same time, so that we have to join them via the logical operator `and`. The first of these tests to see if there is anything present in the input at all, while the second checks if the regex match was successful. If either of these conditions returns False, we display the QMessageBox widget, whose keyword arguments will hopefully be self-explanatory, especially if you deliberately produce an error while running the program to see them live. In case we have valid input, we set the text of the output field by joining the captured groups, capitalising the first word, lowercasing the second, and appending a question mark inside an f-string.

Even if this would now produce the correct output, also for hyphenated compounds like *ice-cream*, it would still lowercase any sentence-initial proper nouns in the output, and still also cannot handle complex subjects. Neither can it handle any cases that would require *do* periphrasis, potentially also involving changing a tensed form, as in e.g. converting *They hated ice-cream.* to *Did they hate ice-cream?*. I leave it up to you to figure out a possible solutions to these issues, so that you could at least partially implement them as an additional exercise or small project.

However, even if you've correctly implemented the invert method, you still couldn't use it at this point without first connecting it to the appropriate signal, which you should do inside the initUI method, ideally immediately after setting up the button:

```
# connect signal to slot
inverter.clicked.connect(self.inversion)
```

Once you've done this, the program is finished, and everything will hopefully work as expected. Note that, because our method doesn't require any arguments, we don't need to use a lambda expression, but can simply pass the method as an argument to connect.

Discussion 54 Creating a Frequency List Editor (a)

The widgets you'll need to import are:

```
from PyQt5.QtWidgets import QApplication, QMainWindow, QTextEdit,
QAction, QPushButton, QLabel, QFileDialog, QComboBox, QMessageBox
```

The first two of these will be required because we're creating an application that is derived from a main window. The QTextEdit widget will be used to display the frequency list, although it would of course be possible to use a QListWidget, too. However, if we used the latter, we wouldn't easily be able to edit any data, for instance to add annotations or delete irrelevant words. The QAction widget will be needed to define actions for loading and saving, the button for triggering the analysis, the label for displaying the file name in the status bar once a file has been loaded, the file dialog for selecting files for loading and saving, the combo box for choosing the sorting options, and the message box for reporting any potential errors to the user. We don't need to import the menu, tool or status bar as widgets because they are components that are automatically available as part of the main window implementation.

Additional PyQt components we require are:

```
from PyQt5.QtGui import QFont, QTextCursor
```

We already used the font object in our last program to set a larger font size, which we'll want to do here again, but we haven't used QTextCursor yet. This component will be required in order to move the cursor inside the text widget to the beginning of the list once it has been output.

The other modules or parts thereof we have to import are:

```
import sys
import os.path
from frequencies_a import Frequency_list
```

As before, `sys` is required in order to interact with the operating system, `os.path` to be able to handle I/O paths, and last, but not least, we shouldn't forget to import our frequency class that will handle all analysis parts for us, although we'll need to define a new output method for displaying the results inside the text widget.

The constructor is very similar to the one in our previous program, apart from the fact that the window size ought to be larger to accommodate all interface components and show a substantial part of the frequency list output. Hence, it ought to look like this, for convenience already including the call to `initUI` which you're supposed implement two steps later:

```
def __init__(self):
        super().__init__()
        # window setup
        self.setFont(QFont("Courier", 12))
        self.setWindowTitle('Frequency list GUI')
        self.setGeometry(30,30,500,800)
        # properties
        self.file = None
        self.base_dir = '.'

        # create interface
        self.initUI()
```

The geometry setting using a width of 500 pixels and height of 800 should definitely show the frequency list in its full width, and a substantial part of the top of the frequency list, but – if necessary – you can still adjust this later, bearing in mind that it will always be possible to enlarge the window manually, too, because we won't implement any size restrictions, nor discuss these in any detail in this book. The variable to hold the file path, as you can see, should ideally be initialised to `None`. The one for the base folder is initially set to a relative path to the current folder as a default, but may be changed later if files are loaded from any other folder.

Setting up the test block should present no problems; it's very similar to the one in our previous program:

```
if __name__ == '__main__':
    app = QApplication(sys.argv)
    win = GUI_frequencies()
    win.show()
    sys.exit(app.exec_())
```

Note, though, that this time I've opted to handle the window title and geometry options inside the constructor, rather than doing this at run-time. Although this will already allow you to run the program, it will still only show you a bare window because we haven't fleshed out and activated `initUI` yet, which is what we'll do next.

Discussion 55   Creating a Frequency List Editor (b)

Adding the main menu, making it part of the program window, and setting up the `File` menu can easily be achieved in these three lines of code:

```
mainMenu = self.menuBar()
mainMenu.setNativeMenuBar(False)
file_menu = mainMenu.addMenu('&File')
```

The two actions should be equally straightforward, provided you list the arguments in the right order because keyword arguments – such as the one for the shortcut – can only appear after the two positional arguments, the menu text and the parent. Hence, the action definitions and connections of signals to slots should look like this:

```
loadAction = QAction('L&oad', self, shortcut='Ctrl+o')
loadAction.triggered.connect(self.load_file)
saveAction = QAction('&Save', self, shortcut='Ctrl+s')
saveAction.triggered.connect(self.save_file)
```

Rather than adding sub-menu items to the `File` menu directly, we can now simply add the actions, which will automatically add both menu items at once, including the descriptions of the shortcuts:

```
file_menu.addActions([loadAction, saveAction])
```

If we wanted to, we could simply use the same method to add these entries as buttons to the tool bar, but since we didn't create any icons for the actions, we'd only get the menu captions displayed there, which isn't really what users would expect. Hence, we'll only add the other two components to the tool bar once we've created it like this:

```
toolbar = self.addToolBar('main')
```

Because we only need to access the currently selected text of the combo box to use as our argument for the sort order of the frequency list object later, this widget also doesn't need to be connected to any signal. The only thing that's essential here is that it's defined as an instance variable of the object because otherwise we wouldn't be able to access the option from any other method. Therefore, the widget declaration, and adding the options, and the widget itself, to the tool bar, can be achieved as follows:

```
self.optsCombo = QComboBox()
self.optsCombo.addItems([
    'n-1',
    '1-n',
    'a-z',
    'z-a',
    'reverse',
    'w_length'])
toolbar.addWidget(self.optsCombo)
```

The button can be created in the same way as the one in our previous program, linked to the appropriate slot, and added:

```
runBtn = QPushButton('Run')
runBtn.clicked.connect(self.analyse)
toolbar.addWidget(runBtn)
```

This now only leaves the status bar and the editor widget to be set up, which can be done like this:

```
status = self.statusBar()
status.addPermanentWidget(QLabel('File:'))
self.fileLab = QLabel()
self.fileLab.setMinimumWidth(200)
status.addPermanentWidget(self.fileLab)

self.output_win = QTextEdit()
self.setCentralWidget(self.output_win)
```

The only two things to note here are probably that the label to display the file name can be set up without giving it any initial string value, and that we shouldn't forget to make the output window our central widget once it's been created.

Discussion 56   Creating a Frequency List Editor (c)

If you followed the syntax example for the getOpenFile method closely, and set the relative path correctly, adjusting it for our purposes shouldn't have been difficult, so that it should look like this:

```
self.file,_ = QFileDialog.getOpenFileName(
        self,
        'Open file',
        directory='../texts',
        filter='*.txt;;*.*')
```

Of course, you should also not forget to use the dummy variable _, either, because otherwise later attempting to extract the base folder and file name will throw an error since the method returns a tuple, rather than just the file path we want. Testing for whether the instance variable for the file path has been set is necessary here because the user may have chosen to abort selecting a file name by either clicking on the Cancel button or pressing the Esc key, in which case an empty file path would be returned, which would in turn lead to an error later. This would now make the rest of the method something like this:

```
if self.file:
    self.base_dir, in_file = os.path.split(self.file)
    self.fileLab.setText(in_file)
else:
    self.fileLab.setText('')
```

There are actually two reasons for why we use os.path.split() here, rather than simply setting the label text to the file path we retrieved from the dialog. The first is that the whole file path may be far too long to display on the label, and we're really only interested in seeing the file name there, anyway. The other is that we can use the path to the base folder to later prime the getSaveFile method to allow us to store the output file in the same folder, or, if we wanted to have a separate folder for results, either create this based on the path to the texts folder or, if it already exists, set it as our output folder. Feel free to implement this option as part of the save_file method later as an additional exercise.

Discussion 57   Creating a Frequency List Editor (d)

We first need to test for the valid file path again because otherwise it would neither make sense to create a frequency list, nor would it be possible in the first place, as this is the one essential argument to its constructor. And of course, if no valid path was provided, we wouldn't want to terminate our program here, but let the user know what the problem was and allow them to pick a different file that can actually be processed.

Creating the object can easily be achieved by accessing the instance variable of our GUI program containing the file path and reading the value in the sort-order combo box that is currently selected, which would default to the first entry in the list stored inside the combo box. Hence, the first line of code after the if 'clause' should be:

```
analyser = Frequency_list(
        input_file=self.file,
        sort_order=self.optsCombo.currentText())
```

Calling the methods of the frequency list object would thus need to look as follows:

```
analyser.create_list()
analyser.make_sorted_list()
```

and emptying the output window would be done via its `clear` method:

```
self.output_win.clear()
```

All that's left to do now is to append each word and associated frequency entry to the text editor window, then move the cursor to the beginning of that window, and set the focus to it in order to activate it, so that we can start moving or scrolling through it immediately:

```
for word in analyser.sorted_list:
    self.output_win.append(
        f'{word:{analyser.longest_word}}\t'
        f'{analyser.words[word]:>{analyser.max_len_number}d}')
self.output_win.moveCursor(QTextCursor.Start)
self.output_win.setFocus()
```

Because the output window will initially be empty, the first line will simply be appended to its beginning. If we hadn't emptied the window first, and if there were already a frequency list displayed, the new list would simply be inserted at the current cursor position. This would obviously give us the wrong result when we later try to save our list to a file because whatever gets saved to that file will be based on the contents of the output window and not the dictionary stored inside the frequency object. You may now ask why we don't simply use the `output_list` method of the frequency object, but this a) isn't possible directly because that method doesn't accept any arguments, so that any user of our module other than ourselves would need to know that they could in fact manipulate the `output_file` instance variable to assign a value retrieved via the `getSaveFile` method to it before calling the `output_list` method, and b) this would then not allow us to edit the contents of the output window before saving the file, which is one of the purposes for having a GUI in the first place.

The `QTextCursor.Start` property that we use as an argument to the `moveCursor` method will automatically have been set to the first position when the editor window was created, and would only be changed if in fact we had moved the cursor somewhere inside the window by clicking inside it or making a selection, which we didn't do because we inserted the text via our method. This could potentially happen if outputting the frequency list took a very long time and the user happened to click anywhere inside the text already written to the output window. However, because we're only creating relatively short lists from single texts, this is unlikely to happen. If you ever encounter this issue, though, you can prevent any user interaction with the text while it's being written to the output window by setting using the `setTextInteractionFlags` method of the editor window with an argument of `False` before you begin writing the list to the window, and then setting it to `True` again once the output has finished.

Discussion 58 Creating a Frequency List Editor (e)

The way we get the file path for the output file is basically identical to how we get the input file path, only using the other method, so we can write:

```
out_file,_ = QFileDialog.getSaveFileName(
    self,
    'Save file',
    directory=self.base_dir,
    filter='*.txt;;*.*')
```

Here, the default original base folder we set in the constructor should be overwritten if we've opened a file from any folder apart from the current one, as we had intended by specifying `../texts` for the folder in the dialog where we retrieved the input file.

If we have a valid file path – which should be the case if the user hasn't cancelled out of the dialog – the only error that should conceivably occur is that we don't have write access to the folder we've selected, just in case we chose an input file from a folder that wasn't located in our user folder. If there's no error, we can open the output file and write out the contents of the editor window like this:

```
out.write(self.output_win.toPlainText())
```

This of course only works provided that we used `out` as a file handle reference. In case we do encounter an error, we can store it in an error variable and then use that inside an f-string that we display as the `text` keyword argument to the message box like this:

```
QMessageBox(
    text=f'{e}!\nSelect a location you have write access to.',
    windowTitle='Output Error',
    icon=QMessageBox.Critical).exec_()
```

We then add a `return` statement to exit from the exception cleanly. If we never received a valid file name, we simply use a `return` statement because this means that the user has cancelled the save operation.

10

Web Data and Annotations

So far, when we've been working with texts, these were stored somewhere on our computer in plain-text format. However, web data is becoming increasingly popular, due to easy access and increasing availability, Python offers the `urllib` package for working with web data/URLs, and Qt even provides components that function as browsers, so that there's nothing that prevents us from tapping into the web as a huge source of interesting and timely data. Hence, in this chapter, we want to learn how to work with data either originating from the web – and predominantly marked up in the form of HTML –, as well as data that contains additional, linguistically motivated, markup in the form of special XML annotations. To be able to understand and work with such data, we first want to develop a general understanding of markup languages, and then see how we can download and process annotated data in various ways.

10.1 Markup Languages

Markup languages provide special ways for indicating different functions of texts or highlighting different parts thereof, so that these texts can be processed and/or rendered in specific ways, such as only extracting and analysing the language produced by a particular character in a novel or play, or visualising such highlighted parts using colour coding, etc. Although the basic concepts behind markup languages as a means of facilitating standardised information interchange date back to the 1960s, and ***Standard Generalised Markup Language*** (SGML) was ratified as an ISO standard in 1986, markup languages really only became popular when ***H****yper* ***T****ext* ***M****arkup* Language (HTML) arrived on the scene in 1992 as the 'language of the web'. Most web pages have since been written in HTML, a relatively limited markup language that is only of equally limited use for enriching documents with interpretative language-oriented information, so-called ***annotations***. Annotations for linguistic or DH purposes nowadays are generally added in the form of ***eXtensible Markup Language*** (XML), a more advanced successor of SGML.

All markup languages use angle brackets (<...>), referred to as ***elements*** or ***tags***, not to be confused with the PoS tags employed for indicating word-class information, for marking up structural and/or linguistic textual components. Angle brackets are ideal for such purposes because they rarely occur in texts themselves, and can therefore easily be recognised. On the rare occasions that they are present in texts, e.g. in mathematical equations, they need to be replaced by so-called ***character-reference entities***, `&lt;` for <, and `&gt;` for >. The other entities that browsers supporting XML need to recognise are `&amp;` for the ampersand (&), `&quot;` for double quotes,

Python Programming for Linguistics and Digital Humanities: Applications for Text-Focused Fields,
First Edition. Martin Weisser.
© 2024 John Wiley & Sons, Inc. Published 2024 by John Wiley & Sons, Inc.
Companion website: https://www.wiley.com/go/weisser/pythonprogling

and ' for apostrophes. For many years, other entities, such as ä for German ä, were commonly used to represent non-English characters in web pages, but as the percentage of web pages not encoded in UTF-8 is dwindling, you're less and less likely to encounter them in the future.

Tags exist as two types, paired ones that may contain other tags or text, or so-called ***empty elements***. The first type always occur in pairs with one tag indicating the start, and one the end of the marked-up stretch, making their general format

```
<tagname>...</tagname>
```

where the end tag is marked by the additional forward slash following the opening angle bracket, immediately preceding the tag name. As with Python variables, tag names cannot have spaces inside them, but may contain underscores, at least in XML, where they can freely be defined, whereas the tag names are completely fixed in standard HTML. Empty elements primarily contain browser instructions or 'non-text information', and no other tags. Their general format is

```
<tag>
```

or

```
<tag/>
```

where the final slash preceding the closing bracket is specific to XML, and may or may not be preceded by a space. An example for such an empty element would be the HTML line break <br> tag.

Both types can contain additional information in the form of ***attribute–value pairs*** linked via an equals symbol, just as in Python keyword arguments. The values need to – like strings in Python – either appear in (complementary) single or double quotes, and can also contain spaces. For paired tags, attributes can only occur inside the start tag. A typical attribute for elements in XML is n, which usually contains a running number for the element type, and for HTML id, which represents a named location inside a document that may also be accessible via scripting or as a specific hyperlink target inside a page.

Let's now first take a closer look at HTML as a simpler markup language before we download and process data from the web.

10.2 Brief Intro to HTML

Properly written web pages are normally divided into two distinct parts, although web browsers tend to be very forgiving and accept much as HTML that isn't really well-formed. The top part consists of a 'header' inside a paired <head>...</head> tag, which essentially contains meta information, such as the page title, the encoding of the page, (links to) style sheets for formatting, or even script elements written in JavaScript. Most of these aren't usually directly visible to the users of the web page, apart from title, which appears inside the title bar of the browser or on tabs, if multiple ones have been opened.

The actual page text is contained inside the `<body>...</body>` tag, for which a number of main text elements are defined. The most important, and frequently occurring of these is the paragraph, `<p>...</p>`. Just like in other types of documents, though, paragraphs that belong together can also be preceded by headings, for which there are six numbered levels defined, and where *n* here always indicates a level number, `<hn>...</hn>`, with 1 being the highest. A more recent addition to HTML are two further tags for marking textual divisions, the division (`<div>...</div>`), which allows us to group multiple paragraphs together into sections, and the `<span>...</span>`, which groups together shorter textual ranges, e.g. for highlighting or other formatting purposes.

Anchor tags (`<a>...</a>`) provide the HTML-typical functionality for hyperlinking, and work both for hyperlinks outside of and within a page. Their form is

```
<a href="URL" [target="..."]>descriptive text</a>
```

The only essential attribute here is `href`, which is short for *hypertext reference*, and specifies the link target, a so-called **uniform resource locator** (URL). A URL most commonly represents a web page or location inside a web page that has an `id` attribute, but may also point to a local file. As with local file paths, such locations may either be absolute or relative.

Lists and tables (`<table>...</table>`) make it possible to summarise information in compact ways. For the former, we can distinguish between two different types, **o**rdered lists (`<ol>...</ol>`) and **u**nordered ones (`<ul>...</ul>`). Ordered ones are automatically numbered, thus implying a hierarchical or sequential order, whereas unordered ones are simply bulleted. List types can also be mixed and nested within each other. Each list element needs to be contained in a list item tag (`<li>...</li>`). Tables are minimally sub-divided into **t**able **r**ows (`<tr>...</tr>`), with nested cells of **t**able **d**ata (`<td>...</td>`), but may also contain further structural sub-divisions in more recent HTML incarnations, such as the current HTML5.

In terms of embedded multimedia content, we can encounter a number of additional tags, such as for images (`<img src='URL' [alt='description']>`), where the **s**ource attribute (`src`) is equivalent to `href` for anchors, though generally pointing to a local URL, and `alt`, if present, provides an **alt**ernative description if images cannot be loaded or for screen readers used by visually impaired users. As of HTML5, audio (`<audio>...</audio>`) and video (`<video>...</video>`) files also have their own tags with a nested `<source src='URL'>...</source>` tag, whereas in older versions, they were linked in via anchors.

Last, but not least, we also have a number of different formatting options. The original two options were the **b**oldface (`<b>...</b>`) and italics (`<i>...</i>`) tags used for direct formatting of text without any notions of semantics involved. However, as endeavours to separate the logic of HTML documents form their formatting increased over the years, the `<strong>...</strong>` tag was invented to replace boldface to indicate some form of emphasis, whereas these days, it's become more customary to format different text passages using spans or other HTML elements with `id` or `class` attributes via internal or external stylesheets that define their appearance. Figure 10.1 shows a sample HTML page that illustrates some of HTML tags and concepts described above.

HTML Download Test Page for Analysis (<h1>)

This is a very simple web page for testing downloads via scripts or download programs and analysing/processing their contents. As such, the following headings and paragraphs will not contain much sensible information, other than providing an indication of the HTML structure, some specific HTML constructs, and the logical textual units of this document. This is the very first paragraph inside the page.

Heading 1.1 (<h2>)

This is the first paragraph (<p>) below heading 1.1., contained in division (<div>) 1 of the main text, as can be seen in the grey background colour.
It contains a single manual line break (<br>) after the preceding sentence, and is the second paragraph in the document. Divisions are used to group related information together to be able to treat parts of documents as sections.

This is the second paragraph below heading 1.1 and the third one inside the document. It doesn't contain any line breaks, but may wrap around automatically if the browser window isn't wide enough.

Heading 1.2 (<h2>)

This is the first paragraph below heading 1.2, contained in division 2 of the main text, as can be seen in the light-green background colour, and the fourth one inside the document.

This is the second paragraph below heading 1.2 and the fifth one inside the document. **This is some bold (<b>) text.**

Heading 1.3 (<h2>)

This is the first paragraph below heading 1.3., contained in division 3, and the sixth one inside the document

This is the second paragraph below heading 1.3 and the seventh one inside the document. *This is some text in italics (<i>).* And this is an example of a span (<span>).

This is the table caption (<caption>) for this simple table (<table>).

Column heading (<th>) 1 inside the table head (<thead>)	Column heading 2
Cell (<td>) 1 inside table row (<tr>) 1	Cell 2
Cell 3	Cell 4

® 2009 Martin Weisser; last edited: Thu 05-Jan-2023 09:50:40

Figure 10.1 Sample HTML page.

We'll later download the page shown above in Exercise 59, and extract the paragraphs from it in Exercise 60. If you'd like to take a sneak preview at the original page, you can do so at https://martinweisser.org/pract_cl/HTML_download_test_en.html, where you can also inspect the page source using the appropriate option in your browser.

10.3 Using the `urllib.request` Module

Web servers work by accepting requests from client applications, such as browsers, and then generating an appropriate response, either by sending data or – if this isn't possible due to some form of restriction – an error message detailing the problem. Common problems are that a specific page wasn't found because a link is outdated, or that access is forbidden, for instance because the content may be stored behind a paywall, i.e. can only be accessed by subscribers.

The urllib.request module provides a convenient way of requesting data from web servers in the form of mainly HTML or XML documents. All we need to do in order to use it is to import it in the usual way, and then call the urlopen function with a (valid) URL as its argument. If no urllib.error.URLError is encountered in the process, a binary http.client. HTTPResponse object is returned that represents the page, and which we can then query for different page properties and data read from it. If an error occurs, we can of course trap the object in an exception as usual, and use its reason property to construct an appropriate message indicating the error.

However, to be able to read the contents using the object's own read method, we need to decode it, for which we need to know its original encoding. The module tries to identify this by analysing the page's headers, i.e. the meta information, and usually allows us to identify the character set (charset) of the encoding using the syntax

```
page.headers.get_content_charset([failobj="utf-8"])
```

where the optional failobj keyword argument makes it possible to specify an assumed default should the method fail to identify the correct encoding. This still leaves the option that our default encoding will not work for reading, but as this will be very rare these days, we can simply trap the error and abort the download if necessary. To decode the page contents, read them in one go, and store them in a string variable for further processing, we can use the syntax

```
contents = page.read().decode(charset)
```

Armed with this knowledge, we'll soon be able to do our next exercise. Before we can embark on this endeavour, though, we first need to discuss how the QMessageBox, which we'll use to flag potential errors and options to the user, can be modified to allow us to provide alternative options to the user.

The message box we used before only made it possible for the user to acknowledge information, but not make any choice as to how to proceed, other than just accepting the information. To do this, we used the message box widget directly, executing and showing it via .exec_ without assigning it to a variable and customising it further than changing the title, the message, or the icon. The exec_ method is actually a method of the QMessageBox parent class QDialog which causes the dialogue to be shown modally, meaning that the program cannot continue until it's closed, and produces a return value once it gets closed via any button click or corresponding action. However, if we create a new instance of the widget and assign this to a variable, we can add further modifications, such as changing the default buttons, setting one button as the default, and actually testing which button was clicked by the user in order to be able to take action accordingly.

To assign a set of new buttons to the dialogue, we have a number of pre-defined options, such as QMessageBox.Yes, QMessageBox.No, QMessageBox.Abort, QMessageBox.Retry, QMessageBox.Ignore, etc., where each time one of these buttons is created, the text following the . is displayed on the button, and we can also assign the return value of exec_ to a variable that will hold the value of the button type we can use in an if clause. These buttons are set via

```
msgBox.setStandardButtons(buttons)
```

where *buttons* holds a union of the button types, which is created by adding a pipe symbol (|) between the button types required. As one of these buttons should normally be active by default if the user presses the Enter key, we can also set this via

```
msgBox.setDefaultButton(button)
```

We now have all the information needed to complete our next exercise, so let's turn to this task.

Exercise 59 Writing a GUI Downloader

Write the GUI program `23_fetch_page_GUI.py`, in which you use the module `urllib.request` to download and save a web page to your computer. This GUI should have a toolbar containing a button to download a URL specified in a `QLineEdit` widget, a label describing the latter, as well as a `QTextEdit` window to be used for logging the download stages or indicate any errors that may arise in the process. Figure 10.2 shows what the GUI should eventually look like.

Figure 10.2 The Downloader GUI.

Begin by setting up the GUI with an additional skeleton for a `fetch_page` method that we'll flesh out later. Because this is not a very complex GUI, we can do the whole setup inside the constructor of the derived window class without a separate `initUI` method. Don't forget to add a test block, so that you'll be able to test the GUI layout before we can actually do any downloads. When you set up the button, also link it to the slot, and do the same for the `QLineEdit` by connecting its `returnPressed` signal. This will allow you to trigger the download either by clicking the button or pressing the `Enter` key once you've typed a URL into the `QLineEdit` widget.

Once you've got the GUI working, start defining the download method.

Begin by setting up a variable for the web address to which you assign the current text inside the `QLineEdit` widget. In case this variable should be empty after the assignment because the user has triggered the download without first typing in any URL, show a simple message box to the user and abort the download.

If there is an address, use the `urlopen` method with the address variable as argument within a `try` block in order to download a byte object of the page and store it in another variable, logging what's happening or happened at each step by outputting suitable messages.

Catch any potential `urllib.error.URLError` in an exception and output it inside a suitable error message in the log window, again terminating the method.

In the next step, let the user know that we're now trying to identify the encoding and page title, then determine the encoding of the page, and try to use it to decode and read the page content into a string variable. Should this fail, use an exception with the `Exception` base class, and output a suitable message that we're aborting the download due to an encoding issue, and terminate the method.

If you've managed to read the page contents, try to extract the title via the content of the relevant tag using a regex search. Otherwise, if there's no title, output a similar message, only indicating that the page has no title.

If a title was found, use it to generate a file name, first removing any extraneous leading or trailing whitespace, replacing any non-word characters in the title by underscores, and adding the extension `html`. Otherwise, use the method `rindex` and the address to find the position of the page name and extract this from the URL to use it as a file name.

Now save the page contents to a file, using this name, but only if it doesn't exist yet. If it does, alert the user, and ask them whether they want to overwrite the existing file using a suitably adjusted `QMessageBox`. If the response is negative, terminate the method again. Don't forget to add suitable error handling to the saving operation in analogy to what we did before in this program. For the sake of convenience, we'll save the file in the same folder this time. If you've managed to save the file successfully, output an appropriate message.

Finally, test the program using the following page:

https://martinweisser.org/pract_cl/HTML_download_test_en.html.

When we download web pages, naturally we also want to extract all or at least part of the text for analysis. To do so, we could of course use our knowledge of regexes, just as we did for finding the page title in the previous exercise. However, as some HTML pages may be rather complex due to the occurrence of lots of attributes and heavily nested elements, it's more advisable to use an existing module that will facilitate a large part of our work.

10.4   Extracting Text from Web Pages

The module I'm talking about is called *Beautiful Soup*, which is already available in its fourth version at the time of writing. You can install it via

```
pip(3) install beautifulsoup4
```

but to import and use it in your programs later, you need to use the abbreviated name `bs4`. To process web pages, you create a `BeautifulSoup` object from each page, which then holds a parsed *tree* of that page. For our purposes, it's sufficient to import this single object using

```
from bs4 import BeautifulSoup
```

Constructing the page object is then straightforward. All you need to do is to provide a page as the first argument to the constructor, and a parser type as the second. Beautiful Soup supports a variety of parser types, but since not all of these come pre-installed, you may need to install them as required. For our next exercise, though, we'll use the pre-installed `html.parser`.

You can use Beautiful Soup both to find specific elements or pieces of text on web pages, as well as manipulate or navigate them. We'll ignore the latter options here because we're only interested in carrying out analyses, and will hence only discuss a few of the options for identifying and extracting text data. The simplest method for finding relevant pieces of text is `find`, which returns the first instance found of a given tag, attribute or text. Apart from simple strings, it also supports using re objects as search terms. It returns None if nothing is found, but if tags or attributes are found, a Tag object, and for text searches – using the keyword argument string –, a NavigableString object. If a potential tag name without angle brackets is provided, find always attempts to interpret the first argument as a tag, and if there's a second argument that's not a keyword argument, this is normally interpreted as an attribute to the tag. It's also possible to use pre-defined HTML attribute names, such as class, id, or name as keyword arguments, although in searches for the class attribute, you need to use class_ as the keyword, since class itself, as you already know, is a Python keyword.

The same arguments can also be supplied to the find_all method, which returns a list of results. This method also allows us to look for lists of tags, as well as to constrain the search using the keyword limit. Once suitable pieces of text have been found using these methods, the text contained inside the individual elements found can be extracted using the get_text method. If all you're interested in is extracting the text from a page, this method can also be applied to the whole tree object.

In our next exercise, we want to use find_all to extract all paragraphs from the web page we downloaded as part of the previous exercise, and simply print these out. However, as – in order to achieve this goal – we need to apply the get_text method to each individual element found to retrieve the text from each element contained in the list, we first need to learn about a more efficient way of transforming these.

10.5 List and Dictionary Comprehension

In order to transform and/or filter all elements in lists, Python offers a highly elegant technique called *list comprehension*. List comprehension makes it possible to generate new, modified lists from existing ones without the need to use one or more nested loops, and is probably best explained through a simple example.

Let's assume that we have an unsorted list of words that we want to transform to lowercase for comparison purposes, but only if they start with a particular letter that we've stored inside a variable called letter. Hence, one part of this task would be a transformation, and the other a filtering operation, where normally filtering should come first. In order to achieve this, we could run a for loop over the original list, and then use a nested if statement to filter out and transform only the relevant words. Schematically, this could look as follows:

```
for word in word_list1:
    if word.startswith(letter):
        word_list2.append(word.lower())
```

However, Python allows us to formulate this much more concisely as a one-liner like this:

```
word_list2 = [word.lower() for word in word_list1
    if word.startswith(letter)]
```

Because we're creating a new list, the complete expression on the right-hand side needs to be enclosed in square brackets. Please note that – in the above example – I've only added a line break for the sake of readability.

In a similar way, we could use the same list and filter to create a dictionary in which every key has its associated lowercase version as a value, only changing the schematic from above slightly to

```
word_dict = {word:word.lower() for word in word_list1
    if word.startswith(letter)}
```

Here of course we'd need to use curly brackets to create the dictionary. Armed with this knowledge, we can now tackle our next exercise.

Exercise 60 Extracting Paragraphs from Web Pages

Write a new program called `24_extract_paras.py`, in which you extract all paragraphs from the web page you previously downloaded.

First, import the required object from the `Beautiful Soup` module.

Open – this time without any error handling – the web page and create a tree object, specifying `html.parser` as your parser.

Now, create a list of paragraphs using *list comprehension*, using `find_all` on the tree and extracting the text as discussed above.

Finally, output this list line by line using a single `print` statement.

Now that we know how to process HTML-annotated data, we can turn towards discussing linguistic annotation using XML.

10.6 Brief Intro to XML

In XML, the tags, unlike in HTML, don't consist of a pre-defined set, but can be created depending on one's needs. Just like our variable names in Python, they should ideally be self-explanatory and reflect the semantics of the structural and/or textual elements we want to mark up. While browsers or other programs that process HTML tend to be very forgiving, there are a few constraints regarding the well-formedness of XML documents. Any well-formed XML document

- needs to start with an XML declaration,
- to have 'container' tag wrapped around contents, e.g. `<text>...</text>`,
- its tags mustn't overlap (e.g. HTML's `<b><i></b></i>` is not valid), and
- empty tags need to have a / before the closing bracket, e.g. `<pause />`, optionally preceded by a space.

The XML declaration looks like this:

```
<?xml version="1.0"? [lang="language identifier"]>
```

Here, the language identifier, en for English, de for German, etc., is optional, as indicated above through the use of square brackets. Further constraints on the validity of XML documents can be imposed via additional rules defined in **Document Type Definitions** (DTSs) or **XML Schemas**, but we won't discuss these here.

For linguistics purposes, the names of paired tags generally reflect linguistic units or concepts, and empty tags represent 'non-words', e.g. punctuation or meta information, although in some PoS tagged data, punctuation marks may be tagged as word tokens using paired tags. To my mind, though, this is absolutely incorrect from a linguistic point of view. Figure 10.3 shows an abridged version of the XML document we'll be producing in our next exercise.

```
<?xml version="1.0"?>
<text id="frankenstein" corpus="GothicNovels" author="Mary Shelley" lang="en">
<paragraph n="1">
Frankenstein, or the Modern Prometheus by Mary Wollstonecraft (Godwin)
Shelley</paragraph>
<letter n="1">
<heading n="1" type="letter">
Letter 1
</heading>
<paragraph n="2">
TO Mrs. Saville, England</paragraph>
<paragraph n="3">
St. Petersburgh, Dec. 11th, 17--</paragraph>
<paragraph n="4">
<sentence n="1">
You will rejoice to hear that no disaster has accompanied the commencement of an enterprise
which you have regarded with such evil forebodings.
</sentence>
<sentence n="2">
I arrived here yesterday, and my first task is to assure my dear sister of my welfare and
increasing confidence in the success of my undertaking.
</sentence>
</paragraph>
...
</text>
```

Figure 10.3   Abridged sample XML document.

In the above sample, you can already see the XML declaration preceding the main document, that we've used `<text>...</text>` as a container tag, included a few `<paragraph>` and `<sentence>` tags, as well as further textual subdivisions you should easily be able to identify. Now that you ought to have a very basic understanding of what XML might look like, we can embark on another exercise.

Exercise 61   Converting Text to XML (a)

Create the program `25_txt_to_xml.py`, in which you convert the text Mary Shelley's Frankenstein into an XML file. The book contains different letter and chapter headings, and all these should be assigned separate tags with running numbers for each heading, as well as a `type` attribute that matches the heading. The same should be done for all paragraphs and sentences contained in them, and also for the particular section types that contain the letters and chapters. As a preliminary step, open the text file and scan through it to see whether you can observe any other details in terms of structure, layout, or formatting that may be relevant to our task.

Set up three integer variables for the running numbers, `n_heading`, `n_paragraph`, and `n_sentence`, initialising each to 0. Also set up a list variable `abbrevs`, which we'll later fill with abbreviations that need to be masked temporarily during the processing, so that the full stops at their ends won't be mistaken for sentence endings.

Next, create a variable for the input file `frankenstein.txt` from your `texts` folder, and derive an output file name for the new XML file from it. The output file is supposed to be written to the output folder again.

Open the input file, of course using appropriate error handling, read in the whole file, splitting it at two or more newlines, and assigning the result to a list of paragraphs. Please note, though, that these paragraphs still contain spurious line breaks that we need to remove later.

Open the output file `frankenstein.xml`, using appropriate error handling.

As a 'header', write the XML declaration and an opening `text` tag containing the attributes `id`, `corpus`, author, and `lang`, along with suitable descriptive values, into the output file.

Now start a `for` loop to iterate over the paragraphs.

Inside the loop, first replace all line breaks by spaces and then collapse all multiple spaces into one.

Next, we need to handle the different types of paragraphs, so set up conditions for the two cases, i.e. letter or chapter headings versus ordinary paragraphs.

We start by testing if one of the former two is identified. Our test should also capture the type of heading and its number using appropriate bracketing that will later allow us to extract the right values from the groups of our (potential) match. If we've found a heading, this indicates the start of a new document section of that particular type, and we need to create a start tag for it, followed by the header element. However, for all but the first of such sections, we also need to add an end tag before the new start tag to close off the section.

For headings, we don't need to identify any sentences within them, so first increase the heading number counter, then check to see if it's not `1`. If it's not, write out an end tag using the value currently stored in `h_type` as its tag name. This variable will contain a value for all non-initial sections because we'll extract it in the following step outside the current `if` block.

Next, create `h_type` and assign the lowercased value of the first matched group to it. Also set up a variable `n_unit`, and assign the value of the second match group to it.

Write out a start tag of the value of `h_type`, using the value currently stored in `n_unit` for the n attribute of the relevant section element. We can do this because all letters and chapters are numbered consecutively, anyway.

Write out the heading element containing the current paragraph text, and, as the value of its n attribute the heading counter you increased earlier, as well as using `n_type`, this time as the value for the element's `type` attribute. Jump to the next paragraph item in the loop because the current one has now been processed.

If we didn't find a heading, this means that we've found an ordinary paragraph, and need to process that. These are a bit trickier because we need to clean up the formatting, mask the abbreviations, split each paragraph into sentences, unmask the abbreviations again before outputting them, and wrap the sentences and the paragraph itself into the right elements.

The cleanup operation required here is quite simple, as it essentially only consists of replacing two hyphens in a row by one hyphen surrounded by spaces, bearing in mind that we need to specify where these hyphens should not occur.

In order to be able to mask the abbreviations, we first need to identify them in the source text and add them to our abbreviations list. This can be done by searching for 2-3 characters followed by a dot in your editor, ideally searching via a regex so as not to find too many sentence endings. However, make sure that the abbreviations you include don't actually occur at the end of a sentence, as is the case at least once.

To do the masking, you can run a loop over the abbreviations list, each time concatenating a regex where the abbreviation precedes a dot, and replacing this dot by an underscore.

Before we can carry out the next step in our exercise, though, we first need to learn about how we can use user-defined functions in complex regex replacements, so let's discuss this now.

10.7 Complex Regex Replacements Using Functions

The replacement slot in the `re.sub` method can not only contain a string, but also a call to a user-defined function that creates the replacement by manipulating the relevant match. This function is implicitly passed the match object as an argument from within `re.sub`, so we can then extract and work with either the whole match or any particular groups contained within the match object. In order to be able to handle the match object appropriately, the function definition needs to be set up to accept this object as its argument. Armed with this knowledge, we can now continue writing our conversion program where we implement such a function to allow us to generate suitably numbered sentence tags that we wrap around all potential sentences we identify.

Exercise 62 Converting Text to XML (b)

To identify and mark sentences within the paragraph, use `re.sub` with a suitable capturing expression that (non-greedily) finds all relevant characters up to and including either a sentence punctuation mark or string (i.e. paragraph) end, and then replaces the captured sentence by a sentence start tag with the running number as attribute, the sentence content, as well as an end tag. To create the replacement, add a user-defined function in the appropriate place inside your program that accepts a match object as argument, extracts the relevant captured group and returns the tagged sentence. To be able to increment the relevant counter variable, you first need to use the statement `global n_sentence` before incrementing the counter, as the counter variable was defined outside the function and use of the keyword `global` makes it accessible inside the function, so that the variable is no longer interpreted as one that's local to it. Unmask all abbreviations again.
Write the paragraph to the output file.
Finally, after the end of the loop, write the end tag of the current section and the `text` container to the output file, but without a line break for the latter.
Test the program and check the result in your editor.

Now that we know how to produce some basic, simple XML, let's investigate how to produce XML in a more standardised format, that of the TEI.

10.8 Brief Intro to the TEI Scheme

Perhaps one of the best known and relatively standardised formats often encountered in XML annotations for linguistics or DH is that based on the proposals of the ***Text Encoding Initiative*** (TEI; https://tei-c.org). The TEI Consortium was founded in 1987 in order to establish guidelines and standards for annotating the many varied forms of electronic data that exist in the Humanities, and has since been publishing a number of these proposals providing XML frameworks for annotation. The current proposal has reached the number 5, and is hence generally referred to as ***P5***. These frameworks comprise different modules, some containing specifications for elements and attributes that are applicable to all types of documents, contained in the *core* module, and some to only particular ones, such as prose, verse, drama, spoken language, and even whole language corpora. We won't be able to go into all of these in detail, but mainly discuss a few relevant element types that will allow us to construct a valid TEI document representing the *Frankenstein* text we annotated previously, the keyword here being *valid* because the TEI framework actually constrains the elements and attributes we may use and where inside a document they may appear. This is quite different from the type of simply well-formed XML we discussed earlier, where we were in complete control over the structure of elements and attributes we wanted to use as long as we followed the basic rules of well-formedness. For further details, you should consult the TEI website listed above, where you can find most of the relevant information, and can also download a PDF of the full P5, bearing in mind that, with its 2021 pages, it's not exactly a quick and easy read.

Any valid TEI XML document should normally start with an XML declaration, even if not all available language corpora actually comply with this. For instance, both the XML version of the original *British National Corpus*, now generally referred to as BNC1994, and the TEI version of the *Brown Corpus* don't follow this rule. The containing element for all such documents is the `<TEI xmlns="http://www.tei-c.org/ns/1.0" xml:lang="en">...</TEI>` tag, where the `xmlns` attribute defines a so-called **namespace** that helps to disambiguate between the specific elements and attributes defined in the TEI framework and any others by the same name that may be defined elsewhere. For instance, the `lang` attribute that follows in the above example refers to the general language attribute defined in the XML specification itself, rather than the one by the same name that is defined in the TEI framework, and is hence prefixed by `xml:`.

The main basic division within any TEI XML document is between metadata about the text, stored inside a header, and the text itself, so we'll discuss these two parts separately in the following sections.

10.8.1 The Header

The mandatory header tag (`<teiHeader>`) comprises various types of information, out of which only the bibliographic description (`<fileDesc>`) is required. The most important sub-elements of this tag are

- the `<titleStmt>`,
- the `<publicationStmt>`, and
- the `<sourceDesc>`.

The first of these normally contains information such as `<title>` and `<author>`, but possibly also the responsibility statement (`<respStmt>`) if there is an editor for a collection, whereas the second and third may contain free-form paragraphs describing the nature of the publication, i.e. what it's supposed to be used for or be a part of – such as a corpus –, and where the material for the file originated – for instance if it was obtained somewhere in digital form or transcribed, etc. For spoken language, the source description should generally also contain `<scriptStmt>` if the material is based on a prepared script, and a `<recordingStmt>` that provides details as to the recording equipment used and the recording itself.

The optional elements relevant for us here comprise the somewhat inappropriately named `<encodingDesc>`, which provides details about where a text may have originated and whether and how it was cleaned up and edited, rather than the actual encoding of the file, which is of course specified as an attribute of the XML declaration, the `<profileDesc>`, which can provide further information about the file's content and languages (`<langUse>`), as well as a text category (`<textClass>`), and details about the state of revision of the document (`<revisionDesc>`), if any need to be documented. Each potential revision should then be indicated through a

`<change>` tag containing when and who attributes specifying the time of change and who was responsible for it, as well as a description of the change inside the tag. In text corpora, particularly important further elements of the profile description may be `<particDesc>` – detailing participants in spoken interactions or the creation of written texts –, `<settingDesc>` – i.e. where interactions took place –, and `<textDesc>`. Figure 10.4 shows the TEI header we'll produce for the TEI version of *Frankenstein* as part of Exercise 63.

```
<?xml version="1.0"?>
<TEI xmlns="http://www.tei-c.org/ns/1.0" xml:lang="en">
<teiHeader>
<fileDesc>
<titleStmt>
<title>
Frankenstein, or the Modern Prometheus</title>
<author>
Mary Wollstonecraft (Godwin) Shelley
</author>
</titleStmt>
<publicationStmt>
<p>
Part of a corpus of Gothic novels
</p>
</publicationStmt>
<sourceDesc>
<p>
Extracted from eBook #84 from Project Gutenberg; https://www.gutenberg.org
</p>
</sourceDesc>
</fileDesc>
</teiHeader>
```

Figure 10.4 TEI header for the document to be produced in Exercise 63.

10.8.2 The Text Body

The main content of a TEI document is enclosed in the `<text>` element, regardless of whether the material is spoken or written, and may also contain optional `<front>` and `<back>` matter elements related to written information, such as imprints or indexes, etc. The main text is generally enclosed in a `<body>` tag, especially if front and/or back matter elements are present. Multiple texts may also be grouped together using the `<group>` or `<teiCorpus>` options, but I would personally advise against using these because it's better for analysis purposes to work with single whole texts if possible, partly because it's the only way of establishing aspects of dispersion – i.e. the distribution of text features – across a corpus.

Within the text body, there are many predominantly structural elements, some of which we've already encountered for HTML, such as `<p>` (paragraph), `<div>` (division), or `<head>` (heading). Divisions may, for instance, carry attributes like type="chapter" or sample="initial", where the values indicate the particular part of a text the sample was taken from, with other options being medial and final. Headings, however, may only occur immediately after the start tags of divisions or other types of grouping elements, such as lists, tables, etc., some of which we'll still discuss later. Linguistic categories at a lower level are `<s>` (sentence), `<cl>` (clause), `<phr>` (phrase), `<w>` (word), `<m>` (morpheme), `<c>` (character), or even more specifically, `<pc>` (punctuation character), which can all have appropriate type attributes characterising their precise nature. Words tags can also contain information about their lemmas in a `lemma` attribute.

For representing written language, and especially for DH purposes, there may be less emphasis on the linguistic level, but it may perhaps be more important to represent other textual properties more faithfully. We won't really have space here to go into all of these in detail, especially not when they concern precise aspects of layout or specific types of rendering that describe manuscripts or original printed editions exhaustively, but we'll predominantly focus on some textual or non-textual elements that may require special handling.

Some of these elements may also contain text, but not follow an ordinary flow text format; instead, their representation may follow a more itemised or tabular structure that could be important to preserve. This is, for instance, the case for lists that are enclosed in a corresponding `<list>` tag with nested `<item>` elements inside it. This is similar to the HTML options for ordered and unordered lists, only that the numbering or specific format for the items would be indicated via an `n` attribute for numbering, while bulleted list would need to be marked up via other attribute options. In lists, we tend to have a simple hierarchy, whereas the `<table>` element represents a more complex logical arrangement of rows (`<row>`) with nested cells (`<cell>`), where the rows of data may be preceded by an optional `<head>` element, which in this case may offer a caption-like description of the table.

While it's likely that attempts will generally be made to preserve the text in lists and tables for the research purposes envisaged in this book, simply marking them up using the appropriate tags, in some cases, it may also sometimes make sense to omit them. In this case, a `<gap>` can be marked and justified using a `reason` attribute. This might, for instance, be done if tables contain little or no textual material, but simply numbers that add little meaning to the text in terms of its semantics. Similarly, a gap may be marked for figures, unless they are really important for retaining the meaning of the text, e.g. in documenting dictionary entries. In order to include them, one would normally use the `<figure>` element, where the `<graphic>` sub-element would include a reference pointer to a URL specifying the file location, and – if present – the `<head>` a caption, and the `<figDesc>` a more detailed textual description of the content of the graphical illustration. As will have become apparent from my referring to the URL pointer, the TEI also offers various means of linking elements together, predominantly using `xml:id` attributes to establish these links, but these are less relevant for us here, although they may be important if different levels of annotation are linked together using so-called ***standoff*** annotation, an advanced topic we again won't discuss here, though.

If it's important to retain information about the exact pagination and layout, including line breaks, it's also possible to use the empty page break (`<pb/>`), or line beginning (`<lb/>`) elements, where the former would normally have an n attribute to indicate the page number. Other layout or typographic features, such as boldface or other types of emphasis that may appear in original manuscripts or printed copies of the text can be indicated via `<emph>` (emphasis) or `<hi>` (highlight) tags, with attributes like `style`, which takes a CSS (Cascading Style Sheets) style definition like `font-style: bold` as its value, or `rend` (e.g. `rend="italic"`).

In prose texts, we often find either direct speech or thoughts of the individual characters participating in the story. These may be represented using the `<q>` (quote) tag, together with a number of descriptive attributes. In order to mark the distinction between direct speech and thought, we can use the `type` attribute with either `spoken` or `thought` as its value. In order to specify who the speaker was or at whom the speech may be directed, the two attributes `who` and `toWhom` can be used. Another way to mark up this type of feature is to use `<said>`, where there is also an option to distinguish between `true` and `false` values for `direct`, so that passages of indirect speech may also be indicated.

The textual structure for verse differs from that of prose. Here, larger structures, such as stanzas, are generally marked up as line groups (`<lg>`), whereas each individual line is enclosed in an `<l>` tag. Even larger groupings, such as into books or cantos can be marked up using standard division tags with appropriate `type` attributes.

For spoken language, there are some additional elements and attributes of note. The most important of these is probably the `<u>` (utterance) tag, which encloses a relatively uninterrupted sequence of speech by a particular speaker and hence corresponds to what is generally better known as a speaker **turn**. Relevant attributes here are `who`, representing the speaker, and `trans` (transition), which indicates whether there has been a break between the preceding turn or whether it follows on without a pause, in which case the attribute value is `latching`, while the remaining two options are `overlap` and `pause`. Other tags also make it possible to indicate specific verbal or non-verbal features or events that may influence the understanding or interpretation of spoken interaction.

It's also possible to add annotations to texts, or represent existing notes, such as footnotes, by using `<note>` tags. If these tags refer to notes existing in the original source text, then a `place` attribute may also indicate where these appear, for instance in the `margin`. As annotations, such notes can be used to indicate any kind of relevant observations on the source text. Another form of annotation that may be used to clarify specific features of texts is to mark up apparent errors in the source, such as typos or errors in learner annotation. The presumed errors can be indicated using the `<sic>` element, and their corrections provided in the `<corr>` tag. However, such types of normalisations also illustrate one of the weaknesses of the TEI scheme, i.e. that there is a proliferation of container elements that may sometimes even refer to one and the same span of text. Perhaps a better solution to the issue of errors would be to use a single correction tag that brackets the normalised part with the original erroneous form being indicated inside an `orig` attribute so that it remains recoverable if necessary. A similar effect could also be achieved by using a single empty element to indicate such corrections. However, both of these forms are not envisaged by the TEI scheme, and are purely my own recommendations on how to potentially streamline the markup, thereby increasing its legibility and processability. Figure 10.5 shows the beginning of the text body for our TEI version of *Frankenstein* that we'll produce in Exercise 63.

```
<text>
<body>
<div n="1" type="letter">
<head n="1">
Letter 1
</head>
<p n="1">
TO Mrs. Saville, England</p>
<p n="2">
St. Petersburgh, Dec. 11th, 17--</p>
<p n="3">
<s n="1">
You will rejoice to hear that no disaster has accompanied the commencement of an enterprise
which you have regarded with such evil forebodings.
</s>
<s n="2">
I arrived here yesterday, and my first task is to assure my dear sister of my welfare and
increasing confidence in the success of my undertaking.
</s>
</p>
...
```

Figure 10.5 Beginning of the text body for the TEI version of Frankenstein.

The XML coding above of course resembles the coding we produced in Exercise 61, but with a few TEI-specific differences you'll be able to understand better after finishing the next exercise. Now that you have a basic idea of what a TEI XML document should look like, we can use this knowledge to modify our previous program so that it will output a TEI version of the text. Essentially, all we need to do in order to achieve this goal is to add the TEI container, a TEI header that we'll fill with some basic information, and adjust the tags that we used previously so that they'll conform to the ones defined in the TEI scheme. As headings in the TEI scheme can only occur immediately after groupings, we cannot simply add them before the paragraphs at the start of the individual letters or chapters, but need to establish proper <div>s that can then be assigned type attributes and numbered consecutively.

Exercise 63   Converting Text to TEI XML

Copy the previous program to one you call 26_txt_to_TEI.py.

Change the variables n_heading to n_header.

Adjust the function make_sentence so that it will output sentences wrapped in an <s> tag, rather than the <sentence> tag we used earlier.

Change the regex substitution for the output filename so that it generates the frankenstein_TEI.xml instead of frankenstein.xml.

Where you previously opened the text element, add TEI and teiHeader start tags to the output.

As the first paragraph in the text consists of two lines that contain the title and author name that we'll need as sub-elements of the <titleStmt> inside the TEI header, extract this from our list of paragraphs by using the pop method of the list object with 0 as an argument, and assign this to a string variable.

Split the resulting string into two lines and store them in a tuple that contains title and author.

Adjust the author information so that the leading "by" is removed.

Now write out the remainder of the <teiHeader> containing a <fileDesc> with the <titleStmt> and its associated information, as well as a <publicationStmt> and <sourceDesc>, both containing descriptive free-form paragraphs to the file. For the latter, you can use Part of a corpus of Gothic novels and Extracted from eBook #84 from Project Gutenberg; www.gutenberg.org, respectively, in order to provide sufficient detail.

Remove the attributes from the <text> element, as we no longer need them because we now have the header containing the relevant metadata.

Add the <body> tag in the appropriate place.

In the next step, adjust the if block where we tested to see if the match succeeded, and if so, first increase the counter for the division and the header, and extract the result of the group match to the h_type variable, but delete the following line because we no longer need n_unit and also no longer have a group to extract from.

If the division number is not 1, write out an end tag for the division because this will need to precede the next division tag we'll set up next.

Now write out a new <div> tag with an n and a type attribute. For the first attribute, simply use the current heading counter because each heading also indicates the beginning of a new division, and for the second, the type that was matched by the regex search, ensuring that the whole value is lowercased.

Write the header tag, along with its number and the content of the paragraph.
Finally, change all <paragraph> tags to <p>, ensure that all opener start tags are closed, run the program, and check the result.
To ensure that your result really conforms to all TEI rules defined in the scheme, you can use the TEI validator at https://teibyexample.org/exist/tools/TBEvalidator.htm if you want to.

Now that you've hopefully got a basic understanding of XML and the TEI scheme, we can move on to our final chapter and discuss how to create basic visualisations for our data.

10.9 Discussions

Discussion 59   Writing a GUI Downloader

By now, setting up the GUI should be pretty straightforward because the decision as to which widget type to derive your own window class from is essentially determined by the fact that we need a tool bar, which is only provided by QMainWindow. Hence, the constructor for our class that we can aptly name Downloader, the skeleton method, and main block could look like this:

```python
def __init__(self):
    super().__init__()
    self.setFont(QFont("Courier", 12))
    self.setWindowTitle('Downloader')
    self.setGeometry(30,30,1000,400)

    toolbar = self.addToolBar('main')
    fetchBtn = QPushButton('Download')
    fetchBtn.clicked.connect(self.fetch_page)
    self.addressBar = QLineEdit()
    self.addressBar.returnPressed.connect(self.fetch_page)

    toolbar.addWidget(fetchBtn)
    toolbar.addWidget(QLabel(' URL: '))
    toolbar.addWidget(self.addressBar)

    self.logEdit = QTextEdit()
    self.setCentralWidget(self.logEdit)

    def fetch_page(self):
        pass

if __name__ == '__main__':
    app = QApplication(sys.argv)
    win = Downloader()
    win.show()
    sys.exit(app.exec_())
```

The window width of 1000 pixels should allow us to view even a slightly longer URL in our navigation bar, and the height of 400 pixels should give us enough space to view any initial logging messages.

Fleshing out the `fetch_page` method is far more complex, but really only because we need to be able to anticipate a number of errors or choices that may either depend on the user or the interaction with the web server or local I/O system. As a first step, you should of course again remove or comment out the `pass` statement.

```
address=self.addressBar.text()
if not address:
    QMessageBox(
            text='No URL provided!',
            windowTitle='Input Error',
            icon=QMessageBox.Critical).exec_()
    return
self.logEdit.append(f'Attempting to download {address} ...')
try:
    page=urllib.request.urlopen(address)
except urllib.error.URLError as err:
    self.logEdit.append(f'Download error.\n{address} {err.reason}')
    return
self.logEdit.append(f'Page {address} successfully retrieved.')
```

If the address bar has been left the empty when the button was clicked or the Enter key pressed inside the navigation bar, we simply display the pre-defined message box with an appropriate acknowledgement for the user. Of course, we shouldn't forget to `return` to the main program when the dialogue has been closed, as we'll need to do every time we've trapped an error.

If an address was retrieved from the address bar widget, we assume that it's a valid URL, alert the user that we're now trying to retrieve data from that URL, and send the request via the `urlopen` function, storing the result in our `page` variable. If an error occurs, we trap it and log it to the logging window, but if not, we log our download success.

Next, we output a message that we're trying to find the encoding and page title, and then start the process of converting the binary data to readable text that we can search through and store.

```
self.logEdit.append('Searching for encoding & page title...')
charset=page.headers.get_content_charset(failobj="utf-8")

try:
    page_content=page.read().decode(charset)
except Exception:
    self.logEdit.append('Unable to decode URL. Aborting download.\n')
    return
```

Before we can decode and read the page contents, we retrieve the charset information from the header information for the page sent by the server. If this isn't successful, we assume and set a default of `utf-8`. As our default may still be wrong, which could lead to a potential decoding error, we can use the base `Exception` class to trap the error, and allow us to create a suitable message and abort the download. We can use the base class in order to avoid having to detect all specific errors that may occur in decoding, since we always want to abort the download if any such error occurs, anyway, in order to avoid ending up with a file we may be unable to read and process properly.

If the previous step worked, we now have the file contents successfully stored in a string variable, and can attempt to save it to our computer. Of course, we could here ask the user to specify a file name by popping up a file dialogue, but because most pages already have meaningful titles that we can use as a basis for a file name, we here choose the option to either use the title stored in the `<title>` tag, adjusting it to a suitable format, or the file name of the web page, which constitutes the final part of the URL. This makes the part where we identify title and output logging messages related to the title and encoding something like this:

```
title=re.search(r'<title>\s*([^<]+?)\s*</title>',
page_content).group(1)

if charset and title:
    self.logEdit.append(f'encoding: {charset}; title: {title}')
elif charset and not title:
    self.logEdit.append(f'encoding: {charset}; no title')

self.logEdit.append('Generating file name ...')
if title:
    title=title.strip()
    file_name=re.sub(r'\W+', r'_', title, re.M|re.S) + '.html'
else:
    file_name=address[address.rindex('/')+1:]
```

In searching for the title, we already try to avoid having any extraneous whitespace in the title text by prefixing the group by `\s*` and also adding this before the end tag of the title. Doing so makes sense because the title tag may, in theory, also contain additional spaces or even line breaks. Of course, it's quite possible that the page has no title tag, and then the `title` variable will simply have the value None after the search. This has an influence on our logging message, so we distinguish between having the information about encoding and title being present or only the encoding being known, each time outputting an appropriate message to the logging window.

In the next step, we generate the file name, either from an existing title we've extracted, or by determining the position of the last forward slash in the URL and then extracting everything from one position behind it. If a title was found before, we use `strip` to remove any extraneous leading or trailing whitespace before replacing all remaining non-word characters by underscores. Using `\W+` here ensures that any special characters the author of the web page may have used to achieve special effects in the title will automatically be converted to underscores along with all spaces, and using the flags also takes care of titles consisting of multiple lines. Using `strip` in the prior step strictly speaking shouldn't be necessary because our regex to extract the title theoretically ought to have excluded all extraneous leading or trailing whitespace, anyway, so this is just an extra precaution that isn't really costly in terms of the computing effort and memory expended.

Now that we've created a suitable file name, we need to ensure that any existing file may not accidentally be overwritten, so we have to check on whether the file (path) exits, and if so, give the user the option to either replace the existing file or abort the operation. Although we don't usually want to replace a file we've already downloaded if we've simply forgotten that we already did so, in some cases this may make sense after all, especially if we know, or suspect, that the page we want to store and process has been updated since we last accessed it. To achieve this, we need to create a customised message box in the way described earlier, which could look like this:

```
if os.path.exists(file_name):
    msgBox=QMessageBox(
            text=f'File already exists!\nOverwrite it?',
            windowTitle='Overwrite warning',
            icon=QMessageBox.Warning)
    msgBox.setStandardButtons(QMessageBox.Yes | QMessageBox.No)
    msgBox.setDefaultButton(QMessageBox.No)
    button_clicked=msgBox.exec_()

    if button_clicked==QMessageBox.No:
        self.logEdit.append('File overwrite aborted.\n')
        return
```

As described above, in order to customise the message box, we first create an instance of it and assign this to the variable msgBox, where we initially only change the text, title, as well as the icon, because this time we don't want to report a critical error to the user, but instead offer alternatives for actions to be taken. To be able to specify the buttons, we use the setStandard-Buttons method, opting for simple Yes and No choices, and setting the default choice to No, assuming that the user won't want to overwrite the file. Only then do we call the message box' exec_ method, assigning the return value, i.e. the user's button choice, to the variable button_clicked. If the default button is triggered, we output an appropriate message to the logging window and abort the storage process. Should the user want to overwrite the file after all, we need to take no further additional action, as the next step in our program will be to try and save the file contents, anyway. Before doing so, we want to again indicate the pending action in the log window, making the final part of the method:

```
self.logEdit.append(f'Attempting to store page {address}...')
try:
    with open(file_name,mode='w',encoding='utf-8') as out_file:
        out_file.write(page_content)
except OSError as err:
    self.logEdit.append(str(err))
    return
self.logEdit.append(f'{address} saved to {file_name}.\n')
```

Attempting to store the contents should obviously involve suitable error handling with outputting any potential error messages to the logging window and aborting. Upon successful saving, the user should naturally be informed of this again.

Discussion 60   Extracting Paragraphs from Web Pages

To be able to use the relevant object, we actually import the one named after the module without spaces, while we need to refer to the module itself by a different, abbreviated, name including the version number of the module, hence writing

```
from bs4 import BeautifulSoup
```

To open the document, and create the tree, we can use a context manager, and thus write

```
with open("./HTML_Download_Test_Page_for_Analysis.html", mode='r',
        encoding='UTF-8') as page:
    tree = BeautifulSoup(page, "html.parser")
```

This time, we don't need the error handling because we know that the page is present in the same folder – unless, of course, we'd saved or moved it elsewhere –, and we also know the encoding because we set this when we downloaded the file in our download program. The only reason why we're using the relative path is that otherwise the file might not be found on Linux systems. To create the tree, we simply create the `BeautifulSoup` object, passing the file handle to it as the first argument, and the name of the pre-installed parser module as the second. The one thing we need to observe here is that the parser name has to be passed as a string.

To create the list of paragraphs from the tree, we use

```
paragraphs = [paragraph.getText()
    for paragraph in tree.find_all('p')]
```

Here, we essentially run a `for` loop over all paragraph elements the `find_all` method identifies inside the tree, immediately passing each paragraph element in turn to the `getText` method, and then writing the resulting text to the newly created list. To output the list in a single line, we can use `join` inside a `print` statement, thus writing

```
print('\n'.join(paragraphs))
```

Discussion 61   Converting Text to XML (a)

When you scan through the text file, you should notice that, from a structural point of view, the text is sub-divided into individual paragraphs separated from each other by two or more line breaks. Most of these are preceded by a heading indicating that what follows is either a "Letter" or a "Chapter", followed by sequential numbers for each category. Unlike the sentences within the paragraphs, these headings don't end in punctuation marks, and consist of single, short units.

Apart from these structural issues, you should also be able to observe that, on the formatting/ layout level, double hyphens that are't surrounded by spaces are sometimes used to represent dashes that generally start parenthetical structures, which is most likely an artefact supposed to represent the convention in the typeset text, as in "There--for with your leave, my sister, I will put some trust in preceding navigators--there snow and frost are banished" (lines 30–31) in the original text. While it's of course no problem for readers of a text to identify this as an issue and deal with it by pretending that there were spaces between the words and the hyphens, while processing a text like this to create frequency lists, etc., this may create issues, so it's best to replace such double hyphens by a space, a single hyphen, and another space. The only problem here is that we cannot simply indiscriminately replace all double hyphens because they also 'anonymise' the years at the end of the dates that occur at the top of each letter, so we need to ensure that the double hyphens aren't in fact preceded by a number. In addition to this, we have a number of abbreviations that interfere with our identification of sentence endings when we want to extract the sentences from the paragraphs and mark them up. To be able to get around this issue, we can mask the dots by replacing them with underscores – which otherwise don't exist in the text – and then changing all underscores back to dots once we've marked up the sentences. We'll need to deal with each of these features in the relevant extraction steps below.

Setting up the counter variables for the individual headings, paragraphs, and sentences, and initialising them the traditional way individually should really no longer represent any problem, but there is in fact a much neater way that allows you to initialise all of them in one line, which is

```
n_heading = n_paragraph = n_sentence = 0
```

This will initially make all values point to exactly the same location in memory, but, since integers in Python are also immutable like strings, each variable will be re-created later with a separate memory slot once it gets augmented. The list of abbreviations essentially comprises basic terms of address, some other abbreviated forms of proper names, and initials, so we can define it as

```
abbrevs = ['Mrs', 'Mr', 'St', 'Dec', 'R.W', 'M']
```

Here, we leave out the final dots so we can later use positive lookbehind to include only dots that follow them when we do the masking.

Setting up the variables for the input and output files should again present no problems. The easiest way to create the output file name is of course to replace the txt extension by xml using regex substitution, making these lines something like this:

```
input_file = '../texts/frankenstein.txt'
pathName, fileName = os.path.split(os.path.abspath(input_file))
basePath, _ = os.path.split(pathName)
output_file = os.path.join(basePath,
                           'output',
                           re.sub( r'txt$', 'xml', fileName))
```

Even though the original extension doesn't occur as part of the file name, it's best to anchor it in view of the fact that you might later want to expand the program where the file name is fixed to one that may be used to convert different files, perhaps even in the form of an object-oriented module where you can also adjust other features to make the program more universally applicable.

By now, reading, opening, and processing files using error handling should have become a routine task for you, so the only thing you need to pay attention to in generating the list of paragraphs from the file is that you use regex splitting and quantify the number of line breaks appropriately, making the whole procedure this:

```
try:
    with open(input_file, mode='r', encoding='utf-8') as in_file:
```

```
        paragraphs = re.split(r'\n{2,}', in_file.read())
except OSError as err:
    sys.exit(str(err))
```

I'll here skip discussing opening the output file because this is, again, standard routine by now, and will continue by describing what happens once the file is open. In the code listed below, I'll also partially omit the indentation required within the `with` block in order to save space. Before we can start processing the individual paragraphs contained in our paragraph list, we should write out the 'header' for the XML file, which of course consists of the XML declaration and the start tag of the `text` element with the attributes listed in the exercise description, making the lines producing the 'header':

```
out_file.write('<?xml version="1.0"?>\n')
out_file.write('<text id="frankenstein" corpus="GothicNovels" '
               'author="Mary Shelley" lang="en">\n')
```

The last statement above was of course only broken into two lines again to be able to represent it within the space provided in this book, and where I'm using the technique that automatically concatenates two strings that occur in sequence. I'll again omit the beginning of the `for` loop, and save space on the indentation.

Assembling the lines of the paragraph currently being processed inside the loop requires two simple regex substitutions, making the following two lines this:

```
paragraph = re.sub(r'\n', ' ', paragraph)
paragraph = re.sub(r' +', ' ', paragraph)
```

To be able to distinguish between headings and non-headings, we first need to check and see if a potential heading is present, so we do a regex search with capturing on the paragraph and assign it to an appropriate variable:

```
match = re.search(r'\b(Chapter|Letter) (\d+)', paragraph)
```

If no match was found, the variable will be set to `None`, so – in our following conditional statement – we can simply check to see if the match was `True` using

```
if match:
```

and increase the heading counter, i.e. write

```
n_heading += 1
```

In the next step, we need to test if the heading number is unequal to 1, which will be the case for all but the first heading. In this case, we would have previously opened either a letter or chapter section, so that the variable `h_type` – for 'heading type' – would be initialised to whatever tag was opened, so our complete condition would look like this:

```
if n_heading != 1:
    out_file.write(f'</{h_type}>\n')
```

For the very first heading, this is of course `False`, so we skip this section. Because we know that our match was successful, we can now extract the two groups that we captured through the bracketing like this:

```
h_type = match.group(1).lower()
n_unit = match.group(2)
```

Because we generally use lowercase tags for the XML elements and values, we also downcase the heading type before assigning the value to the variable. In case you hadn't noticed this, this variable can actually be used in two different places, once as the name for the section element, but also as a value to the `type` attribute that allows us to specify the type of the heading element. Now that we've got all the relevant information, we can construct the section element start tag and the heading element, write them out to the file, and jump to the next paragraph in the list.

```
out_file.write(f'<{h_type} n="{n_unit}">\n')
out_file.write(f'<heading n="{n_heading}" type="'
               f'{h_type}">\n'
               f'{paragraph}\n</heading>\n')
continue
```

Our `else` branch of the condition allows us to handle all other paragraphs. Because we also want to number all paragraphs consecutively, we start by increasing the paragraph counter:

```
n_paragraph += 1
```

In order to change all symbolised hyphens, we can use a relatively straightforward regex substitution where we only ensure that the hyphens to be replaced aren't preceded by any digit representing part of the years indicated at the top of the letters. If something should not precede the match, this of course means that we're using a negative lookbehind expression.

```
paragraph = re.sub(r'(?<!\d)--', ' - ', paragraph)
```

The abbreviations you should have identified through your search in the editor should have led you to construct the following list:

```
abbrevs = ['Mrs', 'Mr', 'St', 'Dec', 'R.W', 'M']
```

To mask these abbreviations, you can run a `for` loop over the list, replacing all dots preceded by one, which of course this time means using positive lookbehind, so that the regex replacement inside the loop should look like this:

```
paragraph=re.sub(r'(?<='+abbrev+r')[.]', '_', paragraph)
```

Here, we simply construct the replacement regex by concatenating the abbreviation and the relevant regex components. To make it easier to see the dot, we use a character class, rather than masking it via a backslash. This is as far as we can get given our current knowledge or regex substitutions, so we need to complete the exercise after having learnt about regex substitutions using functions.

Discussion 62   Converting Text to XML (b)

The user-defined function we use as the replacement argument to the regex substitution, like all user-defined functions, has to be defined at the top of the program, so directly following the variable declarations. To make it immediately obvious what its functionality is, let's call it `tag_sentence`, and its argument `match_object` because this is what will implicitly be passed by the `sub` method. The sentence we want to tag will – inside the main program – be captured by any number of word characters, quotation marks, apostrophes, colons, round brackets, or hyphens that are followed by a major punctuation mark – i.e. one that may end a sentence – that could optionally be followed by a closing double quotation mark, and then either one or more whitespaces or a line end, making the relevant statement

```
paragraph = re.sub(r'([\w, "\':()-]+?[.?!;]"?)(?:\s+|$)',
        tag_sentence, paragraph)
```

The first group in the search pattern needs to be extracted from the match object inside the function and constitutes the sentence text to be wrapped in the sentence tag. However, before we can do so, the sentence counter, `n_sentence`, that we defined at the top of the program ought to be increased, which would normally be a problem because if we use the variable within a function, it will be local to the function itself, i.e. be distinct from the one in the main program. To allow us to reference the latter, we need to essentially re-declare it inside the function, but mark it as belonging to the global scope, which we achieve by using the corresponding keyword. Once we've increased the value of the sentence counter, we can assemble the whole sentence element, making our user-defined function:

```
def tag_sentence(match_object):
    sentence = match_object.group(1)
    global n_sentence
    n_sentence += 1
    return (f'<sentence n="{n_sentence}">\n{sentence}\n'
        '</sentence>\n')
```

As before, to break the line for presentation here, I've split the output string into two individual strings. Note, though, that in order to be able to break the return statement in this way, I've had to use round brackets around it. Once the sentence will have been tagged and returned as a replacement, we need to unmask the abbreviations, which we can easily achieve via

```
paragraph = re.sub('_', '.', paragraph)
```

because we know that all underscores originally correspond to full stops. The paragraph now has the correct form, so we can wrap it into the corresponding element with the counter attribute n, and write it to the file:

```
out_file.write(f'<paragraph n="{n_paragraph}">\n{paragraph}'
    '</paragraph>\n')
```

To write out the remaining two elements, we of course need to decrease the indentation level again, and can then write

```
out_file.write(f'</{h_type.lower()}>\n')
out_file.write('</text>')
```

Discussion 63   Converting Text to TEI XML

Apart from extracting the first paragraph and using the content as part of the TEI header, there isn't too much we actually need to change in the program. The first difference is, of course, that we don't extract the numbers for the letter and chapter sections from their heading texts, instead treating them all as being `divs` of each particular type, but numbering them consecutively. We also change the variable name for the header counter slightly in order to make it reflect the TEI tag. This then makes the initial variable declaration section:

```
n_head = n_paragraph = n_sentence = 0
abbrevs = ['Mrs', 'Mr', 'St', 'Dec', 'R.W', 'M']
```

The abbreviations remain the same, so we can simply keep the second line above. The adjustment in our user-defined function is only minimal, changing the tag name form `sentence` to `s` as defined in the TEI:

```
def tag_sentence(match_object):
    sentence = match_object.group(1)
    global n_sentence
    n_sentence += 1
    return (f'<s n="{n_sentence}">\n{sentence}\n'
        '</s>\n')
```

The regex substitution to generate the output filename becomes slightly more complex because now we don't simply change the extension, but also need to add something to the filename before, so we end up with

```
input_file = '../texts/frankenstein.txt'
pathName, fileName = os.path.split(os.path.abspath(input_file))
basePath, _ = os.path.split(pathName)
output_file = os.path.join(basePath,
                    'output',
                    re.sub(r'\.txt$', '_TEI.xml', fileName))
```

for the relevant lines. Note that the dot should really be escaped here, even if the regex shorthand dot would also match it. Opening the file and extracting the paragraphs remains the same, so the next changes will occur once you've written out the XML declaration. Here, we need to start by writing out the `TEI` and `teiHeader` start tags:

```
out_file.write('<TEI xmlns="http://www.tei-c.org/ns/1.0" '
        'xml:lang="en">\n')
out_file.write('<teiHeader>\n')
```

Again, the first `write` statement is only broken into two lines to make it fit into the available space, but feel free to write it on one line in your program. To prepare the rest of the header information, we start by extracting the first paragraph from the list of paragraphs using the `pop` method, then split the paragraph into the two lines of information containing title and author. All we need to do now before we can write out the remainder of the TEI header is to remove the "by" from "by Mary Wollstonecraft (Godwin) Shelley", so that the whole section then looks like this:

```
initial_para = paragraphs.pop(0)
(title, author) = initial_para.split('\n')
author = re.sub(r'^\s*by\s', r'', author)
out_file.write('<fileDesc>\n')
out_file.write('<titleStmt>\n')
out_file.write(f'<title>\n{title}</title>\n')
out_file.write(f'<author>\n{author}\n</author>\n')
out_file.write('</titleStmt>\n')
out_file.write('<publicationStmt>\n')
out_file.write('<p>\nPart of a corpus of Gothic novels\n'
        '</p>\n')
out_file.write('</publicationStmt>\n')
out_file.write('<sourceDesc>\n')
out_file.write('<p>\nExtracted from eBook #84 from '
        'Project Gutenberg;www.gutenberg.org\n</p>\n')
out_file.write('</sourceDesc>\n')
out_file.write('</fileDesc>\n')
out_file.write('</teiHeader>\n')
```

Removing the attributes from the original text container tag then leaves us with

```
out_file.write('<text>\n')
```

and we can open the body tag:

```
out_file.write('<body>\n')
```

The next thing we need to adjust – inside the loop that runs over the remaining paragraphs – is the regex search, as we no longer have to capture the heading number, making the relevant line

```
match = re.search(r'\b(Chapter|Letter)\b', paragraph)
```

Because it's now no longer necessary to distinguish between letters and chapters, the section for handling the divs actually becomes easier. Here, if we've encountered either a letter or chapter heading, we can simply increase the header counter, and match the heading type to be used as the corresponding attribute in the header tag:

```
n_head += 1
h_type = match.group(1).lower()
```

Next, we need to check and see if the heading counter is unequal to 1, and if so, write out the end tag for the division:

```
if n_head != 1:
    out_file.write(f'</div>\n')
```

We can then write out the division start tag and the header tag, using the same value for the n attribute, i.e. the one currently stored in n_head:

```
out_file.write(f'<div n="{n_head}" type="{h_type}">\n')
out_file.write(f'<head n="{n_head}">\n{paragraph}\n</head>\n')
continue
```

As before, for the division type, we use the value we matched through our regex search, include the paragraph content in the header tag, and then jump to the next paragraph in the list. As the TEI uses p instead of our more explicit `paragraph` tag, change the relevant line to

```
out_file.write(f'<p n="{n_paragraph}">\n{paragraph}</p>\n')
```

Finally, close all open tags:

```
out_file.write('</div>\n')
out_file.write('</body>\n')
out_file.write('</text>\n')
out_file.write('</TEI>')
```

and you're done with the program. Using the validator is an optional component of this exercise, but a highly useful experience, especially if you should end up creating TEI-encoded data more frequently in the future. As an additional advanced exercise, you can also think about how to make both converters that we just completed more flexible and universally usable, perhaps combining them into an object-oriented interface that allows you to select either type of output via an argument, as well as providing options for specifying cleanup operations or dealing with abbreviations that you read in from files.

11

Basic Visualisation

In this chapter, we want to explore basic means of visualisation that go beyond creating output in tabular form, i.e. in the form of graphs or other types of visual illustrations. One of the most common types of data to be used as the basis for such graphics are frequency lists, which is why we'll use these to explore the most useful visualisation concepts here, expanding the scope of what we'll be able to demonstrate through them in the process by making appropriate modifications to our existing module. For instance, as interesting as raw frequency lists may be if we only want to look at individual files or corpora as a whole, if we want to compare frequencies across two or more files, we need to use relative frequencies instead, so we'll also discuss how to create these as we move along.

Producing anything but the simplest graphics merely using the symbols and layouting we've learnt to apply up to now would not take us very far, so we need to rely on more complex libraries written by others to allow us to create effective visual summaries of the different aspects we might want to focus on. These illustrations will be similar to the ones you may be familiar with from spreadsheet applications such as Microsoft Excel® and LibreOffice Calc, although, given the limited amount of space we have here, and this only being an introductory textbook, we'll restrict ourselves to relatively simple graphs. The main library we want to use here is called *Matplotlib*, which allows us to either show images produced by other modules, or various types of graphs that we'll produce directly therein from our own data. We'll start this chapter by taking a brief look at this library.

11.1   Using Matplotlib for Basic Visualisation

Matplotlib is a visualisation library for Python that makes it possible to create both simple and highly complex figures, sometimes also containing multiple subplots. To such figures, you can add different types of axes, grid lines, labels, legends, and titles. They can also be saved to .png format, so that you'll not only be able to display them, but also integrate them into your publications. To install the library, you use

```
pip install matplotlib
```

Python Programming for Linguistics and Digital Humanities: Applications for Text-Focused Fields,
First Edition. Martin Weisser.
© 2024 John Wiley & Sons, Inc. Published 2024 by John Wiley & Sons, Inc.
Companion website: https://www.wiley.com/go/weisser/pythonprogling

Learning how to use the library can be a bit confusing because there are two interfaces, one that is object-oriented and one that isn't. However, as the object-oriented one provides more flexibility, this is the only one we'll be adopting here. In order to do so without embedding into a GUI, which is possible, but won't be discussed in this book, you always need to import the `pyplot` sub-module, which is usually abbreviated to `plt`:

```
import matplotlib.pyplot as plt
```

The main distinction in terms of the components of a Matplotlib plot is between different ***artists*** that are rendered onto a canvas. We don't really need to concern ourselves with the artist objects themselves, but what's more important to us is that they comprise – amongst others – the ***Figure***, ***Axes***, and ***Axis*** objects that we'll actively be manipulating in creating our plots. The figure here acts as a container for the other object types. Apart from the figure, the most important type of object is the `Axes` object, which represents an object that contains a single set of axes you can plot on. To do this for a set of x and y axes in a basic two-dimensional plot, you need to provide this object with a method call for the type of plot you want to create and a set of data in the form of two lists, one for the x- and one for the y-values.

The easiest way to create `Figure` and `Axes` objects is to call the `subplots` function like this:

```
fig, ax1 = plt.subplots(figsize=(10,8.5))
```

This function would also allow us to create multiple `Axes` objects if we specified a number as the first argument, but we'll restrict ourselves to single plots here. However, the keyword argument `figsize` that's passed in the above example allows us to set width and height of the resulting figure directly – in inches – so that we don't need to specify them later using a more elaborate syntax calling the methods `set_figwidth` and `set_figheight` on the `Figure` object. Setting the figure size – unless you want to stick to the default size chosen by the module – is generally something that you'll need to experiment with to be able to show all the axes and possible labels correctly. If you want to work with different size units, such as centimetres or pixels, you need to append `*cm` or `*px`, respectively, to each number. By default, the title for each figure window we produce in Matplotlib is simply *Figure*, followed by the number of the figure. To change the title to something more meaningful, you can use the syntax

```
fig_name.canvas.manager.set_window_title('title')
```

This title will also be used as the recommended filename if you later save the file from within the plot, and any spaces you may have in the string will automatically be replaced by underscores, which is quite neat. Once we have an `Axes` object, we can use the appropriate plotting method on it to create our graph, thus making the syntax

```
axis_variable.plotting_method(
    x_axis_values,
    y_axis_values,
    color='colour')
```

The named argument `color` is actually optional, but if we don't set it here and want to change the default, we need to use the `set_colour` method on the graph variable later, so again this is a more convenient way of controlling the display directly.

There are many options for plotting available in Matplotlib, but we'll discuss only the ones that are – perhaps arguably – the most useful for our purposes, the `scatter`, `plot`, `bar`, and `hbar` methods. The first of these produces individual dots on the graph, the second a continuous line that connects the values, and the final two, bars with different directions, vertical and horizontal, as the `h` of `hbar` indicates. The first three options are shown in an example plot combining multiple subplots in Figure 11.1.

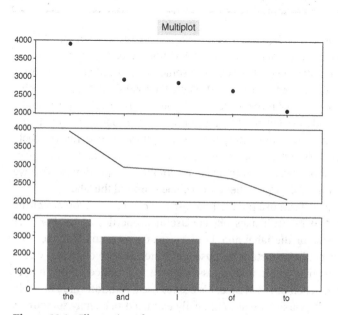

Figure 11.1 Illustration of `scatter`, `plot`, and `bar` methods in Matplotlib.

We'll soon try out all of these graph types in the next few exercises. Before we do so, though, we'll first introduce a few more options for styling the whole plot, and then actually displaying it. As we've already seen before, the individual components of the plot normally make it possible to change their appearance by using methods that start with `set_`. Although the plotting method already makes an attempt to extract suitable values as tick labels for the x- and y-axes – i.e. the markers along these axes –, sometimes this may not provide enough information to easily identify some of the relevant information presented inside the plot. Hence, for instance, we may want to provide a caption for the figure, labels describing the axes, fine-tune the tick marks, etc. Let's start by talking about how to create the axis labels and style them. This can be achieved by using the following syntax, where I provide a non-exhaustive set of options you may want to use:

```
axis_variable.set_xlabel(
    'label',
    color='colour',
    fontsize=value,
    loc='position',
    labelpad=value,
    bbox=dict(
        facecolor='colour',
        edgecolor='colour',
        boxstyle='round, pad=.25'))
```

The above syntax shows the options for setting the label for the x-axis, where the first argument is the only one that is mandatory because there's no point in setting a label without actually providing a value for it. The remaining arguments are simply used to style this label some more, specifying a colour for the text (`color`), how large a font should be used (`fontsize`), where the label should appear relative to the axis (`loc`; defaulting to `center`), the distance (i.e. padding) from the axis (`labelpad`), and a bounding box (`bbox`) to be drawn around the label. Note that the options for the bounding box should be specified as a dictionary with additional attribute–value pairs that also allow you to define the background colour of the box itself (`facecolor`), the colour of its frame (`edgecolor`), and what type of box you want (`boxstyle`). In our example, we use a rounded one with minimal padding, so that we end up with a rectangular box with rounded edges – rather than a circle – around the label.

For styling ticks on the x- and y-axis, we can use the method `set_tick_params` on either the `xaxis` or `yaxis` sub-elements of the relevant axes object. Useful properties to set here are `labelsize` to determine the font size of the label and `labelrotation` to make longer tick labels fit the layout. The latter is especially important because we'll later use the names of words whose frequencies we want to plot as tick labels, and unless we were to produce a huge graph, these words would end up overlapping each other. Hence, it's best to use a rotation value of 90 in order to rotate the words by 90°. On the y-axis, the automatically extracted ticks may sometimes represent values that aren't fine-grained enough to illustrate the frequencies we want to indicate. To fix this, we may need to do two things, first to import another object to handle tick marks, the so-called `MultipleLocator`, and then use this to set intermediate values at regular intervals for the axis. The import should look as follows:

```
from matplotlib.ticker import MultipleLocator
```

and the syntax for the call is

```
axis_variable.yaxis.set_minor_locator(MultipleLocator(value))
```

Last, but not least, we can call the title function on the plot itself to set and style a descriptive caption, i.e. using

```
plot.title(arguments)
```

Here, we need to of course pass a title string as the first argument, and can then use named arguments like `color`, `fontsize`, and `pad` again for some styling and suitable special arrangement. If you want to change the background of the caption, though, instead of using `facecolor` again, which allowed us to set the background colour for the bounding boxes of the labels, here, the argument name is actually `backgroundcolor`. For some, but not all, plots, it may also be useful to include gridlines, which can be achieved via

```
plt.grid(True)
```

Not all of the styling and formatting options described above are of course always necessary, but the reason why I introduced them to you is essentially that you should be able to make your plots as visually pleasing and informative as possible. However, especially the styling should obviously not be overdone unduly, but instead only be used to make the relevant information more prominent and easier to see for potential viewers.

Having covered the representational aspects of creating useful plots, all that remains for me to tell you is how to actually generate the plot, which you do by saying

```
plt.show()
```

This will create a window for you displaying the plot with a toolbar that also allows you to make some changes to the axes, zoom in on interesting parts, etc., but – even more importantly – to save a copy of the plot to a file by clicking on the disk button in the toolbar. However, it's also possible to either save the figure directly without showing it using

```
plt.savefig(filename)
```

or save a copy automatically before showing the plot to explore it interactively using the same syntax. If you want to achieve both tasks, though, it's important to remember to save the file first because if you use `savefig` after showing and closing the plot, the figure may already have been deleted and the resulting file correspondingly be empty. If you save the figure programmatically, it's also possible to use a variety of other common output formats, such as `.jpg`, `.pdf`, or even `.svg`, to name but a few. To find more information about the different features of Matplotlib, you can browse the official documentation at https://matplotlib.org/stable.

Armed with this newly gained knowledge, we can soon embark on our first plotting exercise. Before we do so, however, we first want to make some adjustment to our frequency module to allow us to easily extract the top *n* words. All we need to do in order to achieve this is to add another method that will iterate over the sorted list and extract as many of the top-frequency words as we specify as an argument, and return them as a smaller dictionary that can then be passed to the plotting module, so that it will be able to extract the words and frequencies to plot.

Exercise 64   Adjusting the Frequencies Module to Extract the Top *n* Frequent Words

Before you start writing this method, think about how you could implement it efficiently, how you would call it from another program, and what you need to ensure that it's going to work as expected.

First, make a copy of `frequencies_a.py` and call it `frequencies_b.py`.

Start implementing the method `get_top_n`, passing n as an argument.

Inside the method, first test to see if the sorted list doesn't exist, and if not, create the list, set the sort order to descending frequency, and generate it.

Because we – or any users of our class – may inadvertently set *n* to a value longer than our list of words, ensure that this cannot happen.

Set up the empty dictionary.

Use a `for` loop with `i` as a loop index variable and `range` with `n` as an argument to the right of the `in` operator in the head of the loop. I'll explain the `range` part in the discussion.

Inside the loop, use the index variable to retrieve the word at this index position from the sorted list, use it as a new key inside the new dictionary, and retrieve the value of that word from the frequency dictionary, assigning it as the value to the word in the new dictionary.

Return the new dictionary.

Set up an appropriate test, generating and outputting top-n lists for different values of `n`.

Now that you can generate a dictionary of the top-n words in a file, we can move on to using this option to actually visualise such information in Matplotlib.

Exercise 65   Creating Your First Plot in Matplotlib

Create a new file called `27_Zipf_plot.py`. I'll explain the title once you've actually generated and seen a plot.

Import the Matplotlib plotting function and options for setting more sensible tick marks as discussed above, and also include your adjusted frequency list class.

Generate a frequency dictionary from the file `frankenstein.txt` in your `texts` folder, and extract the top 50 words.

Extract two lists from the dictionary, one for the words that will appear on the x-axis, and one for the frequencies to be plotted against the y-axis, using the appropriate dictionary methods, and assigning them to suitably named variables.

Next, create a figure and one axes object, setting the width of the figure to `10` and its height to `8.5`. Set the window title to `Frankenstein`.

Create a scatter plot on the axis, using the word list for the x-axis and the frequency list for the y-axis, making the resulting dots `blue`.

Set the x label of the axes object to `words`, using `green` as a colour, `14` for the font size, position the label in the centre, and create a bounding box with `ivory` background, `green` edges, and a `round` box style as described above.

Do the same thing for the y-axis label, only using `raw frequency` as label text, and adding a padding of `20` to the label itself, not the bounding box, to add some space between the frequency values and the label.

Set the parameters for the ticks on the x-axis to size `12`, and the rotation to 90°.

For the y-axis, set the minor tick marks to `100`.

Make the title of the plot `'Zipfian Distribution'` (including the scare quotes), turn its background cyan, text orange, and its font size `20`. To set it apart from the plot itself, also pad it by `20`.

Show the plot, interpret it, and also explore the toolbar options to see which ones may be useful.

Change the plot type, first to a line, and then a bar plot. Which type or types do you find most useful, and what are their respective advantages and/or disadvantages?

We've now explored one way of visualising word frequencies in the form of different types of plots generated through Matplotlib. However, Matplotlib can also display content produced by other modules that generate images. How this can be done using another highly popular, though not unproblematic, form of visualisation, **word clouds,** will be discussed in the next section.

11.2   Creating Word Clouds

To be able to create and show word clouds in Matplotlib, we first need to install the relevant module using

```
pip(3) install wordcloud
```

A cloud object is then imported by writing

```
from wordcloud import WordCloud
```

Generating the cloud itself is actually a little easier than creating our plots in Matplotlib because there's a method called `generate_from_frequencies` that directly takes a dictionary as input, so that we don't even need to extract separate lists from the top-n frequency dictionary. As a matter of fact, we can even use the whole sorted frequency dictionary directly because passing `max_words` as an argument when we generate the `WordCloud` object will allow us to restrict the input in this way. The `wordcloud` module would even allow us to generate the cloud from a text without us pre-processing it, but as it uses a very basic form of processing and we know how to do it better, we'll use our own dictionaries. For the full – albeit still rather sparse – documentation of `wordcloud`, see https://amueller.github.io/word_cloud/index.html.

To produce a word cloud from our frequency object, we don't even need to know many more of the arguments that can be passed to the object, but can restrict ourselves to a few basic ones, such as `height`, `width`, and `background_color`. Note, though, that the sizes here are not in inches as in Matplotlib, but pixels instead. With this knowledge, we can simply create a new object, immediately call the method on this, and assign the resulting it to a new variable using this syntax:

```
cloud_variable=WordCloud(
     arguments
     ).generate_from_frequencies(dictionary)
```

Because we don't need to generate any `figure` objects, the remaining statements can all be executed on `plt` directly. To be able to give it a title and to size it, we can – but don't need to – create a figure with a title string and figure size as arguments using the `figure` function. If we don't do this, then the window title will automatically again be Figure + number, and the figure will automatically be scaled. Note also that, whereas we had to set the title separately in the previous exercise because we created both figure and axes objects by calling a different function, this time we can pass the title as the first argument prior to the named one. Next, we can give the plot a title, as we did in our previous exercise, switch off the axis display using

```
plt.axis('off')
```

because we don't need any coordinates for the image, add the image to the plot using

```
plt.imshow(cloud_variable)
```

and finally call the show function again.

Exercise 66   Creating a Basic Word Cloud

Create a new file called 28_basic_cloud.py.
Import the pyplot function and our frequency list object as in the previous program.
Also import the word cloud as described above.
As before, create the frequency list from *Frankenstein* again.
Generate a word cloud from the dictionary in our frequency list object, and assign it to a suitable variable, giving it a white background, making it 800 pixels wide, 400 high, and again extracting the top 50 words.
Create the figure with a window title Frankenstein word cloud, a width of 10 inches and a height of 5.5.
Set the plot title to Word Cloud for Frankenstein, the font size to 15, and add a padding of 15, as well as a bounding box with ivory background and a rounding factor of .45.
Turn off the plot axis, call the imshow function with the word cloud object as argument, and show the whole plot.
Run the program, and interpret the result.

As we saw in Figure 1.1 in our example of the Voyant Tools word cloud representation and frequency information, as well as in the results of the two previous exercises, using raw frequency data can be relatively uninformative and – at worst – misleading. Therefore, in order to improve the output of any program that creates a visualisation of word frequencies, we need to be able to filter out irrelevant items, most of which tend to be the function words we've observed both in our first plots and the word cloud we just produced. We'll explore how to do this in the next section.

11.3   Filtering Frequency Data Through Stop-Words

Researchers in corpus linguistics, information retrieval, and other language-related areas have long realised that the high frequency words we observed in our previous two exercises are not only common to all texts, but also that they essentially stop us from easily interpreting and using frequency lists to gain insights about the nature of texts through distant reading. Hence, these words have come to be known as ***stop words***. And although you may be able to find stop-word lists on the web for different language-processing purposes, there are no standardised lists that would readily fit all purposes. Hence, it's best to construct our own that we can also manipulate according to our needs. As a matter of fact, if you use the word cloud module to generate a cloud from raw text, you can even use the module's built-in list, but this list may be sub-optimal, and relying on such a list created by someone else without knowing what it actually contains takes away some of our control over the data. To give but one example of where this may be particularly problematic, most prefabricated stop-word lists generally include all possible types of function words, including prepositions. However, if you were working on financial texts related to stock market developments or texts that describe climate change, these prepositions might be of extremely high relevance because they may indicate trends – i.e. especially things going up or down – that you do want to recognise while doing some distant reading.

To filter out stop words from our frequency dictionaries, we essentially have two options, either to filter while we produce the dictionary or when we create the output. The former has the advantage that this will not only keep our dictionaries smaller, but that we can then also still easily extract the top *n* more meaningful words, while doing it the other way round, our list would be shortened because we'd initially construct a dictionary of top-n words, and then filter it further, thereby potentially removing all words! Hence, we'll opt for doing the filtering while we produce the list. All we need for this is a list of words that we can read in from a file for convenience, and then exclude any of the items in this list while we generate the frequency dictionary. Let's do this as our next – rather brief – exercise.

Exercise 67   Filtering Our Frequency List

Copy `frequencies_b.py` to `frequencies_c.py`.
Change the constructor, adding another argument for the file containing the stop-word list, a variable for the list, and including a section where the file will be read in, populating the list if it's been specified. We'll assume that this list has one word per line.
Finally, add a way to skip any stop words in the creation of the frequency dictionary, create an initial short stop-word list in the `texts` folder, and test the module. To get some inspiration as to which words you may want to include in your initial list, you can create a frequency list sorted in descending order in your Frequency list GUI, and pick some of the top items.

Such a little change to our module will make a rather big difference to our word cloud, as you'll be able to see once you've created the stop-word list and adjusted our earlier word-cloud program a little, which we'll do as our next exercise.

Exercise 68   Filtering the Word Cloud

Copy `28_basic_cloud.py` to `29_filtered_cloud.py`.
Adjust the frequency list import appropriately.
Add the stop-word file to the object initialisation of the frequency list.
Change the argument to the method generating the cloud to use our object's method to get the top 50 words directly.
Adjust the window and title and caption in a suitable manner and test the module, perhaps iteratively making further changes to your stop-word list.

Once you'll have made all the necessary changes and tested the new word-cloud program, you'll hopefully be able to observe directly that the output becomes far more meaningful. The more function words you identify in the cloud and add to the stop-word list, the more the content words like *father, life, being,* and even some important proper names representing the most important characters will eventually come to the fore. . .

While visualising frequency data for individual files – or perhaps even collections of them – will already allow us to gain insights into single or collected works of particular authors, genres, or eras, being able to compare such data will make it possible to identify important differences between them or notice particular trends, so how to achieve this will be our next topic. However, before we can actually carry out any comparisons properly, we first need to modify our frequency list generators to make the frequencies we extract comparable to each other, so this will also form an important part of our discussion.

11.4   Working with Relative Frequencies

Absolute frequencies and their associated ranks are fine to use in order to gain a first impression of our data in terms of the overall number and/or importance of specific words. In addition, they can also allow us to identify issues in identifying the relevant information, as we've already seen in the previous exercises. However, these raw frequencies don't really tell us anything about the contribution that individual tokens make to a file or corpus in terms of the meaning of this frequency. In other words, unless we can relate the frequency to the overall number of word tokens in the data, we don't really know enough about the effect it may have on the text or corpus. Furthermore, when comparing two or more sets of data to another, this can lead to further issues, as you'll hopefully be able to see in Figure 11.2.

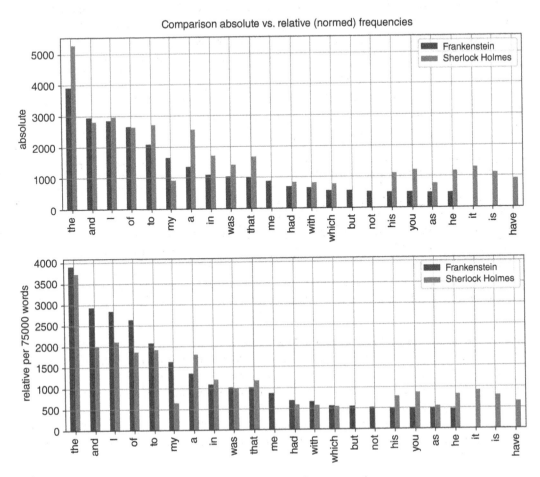

Figure 11.2   Absolute versus relative frequencies in comparing two novels.

Figure 11.2 displays the absolute and relative frequencies of the top 20 files in the novels *Frankenstein* and *The Adventures of Sherlock Holmes*. Don't be confused by the fact that the plot actually contains 24 words; this is simply due to the top 20 words not completely overlapping in the two source files.

Looking at the first few bars in the top graph, you may be tempted to assume that *the* is far more frequent in the Sherlock Holmes novel, *I* slightly more, and the words *and* or *of* a little less so. However, comparing this to the graph in the bottom half of the figure, where the frequencies have been relativised and normed to 75,000 words – which is close to the highest number the two novels have in common –, we can see that, in fact, all of these four words are less common in the second book – sometimes even considerably –, and the misinterpretation based on the absolute frequencies is really only due to the fact that the second novel is longer than the first. In other words, because we haven't factored in the overall length of the novels, the comparison is not only inaccurate, but even misleading. Hence, if anything, we can only judge the contribution of each of the words in the top graph in relation to the other words in the same novel, but certainly not in relation to the same word in the other book. I hope that this illustration has clearly demonstrated to you how important using relative frequencies is in this context, so we can now proceed to adding their calculation to our frequency list module.

Relative frequencies are calculated by dividing the frequencies of the individual words (or n-grams) by the overall number of tokens. If you multiply them by 100, you can turn them into percentages, which already gives you a more useful indication of their importance if you're working with a single file or corpus. When comparing relative frequencies, though, it's more useful to norm them using a more sensible factor, for instance by using a number close to the largest common denominator between the two lists. Hence, if we have three corpora, and – for instance – the largest corpus contains 50,000 words, the second 25,000, but the last one only 1,500, then we could calculate relative frequencies for the first two and multiply these by 1,500, simply keeping the raw frequencies for the third one, so that the frequencies for the first two would become comparable to the third one. For Figure 11.2, I've opted to norm to 75,000 words because the Frankenstein contains 75,234 words, while *The Adventures of Sherlock Holmes* has 105,855 tokens.

Often, less flexible corpus tools simply multiply by fixed frequencies, though, and then report these normed frequencies per *n* thousand or million words, which, however, may end up exaggerating the differences if too high or low a factor is chosen, effectively 'pretending' that there are more or fewer occurrences than are actually possible. From a mathematical point of view, this of course makes no difference, but especially in visualising frequencies, it may potentially be misleading.

In practice, in implementing tools for comparing frequencies, you can simply calculate relative frequencies for all corpora, then set or algorithmically determine the factor, and multiply all data by that factor, even if this is not necessary for the corpus whose number of tokens may be used as a factor. The overall count of all tokens should ideally be determined while creating the list(s) via a counter variable, as otherwise all values need to be summed up later to be able to establish the number of tokens. With this knowledge, we can now easily modify our frequency list generator to calculate and output relative frequencies, including normed ones and percentages, too.

Exercise 69   Adjusting the Frequency List Generator for Relative Frequencies

Copy `frequencies_c.py` to `frequencies_d.py`.
Before you actually make any changes to the program, look through the original version and think about what you may need to adjust and how the program could be used to either generate a frequency list in a file or use it in another module, such as in our frequency GUI.
Add the argument `abs_rel` to the list of arguments for the constructor and set the default to `abs`. Also add a `percent` argument, but set this to `False`.

Inside the constructor, copy the values of this arguments to instance variables.

Add the variable `self.tokens` to the `create_list` method in the appropriate place and also initialise it to 0.

Inside the `for` loop where you iterate over the words, increment the token counter.

Inside the loop that iterates over the sorted list in the `output_list` method, add a new condition that tests if the additional argument is set to `rel`. If this is the case, you need to distinguish between three different sub-options:

a) that the argument for outputting percentages has been activated, in which case you'll want to divide the frequency by the number of tokens and multiply it by 100,

b) that a factor has been provided, so that we need to multiply by the relative frequency by that instead, and, finally,

c) that we only want to output the relative frequency without modification.

Although multiplying by a factor may well result in integer values, there's still a chance that the result could be a floating point number, so that you should change the output format option to `f`. Adjust the `get_top_n` method accordingly.

For convenience and later use, also create an accessor method called `get_num_tokens` that will allow us to extract the number of tokens from the object.

Test the program by generating both absolute and relative frequencies for a file.

Now that we know how to generate relative frequency information, and hence display type distributions in a more representative manner, we can move on to discussing plots that allow us to compare frequencies.

11.5 Comparing Frequency Data Visually

While – as we've seen – plotting simple frequency graphs is fairly easy using Matplotlib, creating plots that contain information bringing together multiple sets of frequency data is considerably more difficult if done adjusting our previous program to accommodate more data. For instance, by default, Matplotlib creates a stacked bar chart if multiple sets of data are plotted as bar charts, as shown in Figure 11.3.

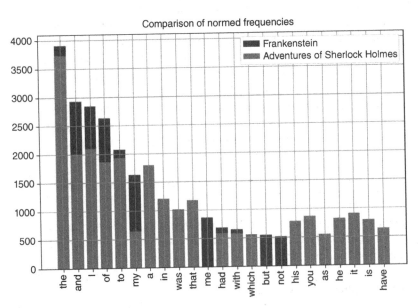

Figure 11.3 Frequency comparison as stacked bar chart.

If you observe Figure 11.3 closely, you'll notice that, even though it's possible to perceive in which book the frequencies for the words are higher, you don't always get to see all the frequency values. For instance, for *a*, *in*, and *that* in *Frankenstein*, we don't see any frequencies, while for *was*, we can barely make out that the frequency is higher. We're also not shown which words are top only in one of the files because the lower values for the other file may simply be hidden 'behind' that particular bar. Hence, what we'd really want to see is a side-by-side plot of the bars like the one I created for Figure 11.2, which is more commonly referred to as a **grouped bar chart**. Creating such a plot using Matplotlib directly, though, is rather difficult because we'd need to calculate the width of the bars, which is still relatively straightforward if you only want to compare two texts or corpora, but would get far more complex if you started adding more files to the comparison.

Luckily, though, there's another Python library that interfaces directly with Matplotlib for plotting, and will perform such calculations for us automatically, thereby making this type of task considerably easier. This library is called **Pandas**, can easily be installed using

```
pip install pandas
```

and is generally imported like this

```
import pandas as pd
```

Pandas was originally designed for financial data analysis, but is today used for more varied tasks in general data science. Its data structures and analysis options are rather similar to the ones found in spreadsheet programs such as Microsoft Excel or LibreOffice Chart. In addition, it offers many built-in import and export options for working with different types of file formats, such as .csv (comma-separated values) or .xlsx. We won't discuss this type of functionality here, but restrict ourselves to only developing the basic understanding of Pandas we need to be able to create our comparison plots. To find out more about Pandas yourself, you can browse https://pandas.pydata.org.

There are three main data types in Pandas, the series (Series), the data frame (DataFrame), and the panel (Panel). A series essentially represents a single, indexed, column of data with a name, while a data frame is a collection of multiple series that share an index, and a panel, in turn, a collection of multiple data frames. Out of these three, only the DataFrame is really relevant to us here because we want to be able to plot multiple series. Conveniently, when constructing a data frame, we can pass a list of dictionaries as arguments and these will automatically be indexed and represented as series, i.e. group of columns, using the following syntax:

```
dataframe_variable=pd.DataFrame([dictionary1, dictionary2])
```

You may now be wondering what happens when a word appears in only one dictionary, but not in the other. In this case, the relevant entry in the series where the word doesn't occur will automatically be set to NaN, short for 'not a number'. Hence, we also don't even need to think about how to create a list of x-axis tick-mark labels that represent all the possible words that occur in either frequency list. Incidentally, the same thing also happened in the earlier example of the stacked bar chart, where I simply passed the keys from each list as x-axis labels and the values as y-axis points when I plotted two bars in a row. Matplotlib automatically used the ones that overlapped without repeating them and added the ones that didn't. Thus, creating our two-dimensional data structure for plotting in general is very easy. Yet there's one single flaw here, which is that the words in this data structure are column headings and not indexes, but we need to create a plot where the words represent the indexes against which the two bars will then be plotted. Instead,

Pandas automatically created two numerical index values for the rows of data. To be able to visualise this better, take a look at Figure 11.4.

```
          the          and            I  ...        it        is      have
0   3897.838743   2927.865061   2841.135657  ...       NaN       NaN       NaN
1   3728.921638   1990.930991   2097.916962  ...  904.7754  782.910585  639.790279

[2 rows x 23 columns]
```

Figure 11.4 Original Pandas DataFrame created from two dictionaries.

I obtained this figure by using the data frame as an argument to the print function, and here you can see that the values from the first dictionary are associated with index 0, and those from the second dictionary with index 1. The printed representation of the data frame is abridged, showing the first and final three columns in the data structure, with the three dots in the middle standing for the columns that have been elided. You can also see this in the summary in square brackets that refers to 23 columns.

Luckily, though, this doesn't really present a problem for us because the data frame can simply be transposed, with the words becoming the index entries and the numerical indexes column headings, yielding the result depicted in Figure 11.5.

```
                 0             1
the     3897.838743   3728.921638
and     2927.865061   1990.930991
I       2841.135657   2097.916962
of      2630.791929   1859.146946
to      2073.530585   1921.496387
my      1628.917777    641.915828
a       1340.816652   1798.214539
in      1077.637770   1198.809693
was     1014.833719    986.254782
that    1001.874153   1167.634972
me       863.306484           NaN
had      681.872558    581.691937
with     652.962756    568.938642
which    556.264455    540.597988
but      547.292448           NaN
not      505.423080           NaN
```

Figure 11.5 Transposed DataFrame.

In order to achieve this, we can either call the transpose method on the data frame object – in which case we'd need to assign the result to a new variable before plotting, or overwriting the old one – or, much more conveniently, use the T property of the object when we do the plotting. The T property is simply 'switched on' by referencing the data frame like this before you call any methods on it:

```
dataframe_variable.T
```

As I already pointed out above, Pandas interfaces directly with Matplotlib, and this goes so far that it even provides a convenient method called `plot` that creates a Matplotlib `Axes` object, at the same time making it possible to specify a number of parameters for the plot as arguments that we'd otherwise need to set separately. This allows us to set up and create a graph in one go, even though it doesn't allow you to fine-tune options for displaying the labels. The most important argument to this method is the `ax` argument, through which you specify where to put your graph in the Matplotlib figure. The other useful arguments you can specify for out purposes are:

a) `kind`: bar, barh, line, scatter, etc. (as available in Matplotlib);
b) `title`: a title for your figure;
c) `figsize`: size of the figure;
d) `grid`: switch grid lines on/off;
e) `rot`: rotation angle for x-axis tick marks;
f) `fontsize`: font size of tick marks;
g) `xlabel`: y-axis label, and
h) `ylabel`: x-axis label.

As you can see from the above list, there are quite a few arguments here that we can use without having to set the plotting parameters in separate statements. However, as useful as this interface may be, it leaves us with less control over the appearance of certain parts of the plot. Thus, for instance, while (g) and (h) are useful for setting the axis labels efficiently, they don't allow us to specify the font size for either label because (f) only sets the size of the tick marks. Neither can we define any extra padding for the y-axis label, so that we may end up with that label being rather close to the tick marks of the y-axis. If we can live without those niceties, though, we can speedily construct a sensible plot, and only make any changes to the styling afterwards, using the relevant setting routines defined in Matplotlib that we discussed earlier.

Armed with this knowledge, we can now embark on our final exercise, where we'll create a plot to compare the frequencies for our two novels side-by-side.

Exercise 70   Plotting Frequency Bars Side-by-Side

Write a new program called `30_grouped_bars.py` in which we'll create the plot for the side-by-side comparison.

Import the relevant items from Matplotlib, Pandas, and our frequency list module.

Define a variable to be able to control the number of words to be extracted easily, setting this to 20.

Create relative frequency lists from both novels.

Get the number of tokens from each list to allow us to determine a factor for normalising the data, storing them in appropriate variables.

Set up another variable for the factor itself, initialising it to 1000.

Determine the lower number of tokens and, using the `round` function with this number as the first argument and `-3` as the second, assign the result to the factor variable.

Get the top *n* words from each list, also using the norming factor.

Create a figure and axes object as before, and set the title of the window to `Grouped bar chart`.

Create a data frame from the two top-n dictionaries, assigning this to a suitable variable.

Plot the transposed data frame as a grouped bar chart using the axes object you created earlier, setting the title to `Comparison of Normed Frequencies`, switching on the grid, rotating the tick marks, setting a font size of `14`, a figure size of `8×7.5` inches, as well as labels for the axes that include information regarding the number of words extracted from each list and the norming factor.

Finally, set the legend of the axes object to a list containing the names of the novels, show the plot, and evaluate it.

In this chapter, we've learnt how to create basic graphs using Matplotlib, the `wordcloud` module, and Pandas, which allowed us to produce visual summaries for illustrating and highlighting different aspects of our data. In the process, we've also covered further important aspects in creating more meaningful frequently lists that can help us gain more insights into the meanings of texts, as well as make these comparable.

11.6 Discussions

Discussion 64   Adjusting the Frequencies Module to Extract the Top *n* Frequent Words

Overall, writing this method should not be too difficult. Essentially, you need to access the sorted list inside the frequency object, extract the first *n* items from this list, use this as a key in a new dictionary, and retrieve the corresponding value from the dictionary that contains the word and its associated frequency. In addition, you need to ensure that the sorted list has been created in the first place, and that it has also been sorted in the right order, which only requires a relatively simple test to see if the sorted list is not empty, and running the appropriate commands if no frequency dictionary exists. To prevent anyone from specifying a larger n than we actually have words in our dictionary, we first test to see how many words there are, which we can do by using `len`. If it turns out that n is larger, we simply set it to cover all words:

```
if n > len(self.words):
    n=len(self.words)
```

However, given your current state of knowledge, you'll probably think of using a *while* loop to generate the index positions that you'll want to retrieve from the sorted list, which is rather inefficient, requiring you to write something like this, assuming that new dictionary is called `top_dict`:

```
top_dict = dict()
i=0
n=5
while i<n:
    top_dict[self.sorted_list[i]]=self.words[self.sorted_list[i]]
    i+=1
```

Instead, to make the above more efficient, we use `range`. As we've previously used functions to control the loop variables, you may now assume that `range` is a function, too, when in fact it's an object that generates a list of integers given the starting and end point for a range of integers as arguments. However, if you leave out the first argument, as usual, the default value is assumed to be 0, so you only need to specify the final range value. Because the numbers generated by `range` exclude the top value and we start at 0, which is also the first index position in the list, we then end up with list indexes from 0 to n-1, which is exactly what we want. Also returning the top-n dictionary, this makes the full method

```
def get_top_n(self, n):
    if not self.sorted_list:
        self.create_list()
        self.sort_order = 'n-1'
        self.make_sorted_list()
    if n > len(self.words):
        n=len(self.words)
    top_dict = dict()
    for i in range(n):
        top_dict[self.sorted_list[i]]=\
            self.words[self.sorted_list[i]]
    return top_dict
```

Discussion 65 Creating Your First Plot in Matplotlib

The imports for the program should be

```
import matplotlib.pyplot as plt
from matplotlib.ticker import MultipleLocator
from frequencies_b import Frequency_list
```

To generate the initial frequency list, we only need to create the object with the file path and descending frequency order as arguments, and call the appropriate methods for creating the dictionary and the sorted list. Strictly speaking, we wouldn't even need to provide the second argument because descending order is the default sort order, anyway, and we also ensure that the list is sorted in descending frequency order if we need to create it inside the method that extracts the top-n words. To extract the top 50 words, we then call that method with 50 as an argument, and extract the words to the list using the `keys` method of the newly created dictionary, and the `values` method to get the frequencies, making this whole section of the program

```
f_list = Frequency_list(
    input_file='../texts/frankenstein.txt',
    sort_order='n-1')
f_list.create_list()
f_list.make_sorted_list()
top_words = f_list.get_top_n(50)
x_words, y_freqs = top_words.keys(), top_words.values()
```

In the final line, we actually generate tuples, but without using any brackets around them. If this is not explicit enough for you, feel free to add these brackets in your code.

Creating the figure and one set of axes at the same time is of course achieved by calling the subplots method on the plot like this:

```
fig, ax1 = plt.subplots(figsize=(10,8.5))
```

Here, the value to the figsize argument of the figure is again passed as a tuple, only that, this time, the brackets are of course mandatory. In order to set the title of the window itself, we use the syntax described above, making this line

```
fig.canvas.manager.set_window_title('Frankenstein')
```

To create the scatter plot, we simply write

```
ax1.scatter(
    x_words,
    y_freqs,
    color='blue')
```

Here, of course we need to pay attention to the fact that the named argument for the colour is spelt the American way because otherwise it won't be recognised. If you've ever dealt with colour strings in HTML or CSS style sheets, you'll probably be familiar with this issue, though.

Setting the labels for the two axes should be relatively straightforward if you've referred to my earlier descriptions, making the relevant lines

```
ax1.set_xlabel(
    'words',
    color='green',
    fontsize=14,
    loc='center',
    bbox=dict(
        facecolor='ivory',
        edgecolor='green',
        boxstyle='round, pad=.25'))
ax1.set_ylabel(
    'raw frequency',
    color='green',
    fontsize=14,
    labelpad=20,
    bbox=dict(
        facecolor='ivory',
        edgecolor='green',
        boxstyle='round, pad=.25'))
```

All you really need to pay attention to here are the different argument names for the types of colour used for the text and the elements of the bounding box, as well as the additional padding that we need for the y-axis, which we generate via the labelpad argument.

Setting the parameters for the x-axis is relatively straightforward, provided you use the right arguments, labelsize and labelrotation:

```
ax1.xaxis.set_tick_params(
    labelsize=12,
    labelrotation=90)
```

In order to adjust the tick marks to be multiples of 100, rather than accepting the automatically assigned steps of 500, you need to set the minor locators as described above, making this line

```
ax1.yaxis.set_minor_locator(MultipleLocator(100))
```

While the previous options were either set for the figure or different parts of the axes object, the title now needs to be set for the plot itself. Here, you need to bear in mind that changing the background colour requires use of the `backgroundcolor` argument, whereas before we used `facecolor` for the bounding boxes, even if we're creating a similar kind of artist. The remaining arguments should be more straightforward again, although you have to pay attention to either use double quotes around the title string or escape the single quotes that are part of the title if you use single quotes to mark the string. The resulting statement should thus look like this:

```
plt.title(
    "'Zipfian Distribution'",
    backgroundcolor='cyan',
    color='orange',
    fontsize=20,
    pad=20)
```

It's now also time to explain the title and the scare quotes within it. The scare quotes are used because what we'll be plotting once we complete the next step does not conform fully with the rules for the distribution of words, also known as ***Zipf's Law***, that George Kingsley Zipf – after whom the distribution is named – expressed. This law states that essentially the frequency of a word in a corpus is inversely proportional to its rank, so that the most frequent word would occur with double the frequency of the second-most frequent word, and the third-most frequent one would then occur with half the frequency of the second-most again, and so forth. This should create a curve that is at first steeply descending and will then peter out at the bottom. As you'll be able to see once we've created the plot like this

```
plt.show()
```

our data does indeed look rather similar to this idealised notion, but does not quite follow the rule of inverse frequency and rank, which is why we use the scare quotes. You can verify this easily when you hover over the top 2 points and look at the frequencies that will be displayed on the right-hand side of the toolbar. If you look closely at the plot, you'll see that, amongst the top 50 words, there isn't a single content word. This fact will also become highly relevant in the next section, where we'll be producing word clouds that of course – just like frequency lists – only really make sense if we're able to filter out less meaningful items. Because we're only looking at the top 50 words, the curve towards the bottom will also not approach 1, as would be the case if we were to plot the frequencies of almost all the words because, in any file or corpus, there will always be some words that occur only once. The technical term for these singletons is ***hapax legomena*** (singular *hapax legomenon*).

When you change the plot to a line plot using the `plot` method, you'll hopefully note that it will become more difficult to see the individual values that were previously easily discernible through the individual dots. Hence, this type of plot is slightly less useful for our particular purpose here, but of course more suitable for showing trends, such as when one's trying to trace changes in word usage over time. By contrast, the `bar` plot will again show the differences in frequency quite nicely, and perhaps also the trend a little better than the scatter plot.

Discussion 66   Creating a Basic Word Cloud

The imports should again be relatively straightforward:

```
import matplotlib.pyplot as plt
from wordcloud import WordCloud
from frequencies_b import Frequency_list
```

In order to create the frequency list, you can simply copy the code from the previous exercise, but can of course exclude everything from after the point where you call `create_list()`. This is because the word cloud module will automatically sort the dictionary before extracting the top 50 words.

Generating the word cloud is easy, and should look like this:

```
wordcloud = WordCloud(
    background_color="white",
    width = 800,
    height = 400,
    max_words=50
    ).generate_from_frequencies(f_list.words)
```

Remember that, here, we need to use the variable for the `WordCloud` object so that we can later set the resulting image using `imshow()`. If you want to, you can also leave out the line where we set the background to white, but I personally prefer not to have the default black background. Creating the word cloud object and immediately calling the method on it may be something that you're not used to, but it saves us an intermediate step. Also note that we need to know what the frequency dictionary inside our frequency list object is called to access it directly. Object-orientation purists would frown upon this because they would probably claim that any object needs to be encapsulated completely, i.e. only allow access to its member variables so that users of the class wouldn't need to know anything about its 'internals', but only which methods to call on it. Hence, if you should ever end up in a position where you'll need to distribute your code to others, you may well choose to write another method that returns the whole dictionary or modify the one that returns the top *n* words so that it returns the whole list if called without an argument. Rewriting it like this would also have the added advantage that we could call this method directly as an argument when we generate the word cloud because we've ensured in our code that all the relevant methods would automatically be called if the frequency dictionary didn't exist. Hence, you could then also save yourself the trouble of writing the line that calls `create_frequency` above, making your code more compact, though possibly also a little less explicit.

Creating the figure and setting the caption should present no real problem, bearing in mind that you need to adjust the `pad` argument inside the instantiation of the bounding box to .45 this time to achieve a nice rounding of the box:

```
plt.figure('Frankenstein word cloud', figsize=(10,5.5))
plt.title('Word Cloud for Frankenstein',
        pad=30,
        fontsize=15,
        bbox=dict(
            facecolor='ivory',
            boxstyle='round, pad=.45'))
```

The remaining three steps should be equally simple, making the final lines:

```
plt.axis("off")
plt.imshow(wordcloud)
plt.show()
```

When you interpret the result, you should again notice that we see a similar effect to the one we observed in our 'Zipfian distribution', i.e. that – in terms of representing the semantic content of the book – the word cloud isn't really informative at all because the most frequent words are only function words. The only thing that we may be able to glean is that the narrator's *I* is rather prominent, telling us that we're dealing with a first-person narrative.

If you run the program repeatedly and observe the plots carefully, you should also notice that the image will be re-drawn with the words appearing in different places, due to the algorithm that calculates the positioning. Hence, if you compare your output with that of a fellow course participant or colleague, it may look fairly different, even if it's presenting the same information. Furthermore, we lose the numerical information regarding the word frequencies, as now, when you hover over any words, all you get displayed are the positions on the x- and y-axes of the plot, as well as a tuple of three values that represent the word's colour as RGB (red, green, blue) values. Hence, we can clearly see that some information is lost because the actual frequency is only indirectly represented through the relative size of the word. In other words, the word cloud is more useful for creating a quick visual impression and – with the appropriate filtering we'll be discussing next – very distant reading of a text, but not as useful for an in-depth analysis.

Discussion 67   Filtering Our Frequency List

There aren't really very many things to do for this exercise. The first thing is adding the new argument to the constructor, copying the argument to an instance variable, and creating the empty list, making the top of the constructor this:

```
def __init__(self,
          input_file=None,
          output_file=None,
          sort_order='n-1',
          stop_file=None):
    self.sort_order = sort_order
    self.stop_file = stop_file
    self.words = {}
    self.sorted_list = []
    self.stop_words = []
```

At the end of the constructor, you should first check to see if a file name has been provided for the stop-word file, and if so, read in the file – of course using appropriate error handling –, and add each word to the list:

```
if self.stop_file:
    try:
        with open(
            self.stop_file,
```

```
                mode='r',
                encoding='utf8') as stop:
                self.stop_words=[l.strip() for l in stop.readlines()]
        except OSError as err:
            raise OSError(err)
```

Hopefully, you'll have noticed that the easiest way to construct the list is to use `readlines` inside a list comprehension structure where you also strip away the line endings as I've done above, and where of course `l` is short for 'line'. To skip the stop words while generating the frequency dictionary, all you need to do is modify the top of the `for` loop where you split the line into words to iterate over, adding a test and skipping to the next iteration if it yields `True`:

```
for word in re.split(r'\s', line):
    if word in self.stop_words:
        continue
```

All that you'll need now is the stop-word list, which you can either create by looking at our previous cloud and thinking about which words you may want to exclude, or by using a list that you can output to the Debug I/O window, modifying your module test to only output the top *n* words, perhaps starting with 30, and then expanding the list until the function words start disappearing.

Discussion 68   Filtering the Word Cloud

Adjusting the frequency list import of course only requires you to change

```
from frequencies_b import Frequency_list
```

to

```
from frequencies_c import Frequency_list
```

and instantiating the frequency list object should now look like this:

```
f_list = Frequency_list(
    input_file='../texts/frankenstein.txt',
    sort_order='n-1',
    stop_file='../texts/stopwords.txt')
```

As stated before, setting the sort order as an argument isn't really necessary, but we'll leave it in for explicitness. Instead of accessing the frequency dictionary directly from outside the module, which, as I told you, object-orientation purists would frown upon, we now actually do call the method, returning the filtered and shortened frequency list dictionary directly as an argument to the word cloud module:

```
wordcloud = WordCloud(
    background_color="white",
    width = 800,
    height = 400,
    ).generate_from_frequencies(f_list.get_top_n(50))
```

Adjusting the title and caption to make them more explicit is very straightforward, resulting in something like this:

```
plt.figure('Frankenstein word cloud (filtered)', figsize=(10,5.5))
plt.title('Filtered Word Cloud for Frankenstein',
         pad=30,
         fontsize=15,
         bbox=dict(
             facecolor='ivory',
             boxstyle='round, pad=.45'))
```

The remainder of the program of course stays the same, so the only changes you might still end up making are those to modify the stop-word list.

Discussion 69   Adjusting the Frequency List Generator for Relative Frequencies

Basically, to turn our current module into one that can also generate relative frequency lists, normed ones, and percentages, there aren't many steps we need to take. If we want to be able to generate both types of frequencies, raw and relative, we need to add another argument to the constructor that allows us to determine this, and then copy that argument into an instance variable inside the constructor. To be able to keep track of the tokens, all we need to do is to add a counter variable to the method that creates the list, initially setting it to 0, and then incrementing it for each token we find. Because it's an instance variable that will be accessible from anywhere within the object, we can then change the method that outputs the value to a file to test for the additional argument and add a new conditional branch that simply divides the raw frequency by the number of tokens before writing the output, bearing in mind that we also need to change the output format to produce floating point results. In the same way, we can integrate the percentages and factor into the methods that produce output, i.e. the one that writes to a file or extracts the top *n* words.

For any other programs that may use the module, such as our frequency GUI, we need to provide a means for setting the relevant arguments and then doing the division when we either use the type frequency in some way or create the output for the particular type inside the program, unless we use the method for writing to a file directly. In this case, the program would need to supply the module with names for input and output files or allow it to generate the latter as the module would do if not provided an argument for the output file.

Because the changes are relatively straightforward, I'll only present the relevant pieces of code here, if necessary embedded in some context. The modified constructor should now look like this:

```
def __init__(self,
    input_file=None,
    output_file=None,
    sort_order='n-1',
    stop_file=None,
    abs_rel='abs',
    percent=False):
    self.sort_order = sort_order
    self.stop_file = stop_file
    self.abs_rel = abs_rel
    self.percent = percent
```

The top of the `create_list` method – also streamlining the initialisation of the relevant variables in the way we learnt earlier – should be modified to the following:

```
def create_list(self):
    self.words.clear()
    self.tokens = self.longest_word = self.max_len_number = 0
```

The first four lines of the loop that runs over the word tokens become

```
for word in re.split(r'\s', line):
    if word in self.stop_words:
        continue
    self.tokens += 1
```

Next, we need to change the head of the `output_list` method to add the potential factor, making it

```
def output_list(self, factor=0):
```

We set the default value for the factor to 0 because we can then use a simplified `if` test later, as, just like `None`, 0 evaluates to `False` in such a test. This now makes the part immediately following the `for` loop inside the method this:

```
if self.abs_rel == 'rel':
    rel_freq = self.words[word]/self.tokens
    if self.percent:
        factor=100
    if factor:
        rel_freq *= factor
    outFile.write(
        f'{word:{self.longest_word}}\t'
        f'{rel_freq:>{self.max_len_number}f}\n')
else:
    outFile.write(
        f'{word:{self.longest_word}}\t'
        f'{self.words[word]:>{self.max_len_number}d}'
        '\n')
```

Note that the lines containing the `write` statements were broken again to be able to display them here. Because we need the relative frequency both for displaying it with or without a factor, we calculate it directly, also in order to simplify the f-strings we'll later use to create the output. If the flag for showing percentages has been set to `True`, we can adjust the factor to 100. Otherwise, we still need to test if a factor has been set, and if so, immediately multiply the relative frequency by it.

The changes we need to make in the other method are of course analogous, only that they have to be integrated into the `for` loop that extracts the top *n* words. As an additional advanced exercise, you could adjust the GUI frequency list generator to allow you to create both forms of output.

Finally, adding the accessor method that allows us to extract the number of tokens should also be quite easy, as all we need to write is:

```
def get_num_tokens(self):
    return self.tokens
```

Discussion 70 Plotting Frequency Bars Side-by-Side

The import section of the program should present no difficulty for you to write, and ought to look like this:

```
import matplotlib.pyplot as plt
import pandas as pd
from frequencies_d import Frequency_list
```

The variable for controlling the number of words to extract would reasonably be called n, so we create and initialise it to

```
n=20
```

In a more flexible program, we'd of course allow the user to control this variable, either via the command line or some form of GUI interface. Creating the two frequency lists is again straightforward:

```
f_list1 = Frequency_list(
    input_file='../texts/frankenstein.txt',
    abs_rel='rel')
f_list1.create_list()

f_list2 = Frequency_list(
    input_file='../texts/adventures_of_sherlock_holmes.txt',
    abs_rel='rel')
f_list2.create_list()
```

All you really need to remember here is that we need to generate relative frequencies to be able to compare the data properly. In a more sophisticated interface, we'd of course provide a more flexible way of selecting the input files. To get the number of tokens for each file, we simply call the relevant accessor methods:

```
tokens1=f_list1.get_num_tokens()
tokens2=f_list2.get_num_tokens()
```

We initialise the factor to 1,000 first, just in case neither file should happen to be larger than the other, in which case this norming factor would make sense because we're dealing with texts that are definitely larger than 1,000 words. This, again, could be controlled in a more complex interface. For the comparison, we then evaluate two options, either that file number 1 is larger than file number 2, or that file number 2 is larger than file number 1. If none of these conditions return True, we simply retain the factor, making the whole section of the program

```
factor = 1000
if tokens1 > tokens2:
    factor=round(tokens2, -3)
elif tokens1 < tokens2:
    factor=round(tokens1, -3)
```

To get the pruned and normed frequency lists, using n and the factor, we now simply write

```
top1=f_list1.get_top_n(n,factor)
top2=f_list2.get_top_n(n,factor)
```

Of course, all the operations where we extract information or data from the two lists could also be written more compactly in tuple notation in a single statement each time, but I've refrained from doing so here to fit everything onto the page. Equally, we could also create list of frequency objects, simply passing in the file paths as arguments, but I leave such tweaks up to you as additional exercises.

The code for preparing the figure for plotting is almost identical to the way we did it last time, with only the window title being different:

```
fig, ax = plt.subplots()
fig.canvas.manager.set_window_title('Grouped bar chart')
```

We next need to create the data frame object like this:

```
df=pd.DataFrame([top1, top2])
```

and can then plot it directly, only bearing in mind that we need to use the T property to use the transposed data frame to fix the index for the y-axis for plotting, making this statement:

```
df.T.plot(ax=ax,
          kind='bar',
          title='Comparison of Normed Frequencies',
          grid=True,
          rot=90,
          fontsize=14,
          xlabel=f'top {n} words',
          ylabel=f'relative per {factor} words',
          figsize=(8,7.5))
```

The arguments I've passed here should be more or less self-explanatory, apart from perhaps the f-strings for the labels, where I've interpolated the information about n and the norming factor, respectively. Unfortunately, we cannot incorporate setting the legend into the above directly, but need to do so separately because otherwise our labels, taken from the transposed column headings would be 0 and 1. We therefore have to set this writing

```
ax.legend(['Frankenstein','Sherlock Holmes'])
```

before we can show the figure with

```
plt.show()
```

exactly as we did before.

When you evaluate the resulting graph, you should now be able to note that all the information we want is directly observable, including which frequency is higher in which novel and which words are uniquely present in the top 20 lists. The latter obviously doesn't mean that they might not occur with a lower frequency, though, only that they don't occur within the most frequent types. The tick marks on both axes are easily legible, but because we used the arguments for the `plot` method for creating the x- and y-axis labels and couldn't control the font size that way, these are rather small in comparison and the y-axis label is closer to the axis than we might want.

12

Conclusion

In this textbook, I've tried to provide you with an overview of the most important techniques in handling electronic textual data in Python in order to carry out linguistic analyses that may provide you with insights into how language works, both from a systemic and/or cultural point of view. Having been exposed to these options, you should now be able to develop your own small applications that can not only help you with your own research, but potentially also contribute towards larger-sized projects in Linguistics or text-oriented DH.

We began by developing some ideas about why it may be useful or necessary for you to be able to write your own programs for such purposes to be able to stay in control of your data and not be 'at the mercy of' tools that others have designed, and which may either be flawed in some way or not provide you with enough options to control all the relevant settings. The latter issue should especially have become clear in the final chapter when we introduced a way of filtering our data by using stop words, a feature that is sadly missing from the Voyant Tools, at least at first glance, which is why the sample analysis I showed you in Figure 1.1 didn't make much sense, at least not from the point of view of textual semantics. Given the skills you now have in using stop-word lists in your own programs, you should definitely be able to produce more meaningful data that can serve as a basis for producing better graphics or investigating the relevant vocabulary further through concordances.

Next, we moved on to cover a few essentials that allowed us to create Python programs on our computer. We first discussed how to install Python, and then learnt how to activate and use the command line in order to verify that the installation had been done correctly. This was followed by a brief discussion of the distinction between editors and IDEs, as well as how to install and configure the preferred IDE for the course.

In Chapter 2, we took our first steps in basic programming, starting with issuing our first statements in the Python Shell, then moving on to learn about variables and data types, as well as covering simple data types and some of the operations that can be performed on them. Towards the end of the chapter, we then discussed how you can actually write proper – yet still very simple – programs, and even comment those in a sensible way to help you understand your code and develop your skills in algorithmic thinking.

The next chapter introduced you to more programming basics, beginning with a discussion of compound data types, especially focussing on lists. Here, we already started dealing with lists of words, something that has since then been one of the most essential forms of dealing with syntactic constructs or lines of text to be processed. Later in this chapter, we looked at how to achieve some basic interaction with both our programs and potential users as a precursor to working with

Python Programming for Linguistics and Digital Humanities: Applications for Text-Focused Fields,
First Edition. Martin Weisser.
© 2024 John Wiley & Sons, Inc. Published 2024 by John Wiley & Sons, Inc.
Companion website: https://www.wiley.com/go/weisser/pythonprogling

control structures such as conditionals and loops. Before focussing on the latter, though, we learnt how to make efficient use of the IDE to help us understand and handle our code better, including the convenient way of starting our programs through the built-in debugger, thereby being able to catch and fix any potential errors efficiently.

Chapter 4 then focussed on slightly more advanced string operations, including how to extract parts of them for morphological analysis and similar tasks. In addition, we learnt how to create better representations for our output through specific formatting options, most notably the highly versatile f-strings.

In Chapter 5, I introduced you to working with data stored on your computer, i.e. the local file system, which we first learnt to navigate and understand. In the next step, we explored how to open, read, and write files, along with anticipating and catching the errors that might occur during this process, finally moving on to how to work with more complex file paths.

In the next chapter, we advanced to more sophisticated string processing techniques, learning how to identify and match complex patterns by means of regexes. This not only provided us with more flexibility in splitting longer strings into words and other components, but also allowed us to write a basic concordancer, one of the most common and useful tools in identifying language patterns and their associated meaning. Along the line, we also found out how to handle more specific errors related to regexes and how to deal with them.

In Chapter 7, we discussed the different aspects of modular programming that allow us to divide our programs into parts that are easier to maintain and use, essentially providing the basis for developing larger-scale and far more useful programs. Here, we not only learnt how to create our own user-defined functions and basic modules, but also how to accomplish the highest level of modularity, object-orientation. As one part of this, we also covered yet another very important compound data type, the dictionary, which allowed us to store and access related information in the form of key–value pairs.

In the next chapter, apart from first creating a simple word list from a file, we put our newly gained knowledge of dictionaries to good use in creating a proper frequency list generator, which we later developed into an object-oriented module with greater flexibility and various options for sorting the list before writing it to a file. As we developed this module, we also explored more complex and sophisticated ways of creating sort keys using lambda functions.

In Chapter 9, we then investigated more sophisticated ways of interacting with data and users by learning how to create basic GUIs. As part of this, we first created a modest interface for turning simple declaratives into interrogatives, but finally also a more complex one to allow us to control the output from our frequency list generator as a first step in providing us with a means to explore the semantics of individual texts through the lens of word – and perhaps later n-gram – frequencies.

The penultimate main chapter introduced us to markup languages, such as HTML and XML, as well as the TEI format for representing language data. This was complemented by a discussion of how to download data from the web, using our very own GUI interface to the `urllib.request` module, how to extract text from such web data, as well as how to convert text files into Simple XML and the TEI format.

Chapter 11 then rounded off the introduction with a brief discussion of useful visualisation techniques based on the frequency information we were able to extract through our frequency list generator, which we also refined further in the process to produce more useful and comparable data. We explored our frequency data through creating basic and more complex charts and word clouds that reflected different aspects of the data we need to be aware of in order to achieve a more meaningful interpretation of the texts we want to work with.

Throughout these chapters, I've not only tried to teach you the essential concepts required at each stage for writing increasingly complex programs in Python, but also to make you aware of the problems and pitfalls that you may be confronted with in analysing textual data on the computer, as well as to show you ways and means of dealing with these issues. In addition, you've hopefully also realised that it's always necessary to critically reflect on potential issues in designing our own programs, and to retain an equally critical perspective on what the libraries and modules provided by other programmers may have to offer, including where their potential weaknesses may lie.

This being an introductory textbook, we've obviously only been able to scratch the surface of what is possible to achieve using the techniques we've learnt here. However, since we've essentially progressed from a beginner's stage to at least an intermediate level through the topics we've explored, I hope to have given you a means to develop your programming skills further by applying them in your own projects, perhaps by expanding on the exercises we've gone through, or by creating your own modules and approaches.

Of course, even though you've gone through an extensive number of exercises, and hopefully learnt something useful from each one of them, it would be an illusion to expect that you can now handle all programming tasks you may encounter in future with ease, but at least you should have gained some degree of confidence in your knowledge and expertise as a Python programmer. However, it's still best to bear in mind that it takes years of practice to really become an expert in this field, so please don't give up once things may end up getting difficult at times.

Appendix – Program Code

01_swap.py

```python
#!/usr/bin/env python3
# 01_swap.py
# Autor: Your name
# Program for swapping two variables,
# to simulate syntactic inversion
# created: date of creation
# last edit: date of last edit

# declare & instantiate words
word1 = 'there'
word2 = 'is'
print('Prior to swapping, beginning of declarative sentence: Word 1 =',
      word1 + '; Word 2 = ', word2)
# temporarily store contents of word1
temp = word1
print('Value of word1 now stored temporarily in temp')
# assign value of word2 to word1
word1 = word2
# assign temp value to word2
word2 = temp
print('After swapping, beginning of interrogative sentence: Word 1 =',
      word1 + '; Word 2=', word2)
```

Python Programming for Linguistics and Digital Humanities: Applications for Text-Focused Fields,
First Edition. Martin Weisser.
© 2024 John Wiley & Sons, Inc. Published 2024 by John Wiley & Sons, Inc.
Companion website: https://www.wiley.com/go/weisser/pythonprogling

02_sentence.py

```
#!/usr/bin/env python3
# 02_sentence.py

words = ['this', 'is', 'a', 'sentence']
print(words[0], words[1], words[2], words[3]+'.')
print(words[1], words[0], words[2], words[3]+'?')
```

03_get_args_argv.py

```
#!/usr/bin/env python3
# 03_get_args_argv.py
# import sys module
import sys

# Output program name from 1st position of sys.argv
print('The program name is ' + sys.argv[0])
# Get 1st word from command line & store in variable word1
word1 = sys.argv[1]
word2 = sys.argv[2]
print('word1:' , word1 + '; word2:', word2)
```

04_get_args_input.py

```
#!/usr/bin/env python3
# 04_get_args_input.py

# Get 1st word from command line & store in variable word1
word1 = input('Please input 1st word...\n')
word2 = input('Please input 2nd word...\n')
# Output words with explanations
print('\nword1: ' + word1 + '; word2:', word2)
```

05_word_comparison.py

```
#!/user/bin/env python3
# 05_word_comparison.py
import sys

word1 = sys.argv[1]
word2 = sys.argv[2]

if word1 == word2:
    print("The words are equal.\nword 1\t" + word1
            + '\nword 2\t' + word2)
```

```
elif word1 < word2:
    print("Word 1 comes before word 2.\nword 1\t" + word1
            + '\nword 2\t' + word2)
else:
    print("Word 1 comes after word 2.\nword 1\t" + word1
            + '\nword 2\t' + word2)
```

06_collect_collocates.py

```
#!/usr/bin/env python3
# 06_collect_collocates.py

collocate = input(
    'Please type in 3 collocates of the verb \'cause\'.\n')
collocates = list()

while len(collocates) < 3:
    if collocate == '':
        collocate = input(
            'No collocate provided!\nPlease type one in.\n')
    else:
        collocates.append(collocate)
        if len(collocates) == 3:
            break
        else:
            collocate = input('Please provide another collocate.\n')
print('\nThe collocates you provided were:\n', collocates)
```

07_uppercasing.py

```
#!/usr/bin/env python3
# 07_uppercasing.py

sentence = input('Please input a complete sentence.\n')
words = sentence.split()
cap_words = []
for word in words:
    cap_words.append(word.upper())
print('The sentence in all-caps is:', ' '.join(cap_words))
```

08_cleanup.py

```
#!/usr/bin/env python3
# 08_cleanup.py
```

```
string = '  word1  word2  '
print('strip method without arguments: >>'
      + string.strip()
      + '<<')
print('replace method: >>'
      + string.replace('  ',' ')
      + '<<')
print('both methods: >>'
      + string.replace('  ',' ').strip()
      + '<<')
```

09_strip_prefix.py

```
#!/usr/bin/env python3
# 09_strip_prefix.py

import sys

prefixes = tuple(sys.argv[1].split(','))
word_string = 'delete destroy disappear disentangle dispel download'
' downsize overload overheat prefer preload reflect repeat unheard'
' unknown understand underwrite upend upload'
for word in word_string.split():
    if word.startswith(prefixes):
        for prefix in prefixes:
            if word.startswith(prefix):
                print('The stem of', word, 'is:', word[len(prefix):])
```

10_negative_to_positive.py

```
#!/usr/bin/env python3
# 10_negative_to_positive.py

negator = 'not'
sentences = "This is not true. It's not a negative sentence."
" You did not make a mistake here."
for sentence in sentences.split('.'):
    if not sentence.endswith('.'):
        sentence += '.'
    indexPos = sentence.index(negator)
    message_pt1 = 'Sentence with negation: ' + sentence
    message_pt2 = ('\nWithout negation: '
                + sentence[:indexPos]
                + sentence[indexPos+len(negator)+1:])

    print(message_pt1, message_pt2, end='\n\n')
```

11_read_file_a.py

```python
#!/usr/bin/env python3
# 11_read_file_a.py

import sys

# store file name as 1st argument from command line
fileName = sys.argv[1]
# try to open file for reading with encoding UTF-8
try:
    file_handle = open(fileName, mode='r', encoding='utf-8')
# on error, output error message & close program explicitly
except OSError as err:
    sys.exit(str(err))

# read all lines from file object
lines = file_handle.readlines()
# close file manually
file_handle.close()
''' process lines in loop, each time generating  a tuple of
line number & line via enumerate() '''
for (num, line) in enumerate(lines):
    # output line number & line, first removing (stripping) line breaks
    line = line.strip()
    print(f'line number {num+1}: {line}')
```

12_read_file_b.py

```python
#!/usr/bin/env python3
# 12_read_file_b.py

import sys

# store file name as 1st argument from command line
fileName = sys.argv[1]
# try to open file via with...as for reading with encoding UTF-8
try:
    with open(fileName, 'r', encoding='utf-8') as inFile:
        # store file contents as string
        fileContents = inFile.read()
# on error, output error message & close program explicitly
except OSError as err:
    sys.exit(str(err))

for (num, line) in enumerate(fileContents.splitlines()):
print(f'line number {num+1:>2d} : {line}')
```

13_read_file_c.py

```python
#!/usr/bin/env python3
# 13_read_file_c.py

import sys

fileName = sys.argv[1]
try:
    with open(fileName, 'r', encoding='utf-8') as inFile:
        for (num, line) in enumerate(inFile):
            print(f'line number {num+1:>2d}: {line.strip()}')
except OSError as err:
    sys.exit(str(err))
```

14_copy_file.py

```python
#!/usr/bin/env python3
# 14_copy_file.py

import sys

(inputFile, outputFile) = sys.argv[1:]
try:
    with open(inputFile,'r', encoding='utf-8') as inFile, \
open(outputFile,'w',encoding='utf8') as outFile:
        for line in inFile:
            outFile.write(line)
except OSError as err:
sys.exit(str(err))
```

15_read_folder_contents.py

```python
#!/usr/bin/env python3

import os

files = []
folders = []

for element in os.scandir():
    if element.is_file():
        files.append(element)
    elif element.is_dir():
        folders.append(element)

if len(folders) != 0:
    print('folders:', end='\n\n')
```

```
    for element in folders:
        print(element.name)
else:
    print('No folders found!')

print('\nfiles:', end='\n\n')
for element in files:
        print(element.name)
```

16_copy_to_folder.py

```
#!/usr/bin/env python3
# 16_copy_to_folder.py

import sys
from pathlib import Path

inputFile = sys.argv[1]

path = Path.cwd()
backupDir = path / 'backup'
outputFile = backupDir / inputFile

if not backupDir.exists():
    try:
        Path.mkdir(backupDir)
        print('New folder', str(backupDir), 'created')
    except OSError as err:
        sys.exit(str(err))
else:
    print(str(backupDir), 'already exists.')

try:
    with open(inputFile,'r', encoding='utf-8') as inFile, \
            open(str(outputFile),'w',encoding='utf8') as outFile:
        for line in inFile:
            outFile.write(line)
except OSError as err:
    sys.exit(str(err))
```

17_simple_patterns.py

```
#!/usr/bin/env python3
# 17_simple_patterns.py

import sys
import re

pattern = sys.argv[1]
```

```
try:
    with open('../texts/sample_sentences.txt', 'r',
            encoding='utf-8') as input_file:
        for line in input_file:
            result = re.search(pattern, line)
            if result:
                (start,end) = result.span()
                print(f'{line[:start]}[{result.group()}]{line[end:]}',
end='')
except OSError as err:
    sys.exit(str(err))
```

18_test_character_classes.py

```
#!/usr/bin/env python3
# 18_test_character_classes.py
import sys
import re

try:
    search_term = sys.argv[1]
    if not re.search('[.\[\\\]]', search_term):
        sys.exit('No character class defined in search_term!')
except IndexError:
    sys.exit('No search term defined!')

try:
    with open('../texts/sample_sentences.txt', 'r', encoding='utf-8') \
        as in_file:
        for line in in_file:
            if re.search(search_term, line):
                lineNew = ''
                start = 0
                for hit in re.finditer(search_term,line):
                    (startPos,end) = hit.span()
                    lineNew += f'{line[start:startPos]}[{hit.group()}]'
                    start = end
                print(f'{lineNew}{line[end:-1]}')
except OSError as err:
    sys.exit(str(err))
```

19_test_regexes.py

```
#!/usr/bin/env python3
# 19_test_regexes.py
```

```
import sys
import re

try:
    search_term = re.compile(sys.argv[1])
except IndexError:
    sys.exit('No search term defined!')
except re.error as e:
    sys.exit(f'Regex error="{e.msg}" in pattern: "{e.pattern}" '
            f'at position {e.pos}')

try:
    with open('../texts/sample_sentences.txt',
            'r', encoding='utf-8') as in_file:
        for line in in_file:
            if search_term.search(line):
                lineNew = ''
                start = 0
                for hit in search_term.finditer(line):
                    (startPos,end) = hit.span()
                    lineNew += f'{line[start:startPos]}[{hit.group()}]'
                    start = end
                print(lineNew + line[end:-1])
except OSError as err:
    sys.exit(str(err))
```

tagger.py

```
#!/usr/bin/env python3
# tagger.py
'''This is a simple module to perform basic PoS tagging using dic-
tionary lookup.'''

import re
import sys

def read_lexicon(lexicon_file):
    '''Read in a lexicon file provided as an argument
    and create a dictionary from it by splitting
    the lines at cola
    and feeding them into the dictionary.'''

    lexicon = {}
    try:
        with open(lexicon_file, 'r', encoding='utf-8') as lex:
            for line in lex:
                line = line.strip()
```

```
                    if line:
                        word, tag = line.split(':')
                        lexicon[word] = tag
        except OSError as err:
            sys.exit(str(err))
        return lexicon

def read_sentences(sentence_file):
    '''Read in a file provided as argument
    and return a list of sentences by adding
    each line to the list.'''

    sentences = []
    try:
        with open(sentence_file, 'r', encoding='utf-8') as sf:
            for line in sf:
                line = line.strip()
                if line:
                    sentences.append(line)
    except OSError as err:
        sys.exit(str(err))
    return sentences

def tag_sentence(lexicon, sentence):
    '''Using a lexicon and sentence as arguments,
    tag the sentence with PoS tags from the lexicon
    and return the tagged sentence.

    arguments:

    :lexicon: a dictionary containing word:PoS pairs
    :sentence: a string containing a sentence'''

    tagged = list()
    sentence = f'{sentence[0:1].lower()}{sentence[1:-1]} {sentence[-1:]}'

    for word in re.split(r'\s+', sentence):
        if word in lexicon:
            tagged.append(f'{word}_{lexicon[word]}')
        elif word.capitalize() in lexicon:
tagged.append(f'{word.capitalize()}_{lexicon[word.capitalize()]}')
        else:
            tagged.append(f'{word}_???')
    tagged_sent = ' '.join(tagged)
    tagged_sent = tagged_sent[0].capitalize() + tagged_sent[1:]
    return tagged_sent

def output_tagged(tagged):
    '''Take a tagged sentence provided as argument
    and output it.'''

print(tagged)
```

20_tag_sentences.py

```
#!/usr/bin/env python3
# 20_tag_sentences.py

from tagger import (read_lexicon, read_sentences, tag_sentence,
    output_tagged)

lex = read_lexicon('../texts/lexicon.txt')
#print(lex)
sentences = read_sentences('../texts/sentences.txt')
#print(sentences)
for sentence in sentences:
    output_tagged(tag_sentence(lex, sentence))
```

word.py

```
#!/usr/bin/env python3
# word.py
import re

class Verb():
    """Class for modelling verbs

    base -- base form: non-optional
    person -- person: default '1'
    number -- number: default 'singular'
    tense_form -- tense form: default 'present';
        options: present, past, present participle
    v_type -- verb type: default 'r' für regular,
        otherwise i (or anything else ;-))"""

    def __init__(self,
                 base=None,
                 person='1',
                 number='singular',
                 tense_form='present',
                 v_type='r'):
        """Constructor"""

        if not base:
            raise NameError('No base form provided!')
        self.base = base
        self.person = person
        self.number = number
        self.tense_form = tense_form
        self.v_type = v_type
```

```python
    def past(self):
        if self.v_type=='r':
            if re.search(r'e$', self.base):
                return self.base + 'd'
            else:
                redup = re.search(r'([dlmnprt])$', self.base)
                if redup:
                    return self.base + redup.group(1) + 'ed'
                elif re.search(r'(?<![aou])y$', self.base):
                    return self.base[0:-1] + 'ied'
                else:
                    return self.base + 'ed'
        else:
            return 'Irregular verb. Not yet implemented.'

    def pres_part(self):
        if self.v_type=='r':
            if re.search(r'e$', self.base):
                return self.base[0:-1] + 'ing'
            else:
                redup = re.search(r'([dlmnprt])$', self.base)
                if redup:
                    return self.base + redup.group(1) + 'ing'
                else:
                    return self.base + 'ing'
        else:
            return 'Irregular verb. Not yet implemented.'

    def present(self):
        if self.v_type=='r':
            if self.number=='singular' and self.person=='3':
                if re.search(r'[cs]h$', self.base):
                    return self.base + 'es'
                elif re.search(r'(?<![aou])y$', self.base):
                    return self.base[0:-1] + 'ies'
                else:
                    return self.base + 's'
            else:
                return self.base
        else:
            return 'Irregular verb. Not yet implemented.'

    def generate_tense_form(self, tense_form=None):
        if not tense_form:
            tense_form = self.tense_form
```

```python
        if tense_form == 'present':
            return self.present()
        elif(tense_form == 'past'):
            return self.past()
        elif(tense_form == 'present participle'):
            return self.pres_part()

class Noun():
    """Class for modelling nouns

    base -- base form: non-optional
    number -- number: default 'singular'
    n_type -- noun type: default 'r' für regular, otherwise i (or
anything else ;-))"""

    def __init__(self, base=None, number='singular', n_type='r'):
        """Constructor"""

        if not base:
            raise NameError('No base form provided!')
        self.base = base
        self.number = number
        self.n_type = n_type

    def plural(self):
        if self.n_type == 'r':
            if re.search(r'(ch|sh?)$', self.base):
                return self.base + 'es'
            elif re.search(r'(?<!f)f$', self.base):
                return self.base[0:-1] + 'ves'
            elif re.search(r'(?<![aou])y$', self.base):
                return self.base[0:-1] + 'ies'
            else:
                return self.base + 's'
        else:
            return 'Irregular noun. Not yet implemented.'


if __name__ == '__main__':
    for v_base in ['star', 'stare', 'brim', 'stun', 'gaze',
                   'rot', 'compel', 'top', 'pop', 'bed', 'cry',
                   'play']:
        try:
            verb = Verb(
                base=v_base,
```

```
                          person='3',
                          number='singular',
                          v_type='r')
              print(f'Base form: {verb.base}; present for person '
                  f'{verb.person}: {verb.present()}')
              print(f'Present participle: {verb.pres_part()}; '
                  f'past participle: {verb.past()}')
              gen_arg = 'past'
              print(f'Current verb form for "{gen_arg}" via '
                  f'generator method: '
                  f'{verb.generate_tense_form(gen_arg)}\n')
          except NameError as e:
              print(str(e))
    for n_form in ['cow', 'calf', 'puff', 'match',
                    'house', 'baby', 'bay']:
          try:
              noun = Noun(n_form)
              print(f'The plural of the noun {noun.base} is: '
                  f'{noun.plural()}')
          except NameError as e:
              print(str(e))
```

21_word_list.py

```
#!/usr/bin/env python3
# 21_word_list.py

import sys
import re
import os.path

words = []
input_file = '../texts/frankenstein.txt'
pathName, fileName = os.path.split(os.path.abspath(input_file))
basePath, _ = os.path.split(pathName)
outputFile = os.path.join(basePath, 'output', 'wordlist_' +
fileName)

try:
    with open(input_file, 'r', encoding='utf-8') as inFile:
        for line in inFile:
            line = re.sub(r'[".,;!?:()\[\]`_-]',' ', line)
            line = re.sub(r'\s{2,}', ' ', line)
            line = line.strip()
            if not line:
                continue
            words.extend(re.split(r'\s', line))
```

```
except OSError as err:
    sys.exit(str(err))

try:
    with open(outputFile, 'w', encoding='utf-8') as outFile:
        for word in sorted(set(words), key=str.lower):
            outFile.write(word + '\n')
except OSError as err:
    sys.exit(str(err))
```

22_frequency_list.py

```
#!/usr/bin/env python3
# 22_frequency_list.py
import sys
import re
import os.path

words = {}
longest_word = 0
input_file = '../texts/frankenstein.txt'
pathName, fileName = os.path.split(os.path.abspath(input_file))
basePath, _ = os.path.split(pathName)
outputFile = os.path.join(basePath, 'output', 'frequency_list_' +
            fileName)
try:
    with open(inputFile, 'r', encoding='utf-8') as inFile:
        for line in inFile:
            line = re.sub(r'[".,;!?:()\[\]`_-]',' ', line)
            line = re.sub(r'\s{2,}', ' ', line)
            line = line.strip()
            if not line:
                continue
            for word in re.split(r'\s', line):
                words[word] = words.setdefault(word, 0) + 1
                if len(word) > longest_word:
                    longest_word = len(word)
except OSError as err:
    sys.exit(str(err))

try:
    with open(outputFile, 'w', encoding='utf-8') as outFile:
        for word in sorted(words.keys(), key=str.lower):
            outFile.write(f'{word:{longest_word}}\t{words[word]}\n')
except OSError as err:
sys.exit(str(err))
```

frequencies_a.py

```python
#!/usr/bin/env python3
# frequencies_a.py
# frequency module that only implements raw frequencies

import re
import os.path

class Frequency_list():

    def __init__(self,
                    input_file=None,
                    output_file=None,
                    sort_order='n-1'):
        self.sort_order = sort_order
        self.words = {}
        self.sorted_list = []
        if not input_file:
            raise NameError('No filename provided! '
                            'Unable to create frequency list...')
        else:
            self.input_file = input_file
            pathName, fileName = os.path.split(
                os.path.abspath(input_file))
            basePath, _ = os.path.split(pathName)
        if not output_file:
            self.output_file = os.path.join(basePath,
                            'output', 'frequency_list_' + fileName)
        else:
            self.output_file = output_file

    def create_list(self):
        self.words.clear()
        self.longest_word = 0
        self.max_len_number = 0
        try:
            with open(self.input_file, 'r', encoding='utf-8') \
                as inFile:
                for line in inFile:
                    line = re.sub(r'[".,;!?:()\[\]`_-]',' ', line)
                    line = re.sub(r'\s{2,}', ' ', line)
                    line = line.strip()
                    if not line:
                        continue
                    for word in re.split(r'\s', line):
                        if len(word) > self.longest_word:
```

```python
                            self.longest_word = len(word)
                        self.words[word] = self.words.setdefault(
                            word, 0) + 1
                        if len(str(self.words[word])) > \
                            self.max_len_number:
                            self.max_len_number = \
                                len(str(self.words[word]))
        except OSError as err:
            raise OSError(err)


    def make_sorted_list(self):
        if self.sort_order=='a-z':
            self.sorted_list = sorted(
                self.words.keys(),
                key=str.casefold)
        elif self.sort_order=='z-a':
            self.sorted_list = sorted(self.words.keys(),
                key=str.casefold, reverse=True)
        elif self.sort_order=='n-1':
            self.sorted_list = sorted(
                self.words.keys(),
                key=lambda word: (-self.words[word],word.casefold()))
        elif self.sort_order=='1-n':
            self.sorted_list = sorted(
                self.words.keys(),
                key=lambda word: (self.words[word],word.casefold()))
        elif self.sort_order=='w_length':
            self.sorted_list = sorted(
                self.words.keys(),
                key=lambda word: (-len(word),-self.words[word],
                                    word.casefold()))
        elif self.sort_order=='reverse':
            self.sorted_list = sorted(
                self.words.keys(),
                key=lambda word: (word[::-1],len(word)))

    def output_list(self):
        try:
            with open(self.output_file, 'w',
                    encoding='utf-8') as outFile:
                for word in self.sorted_list:
                    outFile.write(f'{word:{self.longest_word}}\t'
                        f'{self.words[word]:>{self.max_len_number}d}\n')
        except OSError as err:
            raise OSError(err)
```

```python
if __name__ == '__main__':
    try:
        f_list = Frequency_list(
            input_file='../texts/adventures_of_sherlock_holmes.txt',
            output_file='../output/test_frequency_list2.txt',
            sort_order='n-1')
        f_list.create_list()
        f_list.make_sorted_list()
        f_list.output_list()
    except OSError as f1:
        print('Wrong input or output file provided!',
              str(f1).split(' ')[-1])
    except NameError as f2:
        print(str(f2))
```

minimal_gui.py

```python
#!/usr/bin/env python3
# minimal_gui.py
import sys
from PyQt5.QtWidgets import QDialog, QApplication, QLineEdit

if __name__ == '__main__':
    app = QApplication(sys.argv)
    window = QDialog()
    window.setGeometry(100,100,250,50)
    window.setWindowTitle('Simple Dialogue')
    output_field = QLineEdit(window)
    output_field.setText(sys.argv[1])
    output_field.move(55,15)
    window.show()
    sys.exit(app.exec_())
```

syn_inversion_GUI.py

```python
#!/usr/bin/env python3
# syn_inversion_GUI.py
import sys
import re
from PyQt5.QtWidgets import (QApplication,QMainWindow,
                QHBoxLayout,QVBoxLayout,QLabel,QLineEdit,
                QPushButton,QFrame,QMessageBox)
from PyQt5.QtGui import QFont

class Inverter(QMainWindow):
    """GUI for illustrating syntactic inversion"""
```

```python
    def __init__(self):
        # call constructor of parent/super class
        super().__init__()
        self.setFont(QFont("Courier", 12))
        self.initUI()

    def initUI(self):
        #pass
        # set up container for layouts
        container = QFrame()
        # set container as central widget
        self.setCentralWidget(container)
        # define main & sub-layouts
        main_layout = QVBoxLayout()
        decl_layout = QHBoxLayout()
        interr_layout = QHBoxLayout()
        conv_layout = QHBoxLayout()
        # add sub-layouts to main layout
        main_layout.addLayout(decl_layout)
        main_layout.addLayout(interr_layout)
        main_layout.addLayout(conv_layout)
        # set layout of container as main layout
        container.setLayout(main_layout)

        # define widgets
        self.decl_input = QLineEdit('This is a declarative sentence.')
        self.interr_output = QLineEdit()
        invertBtn = QPushButton('Invert sentence')
        # connect signal to slot
        invertBtn.clicked.connect(self.invert)

        # add widgets to layouts
        decl_layout.addWidget(QLabel('Declarative sentence:\t'))
        decl_layout.addWidget(self.decl_input)
        interr_layout.addWidget(QLabel('Interrogative sentence: '))
        interr_layout.addWidget(self.interr_output)
        conv_layout.addWidget(invertBtn)

    def invert(self):
        parts = re.search(r'^\s*([\w-]+\b)\s(\b[\w-]+\b)(.+?)\.\s*$',
                    self.decl_input.text())
        if self.decl_input.text() and parts:
            self.interr_output.setText(
                f'{parts.group(2).capitalize()} '
                f'{parts.group(1).lower()}{parts.group(3)}?')
```

```
        else:
            QMessageBox(
                text='Please input a complete simple declarative!!',
                windowTitle='Input Error',
                icon=QMessageBox.Critical).exec_()

if __name__ == '__main__':
    # instantiate the program
    app = QApplication(sys.argv)
    # set up window object
    inverter = Inverter()
    inverter.setWindowTitle('Simple syntactic inversion')
    inverter.setGeometry(15,35,750,100)
    # show window
    inverter.show()
    # start program
    sys.exit(app.exec_())
```

frequency_GUI.py

```
#!/usr/bin/env python3
# frequency_GUI.py
import sys
import os.path
from frequencies_a import Frequency_list

from PyQt5.QtWidgets import (QApplication,QMainWindow,
                QTextEdit,QAction,QPushButton,QLabel,
                QFileDialog,QComboBox,QMessageBox)
from PyQt5.QtGui import QFont, QTextCursor)

class GUI_frequencies(QMainWindow):

    def __init__(self):
        super().__init__()
        # window setup
        self.setFont(QFont("Courier", 12))
        self.setWindowTitle('Frequency list GUI')
        self.setGeometry(30,30,500,800)
        # properties
        self.file = None
        self.base_dir='.'

        # create interface
        self.initUI()

    def initUI(self):

        # menu section
        mainMenu = self.menuBar()
```

```
        mainMenu.setNativeMenuBar(False)
        file_menu = mainMenu.addMenu('&File')
        loadAction = QAction('L&oad', self, shortcut='Ctrl+o')
        loadAction.triggered.connect(self.load_file)
        saveAction = QAction('&Save', self, shortcut='Ctrl+s')
        saveAction.triggered.connect(self.save_file)
        file_menu.addActions([loadAction, saveAction])

        # toolbar
        toolbar = self.addToolBar('main')
        #toolbar.addActions([loadAction, saveAction])
        self.optsCombo = QComboBox()
        self.optsCombo.addItems([
                                'n-1',
                                '1-n',
                                'a-z',
                                'z-a',
                                'reverse',
                                'w_length'])
        toolbar.addWidget(self.optsCombo)
        runBtn = QPushButton('Run')
        runBtn.clicked.connect(self.analyse)
        toolbar.addWidget(runBtn)

        # status bar
        status = self.statusBar()
        status.addPermanentWidget(QLabel('File:'))
        self.fileLab = QLabel()
        self.fileLab.setMinimumWidth(200)
        status.addPermanentWidget(self.fileLab)

        # editor window
        self.output_win = QTextEdit()
        self.setCentralWidget(self.output_win)

    def load_file(self):
        self.file,_ = QFileDialog.getOpenFileName(
            self,
            'Open file',
            directory='../texts',
            filter='*.txt;;*.*')
        if self.file:
            self.base_dir, in_file = os.path.split(self.file)
            self.fileLab.setText(in_file)
        else:
            self.fileLab.setText('')

    def save_file(self):
        out_file,_ = QFileDialog.getSaveFileName(
            self,
```

```python
                'Save file',
                directory=self.base_dir,
                filter='*.txt;;*.*')
        if out_file:
            try:
                with open(out_file, mode='w', encoding='utf-8') as out:
                    out.write(self.output_win.toPlainText())
            except OSError as e:
                QMessageBox(
                    text=f'{e}!\nSelect a location you have '
                    'write access to.',
                    windowTitle='Output Error',
                    icon=QMessageBox.Critical).exec_()
                return
        else:
            return

    def analyse(self):
        if self.file:
            # create frequency list
            analyser = Frequency_list(
                input_file=self.file,
                sort_order=self.optsCombo.currentText())
            analyser.create_list()
            analyser.make_sorted_list()
            # clear output window
            self.output_win.clear()
            for word in analyser.sorted_list:
                self.output_win.append(
                    f'{word:{analyser.longest_word}}\t'
                    f'{analyser.words[word]:>{analyser.max_len_
                        number}d}')
            self.output_win.moveCursor(QTextCursor.Start)
            self.output_win.setFocus()
        else:
            QMessageBox(
                text='No input file selected!\nPlease load a file.',
                windowTitle='Input Error',
                icon=QMessageBox.Critical).exec_()
            return


if __name__ == '__main__':
    app = QApplication(sys.argv)
    win = GUI_frequencies()
    win.show()
    sys.exit(app.exec_())
```

23_fetch_page_GUI.py

```python
#!/usr/bin/env python3
# 23_fetch_page_GUI.py

import urllib.request
import re
import sys
import os.path
from PyQt5.QtCore import *
from PyQt5.QtWidgets import (QApplication,QMainWindow,QLineEdit,
            QTextEdit, QPushButton,QLabel,QMessageBox)
from PyQt5.QtGui import QFont

class Downloader(QMainWindow):


    def __init__(self):
        super().__init__()
        self.setFont(QFont("Courier", 12))
        self.setWindowTitle('Downloader')
        self.setGeometry(30,30,1000,400)

        toolbar = self.addToolBar('main')
        fetchBtn = QPushButton('Download')
        fetchBtn.clicked.connect(self.fetch_page)
        self.addressBar = QLineEdit()
        self.addressBar.returnPressed.connect(self.fetch_page)

        toolbar.addWidget(fetchBtn)
        toolbar.addWidget(QLabel(' URL: '))
        toolbar.addWidget(self.addressBar)

        self.logEdit = QTextEdit()
        self.setCentralWidget(self.logEdit)

    def fetch_page(self):

        address=self.addressBar.text()
        if not address:
            QMessageBox(
                    text='No URL provided!',
                    windowTitle='Input Error',
                    icon=QMessageBox.Critical).exec_()
            return
        self.logEdit.append(f'Attempting to download {address} ...')
        try:
```

```python
        page=urllib.request.urlopen(address)
    except urllib.error.URLError as err:
        self.logEdit.append(f'Download error.\n{address} '
                        f'{err.reason}')
        return
    self.logEdit.append(f'Page {address} successfully retrieved.')

    self.logEdit.append('Searching for encoding & page title...')
    '''Determine encoding (charset) & title from header.'''
    charset=page.headers.get_content_charset(failobj="utf-8")

    # read in page using charset info
    try:
        page_content=page.read().decode(charset)
    except Exception:
        self.logEdit.append('Unable to decode URL. '
                    'Aborting download.\n')
        return

    # search for title
    title=re.search(
        r'<title>\s*([^<]+?)\s*</title>', page_content).group(1)

    if charset and title:
        self.logEdit.append(f'encoding: {charset}; title: {title}')
    elif charset and not title:
        self.logEdit.append(f'encoding: {charset}; no title')

    # generate file name
    self.logEdit.append('Generating file name ...')
    # either from title, if found, otherwise address
    if title:
        title=title.strip()
        file_name=re.sub(r'\W+', r'_', title, re.M|re.S) + '.html'
    else:
        file_name=address[address.rindex('/')+1:]

    if os.path.exists(file_name):
        msgBox=QMessageBox(
                text=f'File already exists!\nOverwrite it?',
                windowTitle='Overwrite warning',
                icon=QMessageBox.Warning)
        msgBox.setStandardButtons(QMessageBox.Yes | QMessageBox.No)
        msgBox.setDefaultButton(QMessageBox.No)
        button_clicked=msgBox.exec_()
```

```python
        if button_clicked==QMessageBox.No:
            self.logEdit.append('File overwrite aborted.\n')
            return

    self.logEdit.append(f'Attempting to store page {address}...')
    try:
        with open(file_name,mode='w',encoding='utf-8') as out_file:
            out_file.write(page_content)
    except OSError as err:
        self.logEdit.append(str(err))
        return
    self.logEdit.append(f'{address} saved to {file_name}.\n')

if __name__ == '__main__':
    app = QApplication(sys.argv)
    win = Downloader()
    win.show()
    sys.exit(app.exec_())
```

24_extract_paras.py

```python
#!/usr/bin/env python3
# 24_extract_paras.py

from bs4 import BeautifulSoup

with open("./HTML_Download_Test_Page_for_Analysis.html",
        mode='r',
        encoding='UTF-8') as page:
    tree = BeautifulSoup(page,"html.parser")

paragraphs = [paragraph.getText()
            for paragraph in tree.find_all('p')]
    print('\n'.join(paragraphs))
```

25_txt_to_xml.py

```python
#!/usr/bin/env python3
# 25_txt_to_xml.py
import re
import sys
import os.path

'''This is a short sample program to illustrate how a book can be
converted to XML from a text file. However, in terms of conversion
```

options, it is fairly limited because the file format is possibly
restricted to Mary Shelley's Frankenstein, & the converter therefore
cannot be used universally without adjustments.'''

```python
n_heading = n_paragraph = n_sentence = 0
#abbreviations need to be masked later, so that they don't
# interfere with sentence processing
abbrevs = ['Mrs', 'Mr', 'St', 'Dec', 'R.W', 'M']

def tag_sentence(match_object):
    sentence = match_object.group(1)
    global n_sentence
    n_sentence += 1
    return (f'<sentence n="{n_sentence}">\n{sentence}\n'
            '</sentence>\n')

input_file = '../texts/frankenstein.txt'
pathName, fileName = os.path.split(os.path.abspath(input_file))
basePath, _ = os.path.split(pathName)
output_file = os.path.join(basePath,
                           'output',
                           re.sub( r'txt$', 'xml', fileName))

# read file
try:
    with open(input_file, mode='r', encoding='utf-8') as in_file:
        paragraphs = re.split(r'\n{2,}', in_file.read())
except OSError as err:
    sys.exit(str(err))

try:
    with open(output_file, mode='w', encoding='utf-8') as out_file:
        # write out 'header'
        out_file.write('<?xml version="1.0"?>\n')
        out_file.write('<text id="frankenstein" corpus="GothicNovels" '
                       'author="Mary Shelley" lang="en">\n')
        for paragraph in paragraphs:
            # assemble lines in paragraph
            paragraph = re.sub(r'\n', ' ', paragraph)
            paragraph = re.sub(r' +', ' ', paragraph)
            match = re.search(r'\b(Chapter|Letter) (\d+)', paragraph)
            if match:
                n_heading += 1
                if n_heading != 1:
                    # write out end tag for section type, based on
                    # previous match
                    out_file.write(f'</{h_type}>\n')
                h_type = match.group(1).lower()
                n_unit = match.group(2)
```

```
            out_file.write(f'<heading n="{n_heading}" type="'
                        f'{h_type}">\n'
                        f'{paragraph}\n</heading>\n')
            continue
        else:
            n_paragraph += 1
            paragraph = re.sub(r'(?<!\d)--', ' - ', paragraph)
            # mask abbreviations here
            for abbrev in abbrevs:
                paragraph=re.sub(r'(?<='+abbrev+r')[.]',
                    '_',
                    paragraph)
            paragraph = re.sub(
                    r'([\w, "\':()-]+?[.?!;]"?)(?:\s+|$)',
                    tag_sentence,
                    paragraph)
            # unmask abbreviations again
            paragraph=re.sub('_', '.', paragraph)
        out_file.write(f'<paragraph n="'
                    {n_paragraph}">\n{paragraph}'
                    '</paragraph>\n')
    # write out 'footer'
    out_file.write(f'</{h_type.lower()}>\n')
    out_file.write('</text>')

except OSError as err:
    sys.exit(str(err))
```

26_txt_to_TEI.py

```
#!/usr/bin/env python3
# 26_txt_to_TEI.py
import re
import sys
import os.path

'''This is a short sample program to illustrate how a book can
be converted to TEI XML from a text file. However, in terms of
conversion options, it is fairly limited because the file format is
possibly restricted to Mary Shelley's Frankenstein, & the converter
therefore cannot be used universally without adjustments.'''

n_head = n_paragraph = n_sentence = 0
#abbreviations need to be masked later, so that they don't
#interfere with sentence processing
abbrevs = ['Mrs', 'Mr', 'St', 'Dec', 'R.W', 'M']
```

```python
def tag_sentence(match_object):
    sentence = match_object.group(1)
    global n_sentence
    n_sentence += 1
    return (f'<s n="{n_sentence}">\n{sentence}\n'
            '</s>\n')


input_file = '../texts/frankenstein.txt'
pathName, fileName = os.path.split(os.path.abspath(input_file))
basePath, _ = os.path.split(pathName)
output_file = os.path.join(basePath,
                           'output',
                           re.sub(r'\.txt$', '_TEI.xml', fileName))

# read file
try:
    with open(input_file, mode='r', encoding='utf-8') as in_file:
        paragraphs = re.split(r'\n{2,}', in_file.read())
except OSError as err:
    sys.exit(str(err))

try:
    with open(output_file, mode='w', encoding='utf-8') as out_file:
        # write out 'header'
        out_file.write('<?xml version="1.0"?>\n')
        # TEI container start
        out_file.write('<TEI xmlns="http://www.tei-c.org/ns/1.0" '
        'xml:lang="en">\n')
        # TEI header start
        out_file.write('<teiHeader>\n')
        # the first paragraphs contains two lines that in turn
        #contain title and autor info,
        # so we need to remove this paragraph first and process it
        initial_para = paragraphs.pop(0)
        (title, author) = initial_para.split('\n')
        author = re.sub(r'^\s*by\s', r'', author)
        out_file.write('<fileDesc>\n')
        out_file.write('<titleStmt>\n')
        out_file.write(f'<title>\n{title}</title>\n')
        out_file.write(f'<author>\n{author}\n</author>\n')
        out_file.write('</titleStmt>\n')
        out_file.write('<publicationStmt>\n')
        out_file.write('<p>\nPart of a corpus of Gothic novels\n'
            '</p>\n')
        out_file.write('</publicationStmt>\n')
        out_file.write('<sourceDesc>\n')
        out_file.write('<p>\nExtracted from eBook #84 from '
            'Project Gutenberg; https://www.gutenberg.org\n</p>\n')
```

```
        out_file.write('</sourceDesc>\n')
        out_file.write('</fileDesc>\n')

        # TEI header end
        out_file.write('</teiHeader>\n')

        out_file.write('<text>\n')
        out_file.write('<body>\n')
        for paragraph in paragraphs:
            # assemble lines in paragraph
            paragraph = re.sub(r'\n', ' ', paragraph)
            paragraph = re.sub(r' +', ' ', paragraph)

            match = re.search(r'\b(Chapter|Letter)\b', paragraph)
            if match:
                n_head += 1
                h_type = match.group(1).lower()
                if n_head != 1:
                    out_file.write(f'</div>\n')
                out_file.write(f'<div n="{n_head}" type="{h_type}">\n')
                out_file.write(f'<head n="{n_head}">\n'
                    f'{paragraph}\n</head>\n')
                continue
            else:
                n_paragraph += 1
                paragraph=re.sub(r'(?<!\d)--', ' - ', paragraph)
                # mask abbreviations here
                for abbrev in abbrevs:
                    paragraph=re.sub(r'(?<='+abbrev+r')[.]', '_',
                        paragraph)
                paragraph=re.sub(r'([\w, "\':()-]+?[.?!;]"?)(?:\s+|$)',
                                tag_sentence, paragraph)
                # unmask abbreviations again
                paragraph = re.sub('_', '.', paragraph)
            out_file.write(f'<p n="{n_paragraph}">\n{paragraph}</p>\n')
        # write 'footer'
        out_file.write('</div>\n')
        out_file.write('</body>\n')
        out_file.write('</text>\n')
        # TEI container end
        out_file.write('</TEI>')

except OSError as err:
    sys.exit(str(err))
```

frequencies_b.py

```
#!/usr/bin/env python3
# frequencies_b.py
# frequency list generator with top n extraction

import re
import os.path

class Frequency_list():

    def __init__(self,
                 input_file=None,
                 output_file=None,
                 sort_order='n-1'):
        self.sort_order = sort_order
        self.words = {}
        self.sorted_list = []
        if not input_file:
            raise NameError('No filename provided! '
                            'Unable to create frequency list...')
        else:
            self.input_file = input_file
            pathName, fileName=\
              os.path.split(os.path.abspath(input_file))
            basePath, _ = os.path.split(pathName)
        if not output_file:
            self.output_file = os.path.join(basePath, 'output',
                                    'frequency_list_' + fileName)
        else:
            self.output_file = output_file


    def create_list(self):
        self.words.clear()
        self.tokens = self.longest_word = self.max_len_number = 0
        try:
            with open(self.input_file, 'r', encoding='utf-8') \
                as inFile:
                for line in inFile:
                    line = re.sub(r'[".,;!?:()\[\]`_-]',' ', line)
                    line = re.sub(r'\s{2,}', ' ', line)
                    line = line.strip()
                    if not line:
                        continue
                    for word in re.split(r'\s', line):
                        self.tokens += 1
```

```
                if len(word) > self.longest_word:
                    self.longest_word = len(word)
                self.words[word] = self.words.setdefault(word,
                    0) + 1
                if len(str(self.words[word])) > \
                    self.max_len_number:
                        self.max_len_number=\
                            len(str(self.words[word]))
        except OSError as err:
            raise OSError(err)

    def make_sorted_list(self):
        if self.sort_order=='a-z':
            self.sorted_list = sorted(
                self.words.keys(),
                key=str.casefold)
        elif self.sort_order=='z-a':
            self.sorted_list = sorted(self.words.keys(),
            key=str.casefold, reverse=True)
        elif self.sort_order=='n-1':
            self.sorted_list = sorted(
                self.words.keys(),
                key=lambda word: (-self.words[word],word.
                                    casefold()))
        elif self.sort_order=='1-n':
            self.sorted_list = sorted(
                self.words.keys(),
                key=lambda word: (self.words[word],word.casefold()))
        elif self.sort_order=='w_length':
            self.sorted_list = sorted(
                self.words.keys(),
                key=lambda word: (-len(word),-self.words[word],
                                    word.casefold()))
        elif self.sort_order=='reverse':
            self.sorted_list = sorted(
                self.words.keys(),
                key=lambda word: (word[::-1],len(word)))

    def output_list(self):
        try:
            with open(self.output_file, 'w',
                    encoding='utf-8') as outFile:
                for word in self.sorted_list:
                    outFile.write(f'{word:{self.longest_word}}\t'
                        f'{self.words[word]:>{self.max_len_number}d}\n'
                        )
```

```
            except OSError as err:
                raise OSError(err)

    def get_top_n(self, n):
        if not self.sorted_list:
            self.create_list()
            self.sort_order = 'n-1'
            self.make_sorted_list()
        if n > len(self.words):
            n=len(self.words)
        top_dict = dict()
        for i in range(n):
            top_dict[self.sorted_list[i]]=\
                self.words[self.sorted_list[i]]
        return top_dict

if __name__ == '__main__':
    try:
        f_list = Frequency_list(
            input_file='../texts/adventures_of_sherlock_holmes.txt',
            output_file='../output/test_frequency_list_rel.txt',
            sort_order='n-1')
        f_list.create_list()
        f_list.make_sorted_list()
        top_dict = f_list.get_top_n(100)
        for word in top_dict.keys():
            print(f'{word}\t{top_dict[word]:>10d}')
    except OSError as f1:
        print('Wrong input or output file provided!',
            str(f1).split(' ')[-1])
    except NameError as f2:
        print(str(f2))
```

27_Zipf_plot.py

```
#!/usr/bin/env python3

# 27_Zipf_plot.py
import matplotlib.pyplot as plt
from matplotlib.ticker import MultipleLocator
from frequencies_b import Frequency_list

# generate frequency list object
f_list = Frequency_list(
    input_file='../texts/frankenstein.txt',
    sort_order='n-1')
```

```
    f_list.create_list()
    f_list.make_sorted_list()
    # get top 50 words & frequencies
    top_words = f_list.get_top_n(50)
    # extract words & frequencies to separate lists
    x_words, y_freqs = top_words.keys(), top_words.values()

    # create figure and axes; size: width, height
    fig, ax1 = plt.subplots(figsize=(10,8.5))
    fig.canvas.manager.set_window_title('Frankenstein')
    #fig.patch.set_alpha(0.0)
    #ax1.patch.set_alpha(0.0)
    # bar creates vertical plot, barh a horizontal one
    ax1.scatter(
        x_words,
        y_freqs,
        color='blue')
    ax1.set_xlabel(
        'words',
        color='green',
        fontsize=14,
        loc='center',
        bbox=dict(
            facecolor='ivory',
            edgecolor='green',
            boxstyle='round, pad=.25'))
    ax1.set_ylabel(
        'raw frequency',
        color='green',
        fontsize=14,
        labelpad=20,
        bbox=dict(
            facecolor='ivory',
            edgecolor='green',
            boxstyle='round, pad=.25'))
    ax1.xaxis.set_tick_params(
        labelsize=12,
        labelrotation=90)
    ax1.yaxis.set_minor_locator(MultipleLocator(100))
    plt.title(
        "'Zipfian Distribution'",
        backgroundcolor='cyan',
        color='orange',
        fontsize=20,
        pad=20)
    plt.show()
```

28_basic_cloud.py

```python
#!/usr/bin/env python3
# 28_basic_cloud.py
import matplotlib.pyplot as plt
from wordcloud import WordCloud
from frequencies_b import Frequency_list

f_list = Frequency_list(
    input_file='../texts/frankenstein.txt',
    sort_order='n-1')
f_list.create_list()

wordcloud = WordCloud(
    background_color="white",
    width = 800,
    height = 400,
    max_words=50
    ).generate_from_frequencies(f_list.words)

# creates the figure; allows us to assign window title directly
plt.figure('Frankenstein word cloud', figsize=(10,5.5))
# creates a 'legend'
plt.title('Word Cloud for Frankenstein',
        pad=30,
        fontsize=15,
        bbox=dict(
            facecolor='ivory',
            boxstyle='round, pad=.45'))
plt.axis("off")
plt.imshow(wordcloud)
plt.show()
```

frequencies_c.py

```python
#!/usr/bin/env python3
# frequencies_c.py
import re
import os.path

class Frequency_list():

    def __init__(self,
                 input_file=None,
                 output_file=None,
                 sort_order='n-1',
                 stop_file=None):
        self.sort_order = sort_order
```

```python
        self.stop_file = stop_file
        self.words = {}
        self.sorted_list = []
        self.stop_words = []
        if not input_file:
            raise NameError('No filename provided! '
                            'Unable to create frequency list...')
        else:
            self.input_file = input_file
            pathName, fileName=
              os.path.split(os.path.abspath(input_file))
            basePath, _ = os.path.split(pathName)
        if not output_file:
            self.output_file = os.path.join(basePath, 'output',
                                'frequency_list_' + fileName)
        else:
            self.output_file = output_file
        # if stopword list has been defined...
        # assumes that stopwords are listed one per line
        if self.stop_file:
            try:
                with open(
                    self.stop_file,
                    mode='r',
                    encoding='utf8') as stop:
                    self.stop_words=[l.strip() for l
                                in stop.readlines()]
            except OSError as err:
                raise OSError(err)

    def create_list(self):
        self.words.clear()
        self.longest_word = self.max_len_number = 0
        try:
            with open(self.input_file, 'r', encoding='utf-8') \
                as inFile:
                for line in inFile:
                    line = re.sub(r'[".,;!?:()\[\]`_-]',' ', line)
                    line = re.sub(r'\s{2,}', ' ', line)
                    line = line.strip()
                    if not line:
                        continue
                    for word in re.split(r'\s', line):
                        if word in self.stop_words:
                            continue
                        self.tokens += 1
                        if len(word) > self.longest_word:
```

```
                            self.longest_word = len(word)
                    self.words[word] = self.words.setdefault(word,
                        0) + 1
                    if len(str(self.words[word])) > \
                      self.max_len_number:
                        self.max_len_number = \
                          len(str(self.words[word]))
        except OSError as err:
            raise OSError(err)


    def make_sorted_list(self):
        if self.sort_order=='a-z':
            self.sorted_list = sorted(
                self.words.keys(),
                key=str.casefold)
        elif self.sort_order=='z-a':
            self.sorted_list = sorted(self.words.keys(),
                key=str.casefold, reverse=True)
        elif self.sort_order=='n-1':
            self.sorted_list = sorted(
                self.words.keys(),
                key=lambda word: (-self.words[word],word.
                                   casefold()))
        elif self.sort_order=='1-n':
            self.sorted_list = sorted(
                self.words.keys(),
                key=lambda word: (self.words[word],word.casefold()))
        elif self.sort_order=='w_length':
            self.sorted_list = sorted(
                self.words.keys(),
                key=lambda word: (-len(word),-self.words[word],
                                   word.casefold()))
        elif self.sort_order=='reverse':
            self.sorted_list = sorted(
                self.words.keys(),
                key=lambda word: (word[::-1],len(word)))


    def output_list(self):
        try:
            with open(self.output_file, 'w',
                    encoding='utf-8') as outFile:
                for word in self.sorted_list:
                    outFile.write(f'{word:{self.longest_word}}\t'
                        f'{self.words[word]:>{self.max_len_number}d}\n'
                        )
        except OSError as err:
            raise OSError(err)
```

```python
    def get_top_n(self, n):
        if not self.sorted_list:
            self.create_list()
            self.sort_order = 'n-1'
            self.make_sorted_list()
        # sanity check; if n larger dict, scale n down
        if n > len(self.words):
            n=len(self.words)
        top_dict = dict()
        for i in range(n):
            top_dict[self.sorted_list[i]]=\
                self.words[self.sorted_list[i]]
        return top_dict

if __name__ == '__main__':
    try:
        f_list = Frequency_list(
            input_file='../texts/adventures_of_sherlock_holmes.txt',
            output_file='../output/test_frequency_list_rel.txt',
            sort_order='n-1',
            stop_file='../texts/stopwords.txt')
        f_list.create_list()
        f_list.make_sorted_list()
        top_dict = f_list.get_top_n(20)
        for word in top_dict.keys():
            print(f'{word}\t{top_dict[word]:>10d}')
    except OSError as f1:
        print('Wrong input or output file provided!',
              str(f1).split(' ')[-1])
    except NameError as f2:
        print(str(f2))
```

29_filtered_cloud.py

```python
#!/usr/bin/env python3
import matplotlib.pyplot as plt
from wordcloud import WordCloud
from frequencies_c import Frequency_list

f_list = Frequency_list(
    input_file='../texts/frankenstein.txt',
    sort_order='n-1',
    stop_file='../texts/stopwords.txt')
f_list.create_list()
#top_dict=
#print(len(freqs))
```

```python
wordcloud = WordCloud(
    background_color="white",
    width = 800,
    height = 400,
    ).generate_from_frequencies(f_list.get_top_n(50))

plt.figure('Frankenstein word cloud (filtered)', figsize=(10,5.5))
plt.title('Filtered Word Cloud for Frankenstein',
        pad=30,
        fontsize=15,
        bbox=dict(
            facecolor='ivory',
            boxstyle='round, pad=.45'))
plt.imshow(wordcloud)
plt.axis("off")
plt.show()
```

frequencies_d.py

```python
#!/usr/bin/env python3
# frequencies_d.py
# frequency list generator:
#    uses stopwords
import re
import os.path

class Frequency_list():

    def __init__(self,
                    input_file=None,
                    output_file=None,
                    sort_order='n-1',
                    stop_file=None,
                    abs_rel='abs',
                    percent=False):
        self.sort_order = sort_order
        self.stop_file = stop_file
        self.abs_rel = abs_rel
        self.percent = percent
        self.words = {}
        self.sorted_list = []
        self.stop_words = []
        if not input_file:
            raise NameError('No filename provided! '
                            'Unable to create frequency list...')
        else:
            self.input_file = input_file
            pathName, fileName=\
                os.path.split(os.path.abspath(input_file))
            basePath, _ = os.path.split(pathName)
```

```
        if not output_file:
            self.output_file = os.path.join(
                basePath,
                'output',
                'frequency_list_' + fileName)
        else:
            self.output_file = output_file
        # if stopword list has been defined...
        # assumes that stopwords are listed one per line
        if self.stop_file:
            try:
                with open(
                    self.stop_file,
                    mode='r',
                    encoding='utf8') as stop:
                    self.stop_words=[l.strip() for l
                                        in stop.readlines()]
            except OSError as err:
                raise OSError(err)

    def create_list(self):
        self.words.clear()
        self.tokens = self.longest_word = self.max_len_number = 0
        try:
            with open(self.input_file, 'r', encoding='utf-8') \
                as inFile:
                for line in inFile:
                    line = re.sub(r'[".,;!?:()\[\]`_-]',' ', line)
                    line = re.sub(r'\s{2,}', ' ', line)
                    line = line.strip()
                    if not line:
                        continue
                    for word in re.split(r'\s', line):
                        if word in self.stop_words:
                            continue
                        self.tokens += 1
                        if len(word) > self.longest_word:
                            self.longest_word = len(word)
                        self.words[word] = self.words.setdefault(word,
                                                        0) + 1

                        if len(str(self.words[word])) > \
                            self.max_len_number:
                            self.max_len_number = \
                                len(str(self.words[word]))
        except OSError as err:
            raise OSError(err)

    def make_sorted_list(self):
        if self.sort_order=='a-z':
            self.sorted_list = sorted(
```

```python
                    self.words.keys(),
                    key=str.casefold)
            elif self.sort_order=='z-a':
                self.sorted_list = sorted(self.words.keys(),
                    key=str.casefold, reverse=True)
            elif self.sort_order=='n-1':
                self.sorted_list = sorted(
                    self.words.keys(),
                    key=lambda word: (-self.words[word],word.
                                        casefold()))
            elif self.sort_order=='1-n':
                self.sorted_list = sorted(
                    self.words.keys(),
                    key=lambda word: (self.words[word],word.casefold()))
            elif self.sort_order=='w_length':
                self.sorted_list = sorted(
                    self.words.keys(),
                    key=lambda word: (-len(word),-self.words[word],
                                        word.casefold()))
            elif self.sort_order=='reverse':
                self.sorted_list = sorted(
                    self.words.keys(),
                    key=lambda word: (word[::-1],len(word)))
    def output_list(self, factor=0):
        try:
            with open(self.output_file, 'w',
                    encoding='utf-8') as outFile:
                for word in self.sorted_list:
                    if self.abs_rel == 'rel':
                        rel_freq = self.words[word]/self.tokens
                        if self.percent:
                            factor=100
                        if factor:
                            rel_freq *= factor
                        outFile.write(
                            f'{word:{self.longest_word}}\t'
                            f'{rel_freq:>{self.max_len_number}f}'
                            '\n')
                    else:
                        outFile.write(
                            f'{word:{self.longest_word}}\t'
                            f'{rel_freq:>{self.max_len_number}f}'
                            '\n')
                    else:
                        outFile.write(
                            f'{word:{self.longest_word}}\t'
                            f'{self.words[word]:>{self.max_len_
                                number}d}'
                            '\n')
```

```python
            except OSError as err:
                raise OSError(err)

    def get_top_n(self, n, factor=0):
        if not self.sorted_list:
            self.create_list()
            self.sort_order = 'n-1'
            self.make_sorted_list()
        if n > len(self.words):
            n=len(self.words)
        top_dict = dict()
        for i in range(n):
            if self.abs_rel == 'rel':
                rel_freq = self.words[self.sorted_list[i]]/self.tokens
                if self.percent:
                    factor=100
                if factor:
                    rel_freq *= factor
                top_dict[self.sorted_list[i]]= rel_freq
            else:
                top_dict[self.sorted_list[i]]=\
                    self.words[self.sorted_list[i]]
        return top_dict

    def get_num_tokens(self):
        return self.tokens

if __name__ == '__main__':
    try:
        f_list = Frequency_list(
            input_file='../texts/adventures_of_sherlock_holmes.txt',
            output_file='../output/test_frequency_list_rel.txt',
            sort_order='n-1',
            abs_rel='rel',
            percent=True)
        f_list.create_list()
        f_list.make_sorted_list()
        #f_list.output_list()
        top_dict = f_list.get_top_n(20)
        for word in top_dict.keys():
            if f_list.percent:
                print(f'{word}\t{top_dict[word]:.5f}')
            else:
                print(f'{word}\t{top_dict[word]:.5f}')
    except OSError as f1:
        print('Wrong input or output file provided!',
              str(f1).split(' ')[-1])
    except NameError as f2:
        print(str(f2))
```

30_grouped_bars.py

```python
#!/usr/bin/env python
# 30_grouped_bars.py
import matplotlib.pyplot as plt
import pandas as pd
from frequencies_d import Frequency_list


n=20
f_list1 = Frequency_list(
    input_file='../texts/frankenstein.txt',
    abs_rel='rel')
f_list1.create_list()

f_list2 = Frequency_list(
    input_file='../texts/adventures_of_sherlock_holmes.txt',
    abs_rel='rel')
f_list2.create_list()

# get tokens to determine factor
tokens1=f_list1.get_num_tokens()
tokens2=f_list2.get_num_tokens()

factor = 1000
if tokens1 > tokens2:
    factor=round(tokens2, -3)
elif tokens1 < tokens2:
    factor=round(tokens1, -3)

# get the relative lists
top1=f_list1.get_top_n(n,factor)
top2=f_list2.get_top_n(n,factor)

fig, ax = plt.subplots()
fig.canvas.manager.set_window_title('Grouped bar chart')

df=pd.DataFrame([top1, top2])
df.T.plot(ax=ax,
          kind='bar',
          title='Comparison of Normed Frequencies',
          grid=True,
          rot=90,
          fontsize=14,
          xlabel=f'top {n} words',
          ylabel=f'relative per {factor} words',
          figsize=(8,7.5))

# needed to replace indexes 0 & 1
ax.legend(['Frankenstein','Sherlock Holmes'])
#ax.set_ylabel(fontsize=20)

plt.show()
```

Index

Python Programming for Linguistics and Digital Humanities: Applications for Text-Focused Fields,
First Edition. Martin Weisser.
© 2024 John Wiley & Sons, Inc. Published 2024 by John Wiley & Sons, Inc.
Companion website: https://www.wiley.com/go/weisser/pythonprogling